IRISH
TRADITIONAL
COOKING

DARINA ALLEN

with a foreword by Regina Sexton

KYLE BOOKS

For Aunt Lil
who kindled my interest
in traditional food

This edition published in 2005 by Kyle Books
An imprint of Kyle Cathie Limited
general.enquiries@kyle-cathie.com
www.kylecathie.com

Reprinted 2005, 2006, 2007, 2008

Distributed by National Book Network
4501 Forbes Blvd., Suite 200
Lanham, MD 20706
Phone: (301) 459 3366   Fax: (301) 429 5746

ISBN 978 1 904920 11 3

Text
© Darina Allen 1995

Photographs
© Michelle Garrett 1995
© Kevin Dunne 1995

Darina Allen is hereby identified as the
author of this work in accordance with
section 77 of the Copyright, Designs
and Patents Act 1988.

The Library of Congress Cataloguing-in-
Publication Data is available on file.

The publishers would like to thank Susan
Martineau for her invaluable contribution
to the production of this book.

Design
Tamasin Cole

Printed and bound in Singapore by
Star Standard

Author's Acknowledgements

The research for this book has taken many years and brought me into contact with countless wonderful people who have generously shared their memories and their recipes with me. I would never have been able to complete the task without their support, and am delighted to have made many new and lasting friendships in the process.

I would particularly like to thank Ted O'Sullivan, who charmed me with stories of his childhood on Bere Island; Diarmuid O'Driscoll, who provided fascinating information about eating habits on Cape Clear Island; Charles Haughey who traced a recipe for sorrel pie on his island of Inisvickillaun; Eamonn MacThomáis, who sat and chatted for hours about the food of old Dublin; Charles Nelson of The National Botanic Gardens who authenticated some of my material on vegetables and shared his writings on the gardens of Trinity College.

I also owe a special debt of gratitude to the many people who welcomed me into their homes and showed me, so willingly, how to make the dishes of their childhood. Lana Pringle who gave me the secret of her family Barm Brack; Jo Twomey who painstakingly taught me how to cook on an open fire and took the mystery out of baking in the pot oven or bastible; Bridget Guerin who showed me how to make Bairneach Soup; Jack O'Keeffe whose family originally came from Sliabh Luachra, and who specially drove all the way to Shanagarry to pass on his family recipe for goose blood pudding. A big thank you to these and the many, many more who are mentioned in the introductions to individual recipes. I also want to thank the people who posted me old recipe books, especially early manuscripts and recipe books handed down through generations. They include a manuscript collection begun in the 1730s by the Dillon family of Clonbrock in Co. Galway, the Ballyduff manuscript book from Mocollop Castle, dated 1801; Eliza Helena Odell's recipe book dated 1851; Alice D'Olier's recipes collected from 1893; Annie Kiely's manuscript, dated Cork, 1908. All of these and many others proved to be an extraordinarily rich source of information.

I also want to thank the countless people who wrote to me with recipes, especially Queenie Endersen of Mallow, Co. Cork who wrote wonderfully evocative letters in her own sweeping hand, each of which I treasure; and Margaret Breen of Beaufort, Co. Kerry, who even sent me slips of Cottiers Kale through the post. I was greatly helped by friends in *Bord Iascaigh Mhara* (The Irish Sea Fisheries Board); by the Government Publications Office and the Ulster Folk Museum.

It would not have been possible for me to tackle a book of this scope, stretching back into the past, without expert historical advice. For this I am indebted to Regina Sexton, an enthusiastic young Irish food historian, who authenticated my own research and provided many additional insights of her own. Her exemplary foreword anchors the book firmly in its historical context.

I am deeply grateful to my own extensive team of helpers, my secretaries Rosalie and Adrienne who typed the manuscript. Florrie Cullinane, Fionnuala Ryan, Dolly Benskin, Ber Allen, and Rachel O'Neill tested and re-tested recipes, in many cases venturing into previously unknown territory to taste such unfamiliar items as pig's head, lamb's tails, tripe and drisheen and beggarman's stew.

Very special thanks to Mary Dowey for her generous help and advice and endless encouragement and of course to my long suffering editors Catherine Bradley and Annie Jackson, who remained smiling to the end even though tired and battle weary from trying to extract the final manuscript.

I am especially grateful to Kevin Dunne and Michelle Garrett for the beautiful photographs which have brought my book to life and have captured that elusive Irish feeling, often so difficult to portray.

Heartfelt thanks also goes to my Aunt Lil, to whom this book is dedicated, to my mother Elizabeth O'Connell and my mother-in-law, Myrtle Allen of Ballymaloe House. They all kindled my interest in traditional Irish food and were good enough to share their rich store of fascinating old recipes with me.

Contents

Introduction

*'Cut and Come' Kale growing in the vegetable
garden at Ballymaloe Cookery School*

I had a magical Irish country childhood. I grew up in a tiny village called Cullohill, in Co. Loais, where all the neighbors helped each other during the busiest times of the farming year. Even as children we lent a hand with the haymaking and then took turns to ride home behind the haycock on the horsedrawn cart. Threshing was still done with a steam machine, and I have many happy memories of bringing sweet tea and 'spotted dog' to the men in the fields, and helping to cook the enormous threshing dinner.

At home, almost everything we and our neighbors ate was natural, wholesome food, homegrown or produced in the locality. We even had a Kerry cow and our own hens. Every day, my mother cooked three wonderful meals on the range, which we all tucked into with great relish around the big kitchen table – it needed to be big because there were nine of us. A packet of fig rolls or coconut creams from the shop was a rare treat.

Our summer holidays were spent, not in France or the Caribbean, but on an uncle's farm in Co. Tipperary. For us, as children, it was an absolutely enchanting place – a big working farm on the edge of the bog, where my greataunt churned butter, they killed their own pigs, cured bacon, and made black and white pudding, and my greataunt did all the cooking over a huge open turf fire. The O'Connell family of Noard was virtually self-sufficient up to the early 1960s.

Here I learned the art of cooking in a bastible and how to make a tender 'railway cake' speckled with plump sultanas. Here I learned how to hand-milk a cow, sitting on a three-legged stool with my forehead leaning against the cow's warm stomach. As I write this I remember the sound of the milk squirting into the pail and the cows contentedly eating their ration of sweet hay. When the milking was finished, the milk destined for the creamery was put into tall churns and a few buckets were taken to the dairy to be run through the separator. The ripened cream of several days was then churned into rich golden butter, washed and salted. Greataunt Lil painstakingly showed me how to use the timber butter-hand to shape the butter into little blocks and tiny pats for the house.

It never occurred to any of us that this way of life, which we took so much for granted, was about to come to an abrupt end. I can remember distinctly the day the first packets of instant whip and blancmange came to our village and we couldn't wait to try them. These foods had a glamor and a novelty value which made home-cooking seem dull by comparison. All over Ireland, within just a few years, people began to prize fancy shop-bought goods. When the priest came to visit, for instance, he would always be offered white

One of the free-range hens at Ballymaloe Cookery School

'shop bread' in preference to homemade soda bread. With the rush to embrace a new consumer culture of packaged and canned foods in the name of progress, a whole food tradition was jeopardized in an alarmingly short space of time. Through the 1950s and 1960s, rural electrification brought the added temptation of frozen foods to more remote areas. Official agricultural policy encouraged farmers to intensify to produce maximum yields at minimum cost – to the detriment of flavour, texture and nutritional content.

It was just as the novelty of new synthetic flavours was wearing off, and I was beginning to question the wisdom of this food revolution, that I first arrived at Ballymaloe House, near Shanagarry in Co. Cork. Fresh from hotel school in Dublin, I had heard about a farmer's wife who had recently opened a restaurant in her rambling country house, and was cooking with local produce from her garden and from the sea close by.

It was to be a turning point in my life. In Myrtle Allen I found a cook who believed in following the seasons, growing her own herbs – at a time when this was far from fashionable – and using the bounty of her farm and the Cork countryside to the full. She wrote her menus every day, incorporating fresh produce from the farm and the kitchen garden, and the fresh catch from the fishing boats at Ballycotton. Far from being seduced by convenience foods, she had no time for them at all. I quickly realized she was someone whose philosophy I could identify with. Myrtle was serving parsnips, swede turnips, carrageen moss and tender spears of rhubarb at a time when they would have been considered far too humble for most restaurant menus. The confidence she had in her own local produce, used in season at its best, was an inspiration.

Almost 40 years later, I am still at Ballymaloe, in the lush East Cork countryside. I became a member of the Allen family by the simple expedient of marrying the boss's eldest son. Since then, Ballymaloe House – the first country-house hotel in Ireland – has developed in various directions with the interest and involvement of different family members.

I started Ballymaloe Cookery School in 1983 in a small way, in converted farm-buildings behind our house. Now it has more than doubled in size, and students from all over the world are attracted to a cookery school set amidst fruit, vegetable, and herb gardens with free-range hens, pigs, and even our own Kerry cow in the orchard to remind me of my childhood. Other members of the family run the large farm which still provides Ballymaloe with much of its produce; manage a shop selling the best of Irish craftwork; or are involved in other enterprises under the Ballymaloe umbrella.

During this time, we have built up a network of dedicated food producers who supply the restaurant and the cookery school with naturally reared meat and poultry, home-smoked fish, and stoneground oatmeal. Our cheeses come from the new generation of Irish farmhouse cheesemakers. I have always felt that these wonderful ingredients are best cooked simply, to preserve their true natural flavors. Both Myrtle Allen and I have always been interested in traditional Irish recipes and we have often found at Ballymaloe that recipes handed down from generation to generation produce the most delicious results. Over the years we gradually built up a small collection. About ten years ago, however, I saw that there was an urgent need to

Lana Pringle shows Darina how to make Barm Brack

research more vigorously. With the passing of one more generation, I realized, a whole culinary tradition, with all its fascinating regional variations, was in imminent danger of being lost.

That was the starting point for this book. Writing it has been a labor of salvage, as well as one of love. Early on in my research I wrote to regional newspapers inviting readers to send me old family recipes, and the response was overwhelming. I received wonderful replies which encouraged me to contact people all over the country and set off on a journey of discovery. In Ballyheigue in Co. Kerry I spent a fascinating day with John Guerin and his mother Bridget, learning how to collect bairneachs (limpets) off the rocks for a traditional Good Friday soup. In Co. Monaghan, Granny Toye, well into her eighties, described in vivid detail how to make the boxty pancakes of her youth. Everywhere I met people who were delighted to pass on recipes for dishes that had been an essential part of their lives, along with their recollections.

While traditional Irish cooking stems, in the main, from simple farmers, it also embraces the more sophisticated food served in the grand houses of the Anglo-Irish gentry. The cooks in these households would have been expected to know the rudiments of classic French cooking. They would also have been encouraged to adapt recipes brought back from the Grand Tour, or from India, where the younger sons of many Anglo-Irish families made their career in the army. From the dining-rooms of the great houses to the kitchens of the poorest cabins, and from pagan times right up to the present day, Ireland has had a strong tradition of generous hospitality. The best food was generally for guests, and the warmest hospitality was often to be found in the most humble homes.

In recent years there has been a renaissance on the Irish food scene. Irish chefs have become more adventurous and many have a greater appreciation of quality Irish produce, giving them the confidence to serve Irish food proudly. The most encouraging development has been the emergence of an artisanal food culture – most based in the Cork area, but gradually spreading through other counties. The farmhouse cheesemakers have led the way, but there is also a whole generation of fish smokers, artisan bakers, jam, pickle and preserve makers, and exciting cured-meat producers.

The Slow Food movement has found an enthusiastic following in Ireland; the Eurotoque Association of chefs, which aims to foster the best traditional products of an area, has led the way in supporting and encouraging the artisan food producers and has highlighted the source of the food on menus; and Bord Bia's Feile Bia Scheme has encouraged restaurant and catering businesses to incorporate local food into their menus, so at last there appears to be a growing appreciation of the value of fresh, naturally produced food in season – the wheel is coming full circle. Even as half the country is living on precooked foods from gas-station forecourts, there is a deep craving among growing numbers of people for forgotten flavours and fresh local food. This grass-roots movement is particularly evident in the crowds that flock to the farmers' markets which are springing up all over the country.

I am delighted at this revival of interest in Irish traditional food – the sort of wholesome, comforting dishes that nourished our ancestors for generations and are just as delicious today. I hope my own enthusiasm will encourage more young Irish chefs to include such things as champ and colcannon in their menus, and to cook them with pride – for simple dishes like these have already begun to appear in fashionable restaurants in London and New York. I believe we can learn a great deal from a tradition based around fresh local ingredients, simply and succulently cooked. That is what this book is all about.

Darina Allen

Foreword
The History of Food in Ireland

'The island is rich in pastures and meadows, honey and milk,' wrote Giraldus Cambrensis, the Anglo-Norman historian, who visited Ireland in 1185. Ireland's extensive coastal and inland waterways and rich agricultural lands have always supplied a bounty of varied produce and the country's culinary traditions have been evolving since prehistoric times.

Some 9,000 years ago, when the entire island was a mass of dense woodland cover of pine, birch and hazel, broken only by meandering rivers and streams, Ireland's inhabitants relied totally on the native mammals, birds, fishes and vegetation for subsistence. At Mount Sandel, near Coleraine, Co. Derry, archaeologists have discovered a prehistoric hut containing a central hearth. The area around the hut is dotted with numerous pits containing domestic refuse and debris from the hearth which show that Ireland's earliest hunter-gatherer inhabitants enjoyed a diet of wild pig, fish (including eel), birds and probably eggs and herbs. At another site, at Newferry, Co. Antrim, dated to about 6,000 B.C., there is evidence that fish were preserved by smoking over smudge fires on the river bank. Remains of charred hazelnuts and waterlily seeds have been found, and possibly of apple or pear too. Of course, these early people must also have eaten many foods from the wild such as mushrooms, herbs and tubers, which do not survive in the archaeological record.

All around the Irish coast there are sites known as shell middens, made up of masses of discarded shells. Shellfish, in particular limpets, were much sought after. The remains of fish species such as mullet, wrasse, bass, sole and tope reflect the common practice of inshore fishing and sea mammals, in particular seal, and various seabirds, such as guillemots, were also eaten by people at this time.

Some time between 4,000 and 3,000 B.C. the hunter-gatherer way of life was superseded by a lifestyle and economy based predominantly on agriculture. This was a major milestone in the evolution of Irish food. Domestic cattle, sheep, goat and pig were introduced into the country, as well as cereal crops such as wheat and barley. Woodland was cleared and houses, enclosures and field-systems built. This revolutionized the nature of Irish society, establishing a farming economy which has characterized Irish food until the present day.

The cereals introduced at this time consisted of primitive varieties which were used to prepare porridge and bread. Cattle were exceptionally important because of their milk, meat, hide and, of course, for plowing. From this time onwards, cattle and milk produce were to play an essential role in the story of Irish food. Sheep and goats were reared specifically for wool and milk. Given the value of their secondary products, they would have been eaten less than pig.

The still heavily wooded landscape was admirably suited to pig-rearing. In fact, pigs greatly assisted Ireland's Neolithic farmers because their nosing and rooting helped to prepare the ground for tillage and pasture. Pigs became increasingly important in the diet and during the Bronze Age, around 2,000 B.C., metal cauldrons were introduced for cooking them. However, hunting had not completely disappeared. As the Bronze Age gave way to the Iron Age (around 800 B.C.) there emerged a warrior aristocracy. Bands of young men belonging to this class travelled about the countryside. They survived by hunting and feeding from the wild as part of their initiation into manhood.

The early fifth century A.D. saw the introduction of Christianity to Ireland. Literacy developed from this period onward and many writings of the time provide an invaluable insight into the range and diversity of early medieval Irish food. The two staples of the early Irish diet were cereals and dairy produce. The cereals grown were oats, barley, wheat and rye and these were used to make coarse flat breads and porridge, which were eaten widely. The palatable quality of wheaten bread, compared to that of barley and oats, rendered it the luxury food of Sundays and the first choice of kings and nobles.

Butter was the most popular accompaniment to bread, since the gritty stoneground flour demanded a lubricant to assist in swallowing it. The abrasive nature of the bread and cereal should not be underestimated. Corn was ground in hand-turned rotary querns or large horizontal watermills. Inevitably pieces of stone and grit were ground down and incorporated into the flour. Archaeological excavation of medieval Dublin has revealed that over 80 percent of the skeletons showed signs of dental attrition. With the lack of effective dentistry, these people were left to endure a life of relentless pain caused by exposure of pulp and nerve cavities. Not surprisingly, more cereal was consumed in the form of porridge. Porridge also had the advantage of facilitating the incorporation of nourishing items like milk, butter and eggs.

Ale, brewed from the barley crop, was an important item of the diet and was consumed at any time of day and at main meals. However, judging from the evidence, the beer was decidedly poor. The penitenial monks make frequent reference in their writings to their vomiting after drinking high ale which was gassy and unhygienically produced.

Milk was turned into sour milk drinks, curds, soft and hard cheeses and, of course, fresh and salted butter. Most milk was drunk sour. Unpressed curds were a summer subsistence dish that could be enlivened with hazelnuts, wild garlic, wood sorrel, honey or salted butter.

Meat was an important feature of the diet, particularly for the affluent and aristocratic classes. The meats most commonly eaten were fresh and salted pork and, to a lesser extent, beef, salted beef, mutton, venison and salted venison. Generous cuts of meat were roasted on spits on open fires or boiled in cauldrons.

However, the vast majority of the populace made do with pieces of salted bacon and enjoyed fresh meat only on holy days or at times of great festivals. When this meat was served, it came with at least an inch or two of fat. A diet high in animal fat was both desired and necessary. Early Irish society suffered continuously from the ravages of famine and human and animal plague. Living with the prospect of malnutrition and plague made it imperative for everyone to carry some degree of body fat to help them make it through the hard times.

A supply of honey was important as a sweetening agent and for the production of mead and sweet bragget. Bees were considered to be so valuable in this period that they had a special law tract, *Beccbretha* (Bee Judgements), devoted entirely to their care and bee trespassing activities. Amongst many other things, the law stated that if your bees trespassed into a neighbor's land to gather pollen, then the neighbor was entitled to a proportion of your honey.

Oats, dairy produce and, to a lesser extent, salted meats continued to dominate the diet of most Irish until the widespread adoption of the potato in the eighteenth-century. Between the twelfth- and seventeenth-centuries Ireland was subject to a forceful and recurrent wave of conquest and colonization. The newcomers brought their food traditions with them which served to augment and diversify both the ingredients and cooking techniques of the native Irish.

During the twelfth century the Anglo-Normans introduced the rabbit to Ireland. The cultivation of wheat, peas and beans also increased dramatically under their influence. Maslin (mixed grain) breads of wheat and rye, and bean and pea pottages became established features of the diet in the Anglo-Norman regions of the south and east. The popularity of wheat and maslin loaves was facilitated by the introduction of the built-up oven by the Anglo-Normans and the new monastic orders who came to Ireland in the wake of the conquest.

Anglo-Norman cookery was characterized by an emphasis on spices and the tendency to mix sweet and acid ingredients in one dish. In addition the Anglo-Normans were highly concerned with the aesthetic presentation of food and they used saffron, parsley and sandalwood as food colorants. This tradition was in marked contrast to the milky, bland and coarse diet of the Gaelic Irish. Henry II, who arrived in Ireland in 1171, carried with him a vast assortment of spices and cordials, in addition to an incredible 569 pounds of almonds. The archaeological excavations of thirteenth-century levels of Dublin and Waterford have confirmed that figs, grapes and walnuts featured strongly in the diet, all of which were common ingredients in British medieval cooking. The establishment of new recipes and cooking techniques in Ireland following the Anglo-Norman conquest is evident in the subsequent importation of saffron, pepper and various other spices.

It seems likely that by at least the fourteenth-century there was a fusion of native Gaelic Irish and Anglo-Norman food patterns. By this time, the Anglo-Normans had been assimilated into Irish cultural and social ways. In an atmosphere of cultural blending, culinary exchange was inevitable.

Innovation and change also followed in the wake of the Tudor and Stuart conquests of the sixteenth- and seventeenth-centuries. The Elizabethans and the Jacobeans introduced the pheasant, the turkey and of course, most importantly, the potato. They also carried with them a more sophisticated appreciation of food and cooking. In this period the diet of the English upper classes became decidedly more cosmopolitan. Professional French chefs became a desirable addition to the kitchens of the wealthy, while the wealthy themselves frequented the new and fashionable tea and coffee houses. The conquests in Ireland saw the emergence of an Anglo-Irish gentry class with distinctively rich and varied cuisines.

It is clear that by the seventeenth-century, Ireland boasted a diversity of culinary traditions. The very basic native peasant diet of oats and dairy produce coexisted with the acquired Anglo-Norman and English traditions. A noteworthy feature of this development is that the native Irish diet of the seventeenth-century remained remarkably similar to the early medieval food patterns. In particular, dairy produce retained its place of paramount importance, as described by Fynes Moryson in his 1625 *An Itinerary:* 'They feed most on white meats, and esteem for a great dainty sour curds, vulgarly called by them "bonaclabbe". And for this cause they watchfully keep their cows and fight for them as for their religion and life; and when they are almost starved, yet they will not kill a cow, except it be old and yield no milk.'

Diet varied considerably with social status. While oats and dairy produce formed the nourishment of the peasantry, an abundance of meats and alcoholic beverage, particularly whiskey, was the prerogative of the rich as was the use of tobacco—an expensive and rare luxury at that time. However, this period was one of great transition for the Gaelic lords. Systematically weakened through political, economic and territorial insecurity, they were replaced by a host of English and Scottish newcomers. The decline of the Gaelic order is marked by the appearance of semi-fortified houses on the Irish landscape. The eighteenth-century became the era of the 'Big House' and the great kitchens of these houses prepared a refined cuisine. For example, records show that the wealthy Anglo-Irish Shapland Carew family could afford regular purchases of such luxuries as rump and sirloin steak, Bohea, Hotspur, China and green tea, coffee and chocolate, Seville and China oranges, lemons, melons, raisins and grapes, lump and brown sugar, sugar candy, lobsters and Jamaican rum.

By the nineteenth-century the potato, which had first made its appearance with the Elizabethans, had established itself as the staple foodstuff of one third of the population. It was this overdependence on the potato crop that led to the devastation of the Famine when successive harvests failed in the 1840s. Despite this, the post-Famine diet displayed a noticeable continuity with pre-Famine food traditions. Potatoes and oats still dominated. However, in the latter half of the nineteenth-century Ireland underwent a period of rapid commercialization. As a result a variety of processed goods filtered into rural regions, with grocers' shops becoming a new and exciting feature of most towns and villages. Though the farmer's wife still fed her family with home-produced goods, she also became a regular customer in the local shop, exchanging her eggs for commodities such as tea, sugar, jam and white baker's bread. By the mid-nineteenth century tea was just becoming widely available to the general populace, but initially there was confusion about it: was it a food or was it a beverage? Evidently sometimes it was considered to be both, as is evident from this story, recounted by a woman born in 1863:

> I went to visit an old woman who had lived through the famine. It was at Christmas time—Kitty (the old woman) had great welcome for us, seated us on the ground in front of the fire in the hearth.— She then got a small pot (skillet) into which she put a noggin of water, a half pound of currants, a half pound raisins (her supply for Christmas), a quarter pound of sugar and a handful of dried tea— then hung the pot over the fire until it came to the boil. Then she

broke into this brew half a loaf, removed the pot from the fire and placed it on the one and only three legged wooden stool in the house, gave each of us a wooden spoon to eat our feast out of the pot—including the tea leaves—we enjoyed it.

This account is important in illustrating the period of culinary uncertainty that invariably follows in the wake of the introduction of a new foodstuff. This was also apparent in the twentieth century when imported fruits became more widely available: some people who encountered oranges and bananas for the first time ate them skin and all. Of course, tea was not the sole preserve of the rural classes. So widespread was its popularity that it became, and still is, a fundamental aspect of the Irish psyche. In particular, tea made considerable inroads into the diet of the urban laboring classes in the early twentieth century. Although the First World War had a considerable impact on their diet, as unemployment and food prices soared, tea and white bread were the staples in many households; potatoes and some vegetables seem to have been plentiful enough.

From the late nineteenth century onward there had been a growing commercial food industry in Ireland. But despite access to factory-produced sausages and margarine, the continuing presence of tripe, potatoes and maize porridge in the diet marked the survival of older food traditions. Two recipe books provide an insight into the diets of different social classes around this time. The Clonbrock manuscript book from Castlegar, Co. Galway, offers a taste of the late nineteenth and early twentieth century upper-class diet. Specialities of this house included curried eggs, Viennoise chicken, *pomme chouxcouvert* and Swedish pancakes. A Cork recipe book dating from 1917 describes typical middle-class dishes of the period, such as steak and sausage stew, macaroni pudding and beef and bacon meat rolls.

Apart from eating at home, there was also the alternative of eating out in many of the restaurants or eating-houses (colloquially known as 'ate-in' houses) that became increasingly prevalent in the towns and cities. One such, male-dominated establishment is graphically described by James Joyce in *Ulysses:*

Perched on high stools by the bar, hats shoved back at the tables calling for more bread no charge, swilling, wolfing gobbles of sloppy food, their eyes bulging, wiping wetted moustaches. A pallid suetfaced young man polished his tumbler knife fork and spoon with his napkin. New set of microbes. A man with an infant's saucestained napkin tucked round him shovelled gurgling soup down his gullet. A man spitting back on his plate: halfmasticated gristle: no teeth to chewchewchew it. Chump chop from the grill. Bolting to get it over . . .
—Roast beef and cabbage.

Whether in a domestic or social setting, Irish food throughout the first half of the twentieth century remained overwhelmingly conservative. Much of this restrained attitude to food can be traced to the Great Famine, when the starving cottagers and laborers were forced to exploit the foods of the wild. These were labelled 'famine foods' and in the post-Famine period there was a great reluctance to eat them. In many cases even the sight of these foods evoked memories of suffering and starvation. Traditional dishes like oatencakes, pancakes and various grain preparations which were employed during food shortages became similarly stigmatized. Consequently these home-produced foods and natural ingredients were abandoned in favor of more prestigious shop-bought items. A good square meal of plain food became symbolic of economic comfort and security. Until well into the 1960s the average Irish dinner was the invariable trio of meat, vegetables and potatoes, bulked out with white buttered bread and washed down with lashings of strong tea.

In the 1960s the forces of change again began to exert an influence on Irish food. This was a period of noticeable economic prosperity. The vacation tour industry took many to foreign countries for the first time, where they encountered the exciting diversity of ethnic foods. Slowly Mediterranean and Eastern cuisines were introduced to Ireland and accepted, at least in urban areas. Today a visit to any Irish supermarket will demonstrate the multicultural nature of Irish food.

In addition, there has been an upsurge in indigenous food developments. The Irish food industry has become more confident in the range and quality of Irish products. Agricultural produce and wild foods, such as seaweeds, coarse fishes and shellfish, have earned international esteem. An excellent manifestation of this new-found culinary confidence is the rebirth of the farmhouse cheese industry, which has deservedly won national and international acceptance.

Irish food is as complex as the many cultural, political and economic forces that have shaped Ireland's existence. It is time to broaden our appreciation of Irish food and to realize that the tradition goes far beyond dishes of Irish stew, or bacon and cabbage. Tasty as these dishes may be, the Irish table has a wider diversity of offerings. With unique insight, an Irish food writer has sliced through the cultural complexities of Irish food and has presented us with a varied plate of rich and wholesome delicacies. This book must surely stand as an enormous and timely contribution to the social and culinary history of Ireland.

Regina Sexton

Broths & Soups

Brotchán or broth was an integral part of the diet in early Ireland. Earliest broths were little more than oatmeal boiled with water. Meat was seldom added because it rarely entered the diet of the poor. The broth would have been nourishing, however, because the oatmeal would have been homegrown, as indeed would the vegetables. In coastal areas, seaweeds such as carageen, laver, dulse and sloke would have been added.

Brotchán is referred to in the ninth century text *The Monastery of Tallaght,* where the broth is described as one of the main meals of the penitent monks. On occasion, some milk was added and this was considered a great luxury.

Brotchán Roy

Serves 2

8oz leeks, washed
2 tablespoons butter
2 cups stock or milk or water
1/2 cup oatmeal
salt and freshly ground pepper
pinch of powdered mace
1 tablespoon parsley

One of the most famous of these broths was made with leeks and was called Brotchán Roy *meaning 'A broth fit for a king' (Roy derives from* Rí, *the Irish word for king). This broth is also called* Brotchan Foltchep *after the main ingredients, leeks, possibly the perennial Babington leek a vegetable frequently mentioned in old manuscripts.*

Slice the white and pale green part of the leeks finely. Melt the butter in a saucepan, toss in the leeks, cook for a minute or two, add the liquid, bring to a boil then sprinkle in the oatmeal. Bring back to a boil, stirring all the time, season with salt, freshly ground pepper and a pinch of mace. Cover and simmer for about 45 minutes or until both vegetables and oatmeal are cooked. Add the parsley, boil for a minute or two, then serve.

Note: *There is considerable academic debate about the translation of* foltchep *and it has been variously rendered as leek or onion.*

Mutton Broth

Serves 6

1 lb lean neck of lamb
10oz diced carrot
6oz diced onion
2 leeks, chopped
1 turnip, diced
1 tablespoon pearl barley
salt and freshly ground pepper
7 1/2 to 8 1/2 cups water
chopped parsley

This would have been cooked in a big black pot over the open fire, with bits of scrawny mutton to give it flavor, and a few fistfuls of pearl barley for extra nourishment. It doesn't sound very promising, but this very traditional soup tastes delicious.

Cut up the meat into small cubes. Put all the ingredients except the parsley into a saucepan, season with salt and freshly ground pepper. Add the water, cover and bring to a boil, simmer for 1 1/2 to 2 hours.

Taste and correct the seasoning. Stir in lots of freshly-chopped parsley and serve hot.

Chicken Broth

Serves 8 (approximately)

2 to 3 raw and/or cooked chicken carcases, or stewing fowl, or jointed giblets from the chicken, i.e. neck, heart, or gizzard
15 cups approx. cold water
1 or 2 sliced onions
1 or 2 sliced carrots
few parsley stalks
sprig of thyme
6 peppercorns
salt

Chicken broth was the cure-all in many Irish homes—warm, nourishing and soothing when one was cold or under the weather. It was a particularly valuable remedy for those who were endeavoring to recover from self-inflicted suffering!

I still find a bowl of broth, filled with soggy white bread and butter one of the most comforting things in the whole world.

Chop up the carcases as much as possible. Put all the ingredients except the salt into a saucepan and cover with cold water. Bring to a boil and skim the fat off the top with a tablespoon. Simmer for 3 to 4 hours. Strain and remove any remaining fat. If you need a stronger flavor, boil down the liquid in an open pan to reduce by one-third or one-half the volume. Add a little salt towards the end of the cooking.

Broth will keep several days in the refrigerator. If you want to keep it for longer, boil it up again for 5 to 6 minutes every couple of days; allow it to get cold and refrigerate again. Broth also freezes perfectly.

Nettles made their appearance in Ireland almost six thousand years ago as the first farmers started to cut down forest trees to clear the ground for their crop cultivation.

In the 'Saints' Lives' from the *Book of Lismore* there is a story of how St. Colum Cille came upon a woman cutting nettles to make herself a pottage. She explained that this was her diet until her cow calved, when of course she would have milk, cream, butter and perhaps some cheese.

Stinging nettles still grow in great profusion throughout the Irish countryside. Use gloves when you are gathering them so as not to roast yourself! Maura Laverty in *Kind Cooking* describes how people would draw 'old footless black woollen stockings' over their hands for protection. With their high iron content, nettles were prominent in Irish folk medicine, and like many other wild foods they helped in some small measure to alleviate hunger during the famine.

Nettle Soups

Serves 6 (approximately)

Irish Nettle Soup

Melt the butter in a heavy-bottomed saucepan. When it foams, add the potatoes, onions and leeks and toss them in the butter until well coated. Sprinkle with salt and freshly ground pepper. Cover with a paper lid (to keep in the steam) and the lid of the saucepan, then sweat on a gentle heat for approximately 10 minutes, or until the vegetables are soft but not colored. Discard the paper lid. Add the stock and boil until the vegetables are just cooked. Add the chopped nettle leaves. Simmer uncovered for just a few minutes. Be careful not to overcook or the vegetables will discolor and also lose their flavor. Add the cream or milk and purée. Taste and correct seasoning if necessary. Serve hot.

3 tablespoons butter
2¹/2 cups potatoes, chopped
1 cup onion, chopped
2 medium sized leeks, chopped
salt and freshly ground pepper
4¹/2 cups chicken stock
5oz young nettles, washed and chopped
²/3 cup cream or creamy milk

This recipe, given to me by 90-year-old Lil O'Connell from Co. Tipperary, is quite different to the previous nettle soup recipe. It makes a rich and nourishing broth. Her family lived on a 'strong farm' and ate this broth in late spring every year. The nettles were measured in a 2-pint measure.

Serves 8 (approximately)

Nettle Broth

Cut up the meat and place in a pot with the barley. Cover with the cold water. Bring to a boil and simmer over a low fire for 2 hours. Add the chopped nettles and scallions, and cook slowly for a further half hour. Season the broth to taste.

2lb stewing beef
1 cup pearl barley
10 cups water
5 cups of nettles, chopped
bunch of scallions, chopped
salt and pepper

Watercress Soup

Serves 6-8

3 tablespoons butter
1¼ cups potatoes, peeled and chopped
1¼ cups chopped onion
salt and freshly ground pepper
2½ cups water or homemade
chicken stock
2½ cups creamy milk
2 bunches of chopped watercress
(remove the coarse stalks)

Watercress is frequently mentioned as a foodstuff in the twelfth-century manuscript Agallamh na Seanórach (The Colloquy of the Old Men). *Legend has it that it was watercress that enabled St Brendan to live to the ripe old age of 180! In Birr Castle in Co. Offaly, Lord and Lady Rosse still serve a soup of watercress gathered from around St Brendan's Well, just below the castle walls.*

Melt the butter in a heavy-bottomed saucepan. When it foams, add the potatoes and onions and toss until well coated. Sprinkle with salt and freshly ground pepper. Cover and sweat on a gentle heat for 10 minutes. Add the stock and milk, bring to a boil and cook until the potatoes and onions are soft. Add the watercress and boil with the lid off for approximately 4 to 5 minutes until the watercress is cooked. It will taste soft and tender. Do not overcook or the soup will lose its fresh green color. Purée the soup in a blender or food processor. Taste and add a little more salt and pepper if necessary.

St Brendan's Well at Birr Castle

Irish people love a warm comforting vegetable soup. Ours changes throughout the year, depending on what is in the garden or available in our local shops and markets.

Melt the butter in a heavy saucepan. When it foams, add the potatoes, onions and vegetables and turn them until well coated. Sprinkle with salt and freshly ground pepper. Cover and sweat on a gentle heat for 10 minutes. Add the stock. Boil until soft, about 15 minutes. Do not overcook or the vegetables will lose their flavor. Purée and add creamy milk. Taste and correct seasoning.

Serves 6
Vegetable Soup

4 tablespoons butter
1¼ cups potatoes, peeled and chopped
1 cup peeled diced onions
3½ cups chopped vegetables of your choice,
    e.g. carrot, parsnip and celery
salt and freshly ground pepper
4½ cups homemade chicken stock
²⁄₃ cup creamy milk (optional)

Despite the fact that Ireland has a rich variety of fungi, the common field mushroom (agaricus campestris) *is virtually the only variety that most people will risk eating.* Agaricus campestris *are most likely to appear in unfertilized grassland grazed by sheep or horses; sand dunes are also worth a search if the weather turns warm and humid between July and the end of September.*

This recipe is wonderfully quick and easy to prepare, with a marvellously intense mushroom flavour. Large flat cultivated mushrooms may be used as an alternative and the result is almost as delicious.

Melt the butter in a saucepan on a gentle heat. Toss the onions in it, cover and sweat until soft and completely cooked. Meanwhile check over the mushrooms carefully, wash both caps and stalks quickly and chop very finely. Add to the saucepan and cook for a further 3 or 4 minutes. Now stir in the flour, cook on a low heat for 2 to 3 minutes, season with salt and freshly ground pepper, then add the stock and milk gradually, stirring all the time. Increase the heat and bring to a boil. Taste and add a dash of cream if necessary.

Serves 8-9
Wild Mushroom Soup

3 to 4 tablespoons butter
1 cup very finely chopped onion
1 lb field mushrooms
3 tablespoons flour
salt and freshly ground pepper
2½ cups homemade chicken stock
2½ cups milk

Lucy Madden from Hilton Park in Co. Monaghan, one of Ireland's most charming country house hotels, made this delicious soup for me from the organically grown vegetables in her garden.

Melt the butter in a heavy-bottomed saucepan on a low heat, add the onions and potatoes, season with salt and freshly ground pepper and sweat until soft but not colored. Add the stock and boil for 5 minutes. Snip the lovage leaves into thin strips with a scissors. Put 3 tablespoons into the soup and cook for a further 10 minutes. Serve with a sprinkling of snipped lovage and a little chopped fresh parsley.

Serves 6
Potato, Onion & Lovage Soup

1 to 2 tablespoons butter
3 medium sized onions, very thinly sliced
3 medium sized potatoes, thinly sliced
salt and freshly ground pepper
5 cups good homemade chicken or
    vegetable stock
3 tablespoons lovage leaves

Garnish
Lovage and parsley

Potato & Fresh Herb Soup

Serves 6

4 tablespoons butter
1¼ cups diced onions
1½ lbs peeled diced potatoes
1 teaspoon salt
freshly ground pepper
1 tablespoon in total of the following chopped
fresh herbs: parsley, thyme, lemon balm,
chives and marjoram
3½ cups homemade chicken stock
½ cup creamy milk

This is one of the most delicious of all soups when made with good Irish potatoes and the bonus of fresh herbs which would have been found in a monastery garden years ago. According to Dr Synott of the National Botanic Gardens in Dublin, culinary and medicinal herbs are likely to have been brought from the continent by returning Irish monks during the early Christian period.

Melt the butter in a heavy saucepan. When it foams, add the onions and potatoes and toss them in the butter until well coated. Sprinkle with salt and pepper. Cover and sweat on a gentle heat for 10 minutes. Add the fresh herbs (reserving a little for garnish) and the stock, and cook until the vegetables are soft. Purée the soup in a blender or food processor. Taste and adjust seasoning. Thin with creamy milk to the required consistency. Serve sprinkled with the remaining chopped herbs.

Note: *If you don't have any fresh herbs just leave them out; the soup will still be very good. Dried herbs give too strong a flavor. Fresh parsley is widely available and would be delicious chopped and sprinkled over the top.*

Oatmeal Soup

Serves 4

1 large onion
1 bowlful of cold cooked oatmeal porridge
stock or water to cover
salt and pepper
1¼ cups skim milk

Nina Farren from Tyrone sent me this intriguing recipe for a very old and absolutely basic soup. It dates from an era when the primary function of food was to keep alive. Part of our heritage, but not exactly dinner party fare!

Peel and slice the onion and put in a saucepan with the porridge. Cover with stock, add salt and pepper. Boil until the onion is tender.

Add the milk and boil up again. Taste!

It is probable that peas existed in Ireland as early as the seventh and eighth centuries, as there is a reference to peas in the Brehon laws tract Bretha Déin Chécht. *It is also evident that 'pea pottage' was widespread by 1700 and had replaced bread in the diet of the communities settled by the Anglo-Normans from the twelfth century onwards.*

Peas were not only used in pottage and soup making, but ground pea meal was also used in breadmaking, in times of poor harvests when corn was scarce.

This soup can be made in winter quite successfully with frozen peas, or with dried split green peas which have been soaked. In the latter case, the cooking time will have to be prolonged to an hour.

Melt the butter and sweat the onion gently until soft but not golden. Add the bacon and fry for another 2 or 3 minutes. Pour in the stock, bring to a boil, add the peas and simmer until they are cooked. (If you are using dried peas add them to the cold stock. It is particularly important not to add salt before they are cooked.) Purée, taste and correct seasoning, adding a little sugar and more stock if necessary. Reheat, sprinkle with parsley and serve.

Serves 6
Pea Soup

12oz shelled peas or 4oz dried split peas soaked overnight in cold water
4 tablespoons butter
1¼ cups chopped onion
3 slices bacon, finely chopped
5 cups chicken stock or bacon or ham cooking water
salt, freshly ground pepper and sugar
chopped parsley

This recipe came from the Kitchen Book of Clonbrock:

Boil the pods in water till quite tender with a small handful of green onions and a sprig of mint—pound in the mortar and add the remains of any thick soup, or some good white sauce. Put back into the pan to heat, then pass through a tammy of fine sieve—if the purée is too thick add some stock. When wanted for table to be made hot, but not boiling a pinch of sugar and a pat of fresh butter stirred in just before serving—a few peas added look well.

Green Pea Pod Soup

Wash the peas before steeping (soaking overnight). Next day, prepare and chop the rest of the vegetables and fry in butter for 5 minutes. Add water (or stock) and peas and ham bone. Simmer until all are soft and remove the bone. Rub the soup through a sieve, add flour blended in the milk and boil for 5 minutes, stirring constantly. Season and serve.

Serves 6-8
Pea Soup

1¼ cups dried peas, soaked overnight or longer
onion, carrot, piece of turnip and parsnip, herbs
2 tablespoons butter
5 cups water or stock
ham bone or bacon rind
1¼ cups milk
3 tablespoons flour
seasoning

Serves 8-10

Jerusalem Artichoke Soup

with Crispy Croutons

2¹/₂lb Jerusalem artichokes,
peeled and chopped
4 tablespoons butter
1¹/₄lb onions, peeled and chopped
1¹/₄lb potatoes, peeled and chopped
salt and freshly ground pepper
5 cups light chicken stock
about 2¹/₂ cups creamy milk

Garnish
freshly chopped parsley
crisp, golden croutons

Pheasants have a particular weakness for Jerusalem artichokes, so most country houses with a big shooting estate cultivate a patch, and often treat their shooters to Jerusalem artichoke soup after a morning's sport.

Artichokes are a nuisance to peel, but if they are very fresh you can sometimes get away with just giving them a good scrub.

Melt the butter in a heavy-bottomed saucepan; add the onions, potatoes and artichokes. Season with salt and freshly ground pepper, cover and sweat gently for approximately 10 minutes. Add the stock and cook until the vegetables are soft. Purée and return to the heat. Thin to the required flavor and consistency with creamy milk, and adjust the seasoning to your own taste.

Serve in soup bowls or in a soup tureen. Garnish with chopped parsley and crisp, golden croutons.

If you live near a rocky strand, look out for sea spinach—its shiny green leaves are unmistakeable. It can be cooked exactly like garden spinach and also makes a delicious soup. Not surprisingly, it is full of iodine, minerals and other trace elements, and has an addictive salty tang. As with all marine plants and shellfish it should be gathered from an area where the water is clean and unpolluted.

Melt the butter in a heavy-bottomed saucepan. When it foams add the potatoes and onions and turn them until well coated. Sprinkle with salt and freshly ground pepper. Cover and sweat on a gentle heat for 10 minutes. Bring the stock to a boil and add it with the milk. Bring back to a simmer and cook until the potatoes and onions are soft. Add the spinach and simmer with the lid off for about 3 to 5 minutes, until the spinach is cooked. Do not overcook or the soup will lose its fresh green color. Purée, taste and add some freshly grated nutmeg. Serve in warm bowls garnished with a dollop of whipped cream and some chopped parsley.

Serves 6-8

Sea Spinach Soup

8 to 12oz chopped sea spinach
4 tablespoons butter
1¼ cups chopped potatoes
1 cup chopped onion
salt and freshly ground pepper
2 cups homemade chicken stock
2 to 2½ cups creamy milk
    (¼ cream and ¾ milk)
freshly grated nutmeg

Garnish:
2 tablespoons whipped cream (optional)
freshly chopped parsley

Lobster Soup

I have transcribed this recipe faithfully directly from a receipt book found among the Pakenham Mahon papers at Strokestown Park in Co. Roscommon. It illustrates the extraordinarily sophisticated food that was eaten in the homes of the Anglo-Irish gentry in the late eighteenth century. The lobster would have been brought specially from the coast by pony and trap over sixty miles on bumpy roads.

Make a good stock of variety of fresh meats a bit of lean bacon and vegetables particularly celery. Have ready the shells of three good lobsters their coral and the red part that sticks to the shells pounded together as fine as you can, strain and skim the stock, then put in the Lobster, boil it very well for a quart of an hour, strain it through a thick sieve or towel add the crust of a French roll cut in small pieces and let it simmer 'till the bread is soft. You may thicken it with a quart of a pound of fresh butter and a spoonful of flower browned if you chose and some put in the fish of the Lobster cut in pieces.

This receit was got from a gentleman who brought it from Germany as the method of making cray fish soop there. We substituted lobster and I think it was the best soop I ever saw.

Cocklety Soup

Serves 6

Cockles have formed part of the Irish diet since earliest times. Archaeological remains have been found at early historic sites such as Oughtymore, Co. Derry, Park Cave, Co. Antrim and Potters Cave, Co. Antrim. Cockles formed the mainstay of the diet along the coastal regions during the great potato famine of 1845. The Congested District Board Records also tell of how cockle gathering was widespread around Donegal on the eve of the great famine.

4 dozen cockles
1 to 2 tablespoons water
2 tablespoons butter
1 small onion, finely chopped
1 stick chopped celery
3 tablespoons flour
2¹/2 cups creamy milk
¹/2 cup heavy cream
1 to 2 tablespoons chopped parsley
salt and pepper

Wash and scrub the cockles well in several changes of water, to get rid of the sand and grit. Then put them in a large saucepan with a tablespoon or two of water, cover and steam for 4 to 5 minutes until the cockles are open. Discard any that do not open. Strain the cooking liquid and set aside. As soon as they are cool enough to handle, remove the cockles from their shells.

Melt the butter in a saucepan. Add the onion and celery and sweat over a gentle heat until soft but not colored. Stir in the flour, then add the strained cockle juice and milk. Cook for a minute or two, stirring all the time, until the soup is smooth and silky. Add the cream and chopped parsley and season with salt and freshly ground pepper. Simmer gently for 10 minutes. Finally add the cockles.

Bairneachs (limpets)

On Cape Clear *bairneachs* were regarded as 'poor people's food' and there was a *sean fhocal* (old saying) 'Avoid the public house or you will end up eating *bairneachs*'. There was a special device for getting the bairneachs off the rocks and it was called an *eisitean*. It was a bit like a chisel and was made by the blacksmith.

If there was a weed growing on the *bairneach,* that was prized. It might be a type of *trapain* or *dulamain* or green shiny stuff, but it was nevertheless left on the shell and it added to the flavor of the soup after boiling. They didn't call it Bairneach Soup on Cape Clear, but *Saile Bairneach*—the word *saile* comes from the Irish word for seawater.

Bairneach Soup

Serves 6 (approximately)

Bairneach is the Gaelic name for limpet (a conical shellfish with a grooved shell). I had never picked bairneachs so I was intrigued to discover how to prize them off the rocks. John Guerin, from Ballyheigue in Co. Kerry, remembered the best spot to find the choicest bairneachs; it was down a long boreen and in July the hedges were full of wild flowers. Suddenly there below us was the mouth of the Shannon harbor. The water sparkled in the morning sun and the flat, sloping rocks were speckled with limpets and seed mussels. Like lightning, John was down on his hands and knees, slicing the bairneachs off the rock with a quick flick of the chisel. I got the hang of it after a few attempts. I soon realized the truth of the expression 'sticks like a limpet'. If you hesitate the limpet, forewarned, tightens its grip and is simply unmovable, so speed in your attack is of the essence!

4¹/2lb bairneachs (limpets)
3¹/2 cups cold water (Bridget says you should put in a sup of salt water)
2 tablespoons flour
butter

Don't wash the *bairneach* first. Put them into a saucepan, add water, bring to a boil and simmer for about 10 minutes. Pour off the liquid and save.

Put the *bairneachs* out onto a dish. Pick off the shells and discard. Then de-horn the *bairneachs*. To do this catch the two small protruding tentacles and draw out the trail—it looks like a long thin string.

Strain the liquid gently back into the saucepan, keeping back any sand. Add the *bairneachs*, bring to a boil and simmer for 30 to 45 minutes. Whisk the flour into ²/3 cup water; pour into the boiling liquid, whisking all the time. Allow to thicken and stir in a big lump of butter.

The mussels I use for this soup come from the clean waters of Kilmackillogue harbor on the Beara Peninsula. Clare Connery, in her excellent book In an Irish Country Kitchen, *maintains that saffron was widely used throughout the eighteenth century to add color to mussel soup.*

Put the wine, shallots, garlic, herbs, saffron or curry powder and pepper into the saucepan, add the mussels, cover and steam open in the wine and flavorings. Shell the mussels and place them in a bowl. Discard the shells. Strain the mussel cooking liquor into an enamelled or stainless steel saucepan and rapidly boil it down over high heat to concentrate its flavor. Taste it frequently as it boils. You may find that if you reduce it too much, the salt content will be overpowering.

Thicken the mussel liquor with the roux shown here to attain a thickish liquid. Add the boiling milk to thin out the soup to a light consistency. Just before serving, add mussels and a little cream. Decorate with chopped parsley or chervil.

Serve croutons separately.

Serves 8

Ballymaloe Mussel Soup

8 to 10lb scrubbed mussels
2 cups light dry white wine
8 tablespoons chopped shallots, or very finely chopped onion
1 clove garlic, mashed
8 parsley sprigs, $^1/_2$ bay leaf,
    $^1/_4$ teaspoon fresh thyme leaves,
    a sprig of fresh fennel
a good pinch of saffron or
    $^1/_4$ teaspoon curry powder (optional)
$^1/_8$ teaspoon ground pepper
Heavy cream

Roux
5 tablespoons butter
$^1/_2$ cup flour
$2^1/_2$ to 5 cups boiling milk

Garnish
croutons and chopped parsley or chervil

Serves 6-8

Oyster Soup

Oysters are one of the oldest foodstuffs in Ireland: there is archaeological evidence of their use from the Later Mesolithic period (Middle Stone Age from c.5,500 B.C. onward). Exploration and excavation around Cork harbour has uncovered at least 20 major shell middens which include substantial quantities of oyster shells.

According to Edward MacLysaght, who edited The Kenmare Manuscripts, *in Dublin in the years 1753-4 it was possible to purchase as many as one hundred oysters for two shillings.*

This old recipe, which came from Ballymoney in Co. Antrim, was obviously made when oysters were cheaper and more plentiful than they are nowadays.

2 large potatoes
36 fresh oysters
3 tablespoons butter
4oz salt pork, diced
4 cups milk
1 bouquet garni
salt and freshly ground pepper
chopped parsley

Cook the potatoes in boiling salted water until just tender. Open the oysters into a sieve over a bowl. Melt a little butter and fry the diced belly of pork over a gentle heat until just tender. Bring the milk to a boil with a *bouquet garni*, turn off the heat and infuse for a few minutes. Peel the cooked potatoes and mash in a saucepan with the milk. Add the pork as soon as it is tender, and season to taste. Bring to a boil stirring all the time. Add the oysters and their liquid and simmer for a few minutes. Adjust seasoning and stir in the remaining butter. Serve at once sprinkled with chopped parsley.

Beef kidney makes a particularly rich and delicious winter soup which always brings back memories of the delicious dinners my mother had ready unfailingly for us, when we raced up the hill from Cullohill National School at 12 o'clock each day.

Peel the kidney, remove all the 'plumbing' and cut into small dice. Put them into a bowl, and cover with cold water with a good pinch of salt. Allow to soak while you prepare the vegetables. Drain the kidney and dry on paper towels. Toss in lightly seasoned flour. Melt the butter in a saucepan, add the kidney and vegetables and toss for a minute or two in the butter. Season with salt and freshly ground pepper, add the beef stock, bring to a boil and simmer until tender (45 minutes to 1 hour).

Before the days of blenders and food processors, the soup would have been painstakingly rubbed through a sieve at this point, but nowadays you can simply process it for a minute or two (saving a little kidney for garnish). Serve piping hot with chopped parsley and a few croûtons.

Serves 6-8

Kidney Soup

12oz beef kidney
1 cup chopped onion
1³/4 cups chopped carrot
1 white turnip, finely chopped
3 sticks celery, finely chopped
seasoned flour
4 tablespoons butter
salt and freshly ground pepper
7¹/2 cups beef stock
chopped parsley and croutons to serve

This recipe would have been used for the giblets of all sorts of fowl in earlier times, when not a scrap of food was ever wasted. This particular recipe came from near Two Mile Borris in Co. Tipperary. The dumplings, simmered in the tasty broth, made a soup sustaining enough for a man out plowing or sowing crops.

Put the giblets (neck, head, flying wings, feet, gizzard, heart) into a pot with the chopped onion, carrot, parsley and thyme. Cover with cold water, bring to a boil and simmer for about 2 hours.

While the broth is cooking make the dumplings. Mix all the ingredients together and make into a pliable dough, adding a little milk if the mixture is too dry. Form into a roll and cut into eight pieces.

Add the dumplings to the broth. Season with salt and freshly ground pepper and simmer for 30 minutes or until the dumplings are tender!

Sprinkle with chopped parsley and serve in old fashioned soup bowls.

Note: *Nowadays it might be advisable to remove the head and feet before serving, unless you want to risk a mutiny!*

Serves 4 (approximately)

Giblet Soup with Dumplings

Soup
giblets from 1 goose or several chickens
1 large onion, chopped
1 carrot, chopped
sprig of parsley
sprig of thyme
cold water

Potato Dumplings
2 cups cooked mashed potatoes
2 cups flour
1/2 teaspoon baking powder
1/2 teaspoon mixed herbs (optional)
1 small onion, minced finely
pepper
salt
a little milk

Eggs

There is a popular legend in Irish folklore that hens were introduced into Ireland by the Danes, but it is impossible to ascertain whether this is really so. However, we know from the eighth-century Brehon Laws that hens and geese were a regular sight around most farmsteads. The ninth-century *Monastery of Tallaght* indicates that in the rigidly sparse diet of the extreme penitent monks, the *Célé Dé*, "dry eggs" are permitted.

Eggs continued to be a staple food into more recent times. In John Dunton's *Letters from Ireland* in 1698, he recounts a dinner he enjoyed in Dublin of 'salt fish and eggs, hen and bacon and rabbits'. Throughout the nineteenth and early twentieth centuries, the poultry trade reached its peak in Ireland. In rural areas poultry rearing was considered exclusively women's work. The women bartered the eggs with the village or town grocers in return for luxuries such as tea, sugar and tobacco. This domestic industry, dominated by women, was of immense economic importance in contributing to paying the rent and running the household.

While the hens cared for themselves during the day, often roosting in nearby trees and hedges, they were always housed at night to protect them from predators. In some cottages, the hens spent the night on a rope or pole, hung across the kitchen from eave to eave, and they laid their eggs in nesting baskets of woven straw or rushes.

Easter Eggs

Even though Easter is the most important Christian festival, the word Easter is linked to the pagan cult of the Saxon goddess of spring, Eostre. The eggs universally associated with Easter are ancient symbols of spring, rebirth and resurrection.

It seems to me likely that the Easter egg tradition is also rooted in the ancient custom of Lenten fasting, which was common to both Eastern and Western Christendom. The last eggs were eaten up in the form of pancakes on Shrove Tuesday, but as the hens didn't know it was Lent, they went on laying! The surplus of eggs which accumulated was enjoyed at Easter in all sorts of different ways.

In Ireland, traditionally, some were hard-boiled with natural dyes, such as herbs, flowers, lichen or onion skins, to colour their shells. Eggs laid on Good Friday were considered blessed and these, marked with a cross, were cooked for breakfast on Easter Sunday. Everyone was expected to eat their share of eggs in one form or another, and anyone who couldn't manage at least two or three was considered to be very feeble.

Fried Eggs

In 1732, Mrs Mary Delaney, who was the wife of Patrick Delaney, the Dean of Down, wrote of her husband 'the greatest feast to him is fried egg and bacon'.

Crispy at the edges and soft in the center, fried eggs are probably the most common way of cooking eggs in Ireland—and they can be utterly delicious if one starts with a perfectly fresh free-range egg. Cook it in sizzling bacon fat, olive oil or even pure beef dripping, and serve immediately. The same thing is a travesty when a stale battery-produced egg is cooked in cheap oil. Sadly superlative fried eggs, simple as they sound, are 'as rare as hen's teeth' nowadays.

Heat a little pure bacon fat, butter or olive oil in a frying pan. When it is just about sizzling, break in the eggs, one at a time, but don't overcrowd the pan. Cook over a low heat if you like the eggs soft underneath, or on a higher heat if you like them crispy. Cook until the white is just set but the yolk soft. Baste with hot fat if you like the top filmed over, or cover the pan with a lid. Flip them over gently with a fish slice if that's your preference. Serve immediately on warm but not hot plates.

Buttered Eggs

One of the most exciting things I have discovered while working on this book is Buttered Eggs. This traditional way of preserving eggs for the short term is likely to have originated in the nineteenth century. At this time, Ireland was exporting an astonishing number of eggs to Britain, where there was a great demand for eggs. For example, in 1850 Ireland exported eleven million eggs annually and this figure rose to forty million by 1900.

This practice deserves to be more widely known for the wonderful flavor and texture it produces. Anyone who has their own hens can try it. The crucial thing is that the eggs must be collected from the nest as soon as they are laid, and their shells rubbed with a thin layer of butter while they are still warm. This seals in the freshness, so the albumen stays soft and curdy when boiled or poached. Buttered eggs are a great speciality in Cork and are still sold in the Old English Market in Cork city.

Eggs have always been popular in the Irish diet; hen's and geese eggs are the main types mentioned in early Irish sources. The ninth century-poem Marbán Gúaire *celebrates them in glowing terms:*

... delightful feasts come ...
A clutch of eggs, honey, mast
... sweet apples ...

My mother used to make this tasty egg snack for us when we were little, particularly if we were feeling fragile. As far as I can gather it was very common throughout Ireland. Eamonn Mac Thomáis, Dublin's popular social historian, remembers it as 'Gug-gug'.

Bring a small saucepan of water to a boil and slip the egg in gently. Bring the water back to a boil and cook for approximately 4 minutes. Meanwhile warm a teacup. (My mother usually did this with hot water from the kettle kept ever boiling on the side of her Aga oven.)

Pop the egg into an egg cup as soon as it is cooked. Remove the top and spoon out all the inside into the warm dry cup. Chop with a spoon and immediately add about 1 tablespoon of soft white breadcrumbs, a lump of butter and pepper and salt to taste. Eat immediately with a teaspoon.

Serves 1

Egg in a Cup

1 fresh egg
white breadcrumbs
butter
salt and freshly ground pepper

Buttered Eggs

Boiled Eggs & Dippies

2 fresh eggs
salt and freshly ground pepper
a few pats of butter
1 slice of fresh white bread, not presliced

Mothers all over Ireland cut up fingers of toast for children to dip into soft boiled eggs. In my husband Tim's family they were called soldiers, but we called them dippies.

Bring a small saucepan of water to a boil and gently slide in the eggs., Bring the water back to a boil and simmer gently for 4 to 6 minutes, according to your taste. A four-minute egg will be still quite soft. Five minutes will almost set the white while the yolk will still be runny, and six minutes will produce a boiled egg with a soft yolk and solid white.

Meanwhile toast the bread, cut off the crusts and spread with butter. Cut in fingers. As soon as the eggs are cooked, pop them into egg cups, put the dippies on the side and serve with a pepper mill, sea salt and a few pats of butter.

Oven Toasted Cheese

Serves 2

2 slices of white bread
1 egg, preferably free range
1 cup (4oz) grated Irish cheddar cheese
1/2 to 1 teaspoon English mustard
salt and freshly ground pepper

When my children were small this superior toasted cheese often saved the day if they were ravenously hungry. It is made from ingredients that are nearly always to hand.

Butter the bread and place the buttered side down on a baking sheet. Whisk the egg in a bowl with a fork, add the grated cheese and the mustard and season well with salt and freshly ground pepper. Spread this mixture evenly on to both the slices of bread and bake in a hot oven (450°F) for about 15 minutes, or until puffy and golden on the top.

Note: *a teaspoon of chopped chives or a few tiny dice of crispy bacon are also delicious added to the mixture.*

This recipe comes from Nina Farren from Co. Tyrone, who was taught how to make it by her grandmother.

Irishman's Omelet

4oz bacon
1 cup chopped onion
2 medium sized potatoes, peeled, boiled and diced
1 tablespoon chopped fresh parsley
2 teaspoons chopped fresh chives
salt and freshly ground pepper
2 tablespoons lard or butter
2 eggs, beaten

Trim any rind from the bacon and cut into tiny pieces. Fry the bacon until crisp and remove to a plate. Sweat the onion for a few minutes in the bacon fat, add the diced potato, bacon, freshly chopped herbs and seasoning to the pan. Stir in the well-beaten eggs and cook over a gentle heat until the eggs are set.

Flip over onto a hot plate and serve immediately.

Serves 1

Kidney Omelet

A trip to Dublin with my father was a stupendous treat when I was a child; the occasion was sometimes a rugby match or a visit to see my mother in the Baggot Street Nursing Home and inspect the latest addition to the family. Absolutely everything was exciting but what I looked forward to more than anything else was a meal 'in a hotel' before our long journey home. Often it was the Clarence on Wellington Quay where the distinguished looking silver-haired maître d'hôtel, Willie James, led us to our table in his tail coat and starched shirt with butterfly collar. Affable Paddy Gannon invariably served our table with that wonderful old-fashioned courteous service that is almost impossible to find nowadays. I ordered the same menu almost every time, kidney omelet followed by crispy fried plaice. I don't remember what I ate for dessert—I expect it must have been ice cream—but it is the flavor of the tender kidney omelet that remains with me.

1 lamb's kidney
a little butter
1 teaspoon freshly chopped parsley
2 eggs
2 teaspoons water or milk
salt and freshly ground pepper
2 teaspoons clarified butter or olive oil

Clean and dice the kidney, cook gently in a little butter, add most of the chopped parsley and keep warm.

Warm a plate in the oven. Beat the eggs with the water or milk in a bowl with a fork or whisk, until thoroughly mixed but not too fluffy. Season with salt and freshly ground pepper. Put the plate beside the cooker.

Heat a 9-inch non-stick omelette pan over a high heat and add the clarified butter. As soon as it sizzles, pour in the egg mixture. It will start to cook immediately, so quickly pull the edges of the omelet towards the center with a metal spoon or spatula, tilting the pan so that the uncooked egg runs to the sides. Continue until most of the egg is set and will not run any more, then leave the omelet to cook for a further 10 seconds to brown the bottom. Spoon the cooked kidney in a line along the center.

To fold the omelet: Flip the edge just below the handle of the pan into the center, then hold the pan almost perpendicular over the plate so that the omelet will flip over again, then half roll half slide the omelet onto the plate so that it lands with the folds underneath. (It should not take more than 45 seconds in all to make the omelet.)

Serve immediately on the warm plate, garnished with a little parsley.

Fish

I now live within sight of the sea, but when I was a child our family used to live in Co. Laois in the midlands, just about as far from the sea as it is possible to be in Ireland.

Fish, when we could get it, was eaten on Friday —a fast day. Whatever was available that day was dropped off in our village by the bus traveling from Dublin to Cork. Plaice, our favorite, was not always there. Smoked haddock, or red fish as it was called, was a certainty; we could always see the luminous orange fillets packed in a timber box. Whiting arrived almost every week in season, and although we found it less interesting than plaice, it could be tender and melting when fried in a coating of flour, egg and breadcrumbs or steamed in the old-fashioned way between two plates. This was a common way of dealing with whiting before ovens were widespread.

Baked Cod

Serves 6

with Cream & Bay Leaves

6 pieces of cod (allow approx. 4oz approx. filleted fish per person)
2 tablespoons butter
1 tablespoon finely chopped onion
salt and freshly ground pepper
3 or 4 fresh or dried bay leaves
light cream to cover the fish
approx. 1¼ cups roux
(see page 40)

In the olden days milk was put into skimming bowls in the cold dairy to set so there was always some rich thick cream that could be spooned off the top to add a little extra savor to a dish. Cooking in cream or creamy milk can transform even the dullest white fish into a feast. A mixture of fresh herbs (e.g. parsley, chives, fennel and thyme leaves) can be used instead of the bay leaves.

Melt the butter in a sauté pan just wide enough to take the fish. Fry the onion gently for a few minutes until soft but not colored. Put the cod in the pan and cook on both sides for one minute. Season with salt and freshly ground pepper. Add bay leaves. Cover with light cream and simmer with the lid on for 5 to 10 minutes, until the fish is cooked. Remove the fish to a serving dish. Bring the cooking liquid to a boil and lightly thicken with roux. Taste and correct the seasoning. Coat the fish with sauce and serve immediately.

This dish can be prepared ahead and reheated, and it also freezes well. Reheat in a moderate oven 350°F for anything from 10 to 30 minutes, depending on the size of the container.

For a whole meal in one dish, pipe a ruff of fluffy mashed potato around the edge.

Fluffy Mashed Potato

Serves 4

2lb unpeeled potatoes, Russet or Yukon Gold
salt
1 cup creamy milk
1 or 2 egg yolks or 1 whole egg and 1 egg yolk
2 to 4 tablespoons butter

Scrub the potatoes well. Put them into a saucepan of cold water, add a good pinch of salt and bring to a boil. When the potatoes are about half cooked (about 15 minutes for 'old potatoes'), strain off two-thirds of the water, replace the lid on the saucepan, put onto a gentle heat and allow the potatoes to steam until they are cooked.

Peel immediately by just pulling off the skins, so you waste as little as possible. Mash while hot. (If you have a large quantity, put the potatoes into the bowl of an electric mixer and beat with the paddle.)

While the potatoes are being peeled, bring the milk to a boil. Beat the eggs into the hot mashed potatoes, and add enough boiling creamy milk to mix to a soft light consistency suitable for shaping; then beat in the butter, the amount depending on how rich you like your potatoes. Taste and season with salt and freshly-ground pepper.

Note: *If the potatoes are not peeled and mashed while hot and if the boiling milk is not added immediately, the fluffy mashed potato will be lumpy and gluey.*

Only egg whites are fine and will make a delicious light mashed potato.

Like many old-fashioned foods which have been almost forgotten, cod's roe is cheap and delicious. It still turns up between January and April in many fish markets and is well worth looking out for. Cod's roe is also sold smoked.

Serves 4-6 (depending on size of roe)

Cod's Roe

a cod's roe or shad
seasoned flour
beaten egg
fine white breadcrumbs

Rinse the cod's roe gently in cold water and then tie it loosely in muslin. Choose a saucepan just large enough to fit. Cook the cod's roe in boiling salted water for 20 to 30 minutes, depending on the thickness. It should be firm to the touch. Drain, put on a plate and cover with another plate to weigh it down slightly. Cool and refrigerate overnight.

Next day, cut the roe into ¾ inch thick slices. Dip each slice into seasoned flour, add the beaten egg, then the breadcrumbs. Fry the slices in bacon fat or melted butter until crisp and golden on both sides. Serve with some crisp slices of bacon and a few fried potatoes, or simply bread and butter.

Cod's roe is also good dipped in a batter and deep-fried until crisp.

Baked Cod with Cream & Bay Leaves

Whiting

Serves 1

Steamed between Two Plates

1 whiting or flounder fillet
milk
a few dabs of butter
flour well seasoned with salt and pepper
2 pyrex plates

Bring a saucepan of water to a boil. Dip the fillet of fish in seasoned flour. Rub the base of one plate with butter, place the fish on top. Season with salt, pepper, and add a few dabs of butter. Pour a little milk around the fish, enough to come about one-third of the way up the fillet. Cover with the second plate and place on top of the saucepan. Keep the water boiling underneath. The fish will cook in 8 or 10 minutes, depending on the thickness of the fillet.

Scalloped Pike

Serves 4-6

This recipe, from the Kitchen Book of Clonbrock, *was signed by 'Charley'.*

3lb of fish
2 tablespoonfuls of Anchovy Sauce
2 tablespoonfuls of Worcester Sauce
Cayenne and mace to taste

Boil the pike or other fish. Pull it to pieces and take out all the bones. Make a roux sauce (see below). Add the sauces, cayenne and mace to season the finished sauce.

Keep stirring the sauce until it boils. Mix the fish with it and place it in a pie dish, or scallop shells with bread crumbs. Dab little bits of butter over the top and bake.

To make the Roux

4 tablespoons of butter
2 tablespoonfuls of flour
2 cups of milk
Salt and pepper or other seasoning

Melt the butter over a low heat in a saucepan. When it is quite liquid, add the flour, mixing thoroughly to form a smooth paste. Cook gently for 2 minutes.

Remove from heat and add the milk a little at a time, stirring well to remove all lumps from the mixture.

Return to heat and cook very gently, stirring all the time until the sauce has thickened. Season to taste.

Pollock

'Thim's not company fish', remarked the Irish R.M.'s housekeeper of pollock, 'but very good nonetheless.' This tribute comes from '*The Boat's Share*' in *Some Experiences of an Irish R.M.* by E.C. Somerville and M. Ross.

Tommy Sliney was a much loved character from Ballycotton who sold fresh fish from his donkey and cart in the neighboring villages and on the pier in summer. Everyone, including children, loved Tommy and in truth he gave away more fish than he ever sold. He explained to me once why pollock—not known for its distinctive flavour — was so popular:' 'tis because it doesn't taste of fish Missus.' Of course! Fish and fasting were inextricable in people's minds because of the obligatory Friday fast.

Traditionally Pollock was boiled or fried.

Fried Pollock

Serves 2

Gut and fillet a perfectly fresh stiff pollock. Cut into generous helpings and salt each portion well. Melt a little butter in a frying pan, dip the fish in flour and shake off the excess. Cook until golden brown on both sides. Eat with lots of brown soda bread and tea.

Herrings

The herring featured prominently in the diet of the Irish from the medieval period through to the early twentieth century. The fish was an indispensable item for two main reasons: firstly, although it could be eaten fresh, it preserved well and proved a most valuable food item for the long lean winter and early spring seasons. Secondly, it was invariably linked with the numerous Christian days of fast and abstinence. The documentary record indicates that, by the fourteenth century, herring was an integral and prevalent item in the Irish diet. In 1306 Scottish fishing fleets were trading in herring which was destined for sale in the Dublin and Drogheda fish shambles; while in 1403 John Slene of Rush exported as many as four thousand salted herring to England.

Its popularity as a foodstuff endured through the eighteenth and nineteenth centuries. Arthur Young, writing in the 1770s, notes that the poor of Wexford ate 'herrings and potatoes', while of the Limavady region he writes: 'the poor live on potatoes, milk and oatmeal with many herrings and salmon.'

During the eighteenth and nineteenth centuries, the bland Irish diet of potatoes and buttermilk welcomed the salty smoked flavor of herrings. Barrels of pickled herrings were commonplace in wealthy households, while in the homes of the poor a number of gutted and salted herrings were hung from the rafters as 'winter kitchen'.

Up until the early twentieth century, the herring was an important part of the Easter Sunday festivities. In a number of towns the butchers, who had little sale for their meat in the Lenten period, celebrated the arrival of Easter by holding a funeral-like procession of a herring—the staple of the church-abiding community during the forty days of Lent. Henry Morris describes the custom as it took place in Dundalk in 1902:

> They [the butchers] got big long rods and walked through the town…beating the poor herring until hardly a fin was left. On reaching the bridge they hurled the horrid herring into the water with insult and hung up a quarter of lamb decorated with ribbons and flowers in its place.

Huge bubbling shoals of herring were a common sight off the Irish coast until relatively recently. Women gutted and salted the fish onshore—these were then packed into barrels for sale by fish merchants and 'cadgers' who transported the herrings right into the heart of the country. My mother remembers as a child in Johnstown, Co. Kilkenny in the early 1930s, a man coming round selling herrings from a pony and cart on Thursdays. They'd hear the clip, clop of the pony's feet on the road once he left the neighbors' house. At the sound of 'fresh herrings, fresh herrings', they'd run to their mother for money and race out to buy the fish. Many farmers also bought a barrel of salted herrings to see them through Lent.

In earlier times a sort of dip or relish was made from dried and salted fish and this 'kitchen' often provided the only condiment when times were bad. There was an old cautionary saying 'Dip in the dip and leave the herring for your father'.

Unfortunately herring stocks off the coast of Ireland have decreased dramatically due to over-fishing and are now the subject of government quotas.

42

Pickled Herring or Mackerel

Serves 8-10

Another tasty recipe for preserving herring or mackerel.

8 fresh herring or mackerel
2 cups very ripe tomatoes,
peeled and sliced
²/₃ cup wine vinegar
²/₃ cup dry white wine
3 sprigs of fennel
¹/₂ bay leaf
¹/₂ cup sliced onion
2 teaspoons sugar
¹/₂ teaspoon mustard seed
1 teaspoon salt
freshly ground black pepper

Gut and wash the fish. Put all the ingredients for the pickle into a casserole. Cook until reduced by half. Put in the fish, cover the pot and simmer gently until the fish are just cooked, about 10 to 15 minutes.

Serve warm with new potatoes or cold as a starter or salad.

The Cork historian Ted O Súilleabháin told me about this method of cooking mackerel, herring and bream which he remembers from his childhood on Bere Island off West Cork. The fish was spread over a pair of tongs and cooked until the skin was crisp on the underside. People said they 'never tasted the likes of them cooked any other way'.

There is a lovely description in *An tOileán a Bhí* by Máire Ní Ghuithín, published in 1978 by An Clochomhar Teoranta, about cooking the mackerel in exactly the same manner on the Great Blaskets:

> *Chuirtí maircréal úr a róstadh ar on dtlú. Leathaítí an maircréal trasna na tlú taobh an chroicinn in airde. Nuair a bheadh on maircréal rósta ón dtaobh thíos dhéanfá é a iompú ansin ar an dtlú le scian. Chroithfeá gráinne salainn mhín air agus gráinne piobair and do réir mar a bheadh on taobh eile ag róstadh bheadh on salann ag leá tríd síos.*
>
> *Bhíodh an-dhúil ag na stróinseirí a bhíodh ag fanacht againn san oilean sa mhaircréal úr no deargán úr rósta ar an dtlú mar seo. Deiridis to mbíodh blas éigin faoi leith air…Dheanfá maircréal buí a róstadh ar an dtlú sa tslí chéanna.*

According to Ted O'Súilleabháin, the islanders would split the mackerel down the back, open it out and pull out the bones so the two fillets were still attached at the belly. The fish was laid crossways over the two bars of the tongs, flesh side down, skin side upwards. It was then held over the open fire to cook. When the fish appeared to be done on one side it was turned with a knife and seasoned with salt and pepper. It was then held over the fire until the skin side was brown and crispy. This was called 'roasting fish' by the locals, but in fact it was really barbecuing before the word was even coined!

Puffins were also cooked in the same way on the Great Blaskets.

Herrings, mackerel or bream
cooked on tongs over the open fire

Serves 8
Soused Herring or Mackerel

8 herrings or mackerel
1 thinly sliced onion
1 teaspoon whole black peppercorns
6 whole cloves
1 teaspoon salt
1 teaspoon sugar
1¹/4 cups white wine vinegar
1 bay leaf

Gut, wash and fillet the herrings or mackerel, making sure there are no bones. Roll up the fillets, skin side down and pack tightly into a cast iron casserole. Sprinkle over the onion slices, peppercorns, cloves, salt, sugar, vinegar and a bay leaf. Bring to a boil on top of the cooker. Put into a very low oven, 275°F, and cook for 30 to 45 minutes.

Allow to get quite cold. Soused herring or mackerel will keep for 7 to 10 days in the fridge.

Red Herrings

Red herrings were herrings that had been salted and heavily smoked. They needed to be soaked in several changes of water before being cooked, often over the embers of the turf fire. They were very tasty eaten with lots of potatoes, and were often washed down with a big mug of buttermilk to quench the thirst.

Whitebait or Sprats

Every year in late summer the sea suddenly boils with tiny whitebait. They can be caught by the bucketful and are irresistible when they are tossed in seasoned flour and fried until crisp. Sprats make their appearance off the coast of Ireland just after Christmas for two or three weeks. They are cheap and delicious and are also good soused or smoked.
In many parts of the country, specially erected wickerwork head weirs were erected to take the sprat.

Estyn Evans in Irish Folkways *points out that in Donegal sprats constituted the chief food of the peasantry during three or four months of the year. In late summer they were taken from the water in buckets and sieves and the mackerel that were closely pursuing their prey were caught almost as easily.*

whitebait or sprats
flour, seasoned with salt
and freshly ground pepper
lemon segments

Heat good quality oil in a deep fryer until good and hot. Toss the fish, a few at a time, in the seasoned flour and shake off the excess. Cook in small batches until crisp and golden. Drain on paper towels. Serve immediately with segments of lemon.

Some people dip the fish first into milk and then flour.

To preserve sprats

In the Shapland Carew Papers *which detail the accounts of the wealthy Carew family of Castleboro in Co. Wexford, there is an entry for 18 February 1773 which records that a 'kegg of red sprats' was delivered to the estate.*

This recipe, which preserves sprats like anchovies, comes from the Mocollop Castle Cookbook *of 1801:*

> To a peck of sprats put 2lb of common salt ½lb of bay salt, 1lb of saltpetre, 2oz of salt prunella, a little bole almoniac, put a layer of this compound in a cag and then a layer of sprats and so on till they are all in, press them down very hard and then cover 'em quite close, let 'em stand six months when they may be used, before you use them let 'em be washed in a strong pickle not to let the smallest amount of pickle remain and then repack them with some fresh compound the same as the first.

Mackerel

In his work *Strong Tea*, John B. Keane eulogises the splendor of mackerel:

> Years before the advent of chip-shops and snack-bars, they sailed in silver armadas through the blue seas of Munster, celestial in design and remarkable humility, proud indeed to show that when God made mackerel, he made them for poor people and if they did nothing more, they kept many a small boy with curls upon his head away from death's door in the horrendous years of the famine.

Every summer the arrival of the mackerel into Ballycotton, our local fishing village, is eagerly awaited; around late July or early August huge shoals sweep around the coastline. Word goes round the village like wildfire that the mackerel are in, and men, women and children of all ages race to the pier with fishing rods, lines and hooks. The water churns with hungry mackerel feeding on the sprats. Anyone can dangle a line over the end of the pier and catch a fish. I once did, but was so horrified to see it wriggling on the end of the line that I couldn't kill it, so I never tried again!

My husband Tim remembers going out in the early 1960s with a local fisherman to catch mackerel which they promptly cooked on the boat's stove, fired with coal they dredged up from the bottom of the sea. He assures me that no mackerel ever tasted better. This poached mackerel recipe is a more sophisticated version, but it uses the same basic cooking technique.

First make the sauce. Beat the egg yolks in a bowl with the mustard and finely chopped herbs. Bring the butter to the boil and pour it in a steady stream onto the egg yolks, whisking continuously until the sauce thickens to a light coating consistency. Keep warm in a bowl over hot water (not stainless steel).

Cut the heads off the mackerel, gut and clean but keep whole. Bring the water to the boil and add salt and the mackerel. Bring back to boiling point, cover and remove from the heat. After about 5 to 8 minutes, check to see whether the fish are cooked. The flesh should lift off the bone. Remove the mackerel on to a plate, scrape off the skin and carefully lift the fillets off the bones and on to a serving plate. Coat carefully with warm sauce. Serve with a good green salad and perhaps some new potatoes.

Serves 6

Mackerel in Salt Water

Poached Mackerel with Green Sauce

6 very fresh mackerel
5 cups water
1 teaspoon salt

Green Sauce
2 egg yolks (preferably free-range)
1 teaspoon French mustard (we use Maille mustard with green herbs)
2 tablespoons mixed finely chopped chives, fennel, parsley and thyme
12 tablespoons (1½ sticks) butter

When Coquebert de Montbret travelled to Kinsale in 1790, he described the meal of a fishing family as follows: 'on the grill over the live coals, they are allowed to cook their mackerel, some mussels and red potatoes with their white eyes'.

Ballycotton people say 'The sun should never set on a mackerel'. Certainly fresh mackerel cooked in this time-honored fashion is utterly delicious.

First make the parsley butter. Cream the butter and stir in the parsley and a few drops of lemon juice. Roll into butter pats or form into a roll and wrap in wax paper or aluminum foil, screwing each end so that it looks like a cracker. Refrigerate to harden.

Heat the broiler pan. Dip the fish fillets in flour which has been seasoned with salt and freshly ground pepper. Shake off the excess flour and then spread a little butter with a knife on the flesh side, as though you were buttering a slice of bread rather meanly. When the broiler pan is quite hot but not smoking, place the fish fillets butter side down on the pan; the fish fillets should sizzle as soon as they touch the pan. Turn down the heat slightly and let them cook for 4 or 5 minutes on that side before you turn them over. Continue to cook on the other side until crisp and golden. Serve each fillet on a hot plate with some slices or pats of parsley butter and a segment of lemon.

Parsley butter may be served directly on the fish, or if you have a pretty shell, place it at the side of the plate as a container for the butter. Garnish with parsley and a lemon wedge.

Note: Fillets of any small fish are delicious pan broiled in this way. Fish under 2lb such as mackerel, herring and trout can also be broiled whole on the pan. Fish over 2lb can be filleted first and then cut across into portions. Large fish 4 to 6lb can also be broiled whole. Cook them for about 10 to 15 minutes on each side and then put in a hot oven for another 15 minutes or so to finish cooking.

Serves 4

Pan Broiled Mackerel

with Parsley Butter

8 fillets of very fresh mackerel
seasoned flour
small knob of butter

Parsley Butter
4 tablespoons butter
4 teaspoons finely chopped parsley
a few drops of freshly squeezed lemon juice

Garnish
8 lemon wedges
parsley sprigs

Baked Lemon Sole or Plaice
with Herb Butter

Serves 4

4 very fresh plaice or lemon sole on the bone
4 to 8 tablespoons butter
4 to 6 teaspoons mixed finely-chopped
fresh parsley, chives, fennel
and thyme leaves
salt and freshly ground pepper

Both lemon sole and plaice are abundant around the coast of Ireland and are sought after for their meltingly tender flesh. A splendid extract from Ulysses *by James Joyce:*

> Wouldn't mind being a waiter in a swell hotel. Tips, evening dress, half naked ladies. May I tempt you to a little more filleted lemon sole, miss Dubedat? Yes, do bedad. And she did bedad. Huguenot name I expect that. A miss Dubedat lived in Killiney I remember. Du, de la, French. Still it's the same fish, perhaps old Micky Hanlon of Moore street ripped the guts out of making money, hand over fist, finger in fishes gills, can't write his name on a cheque, think he was painting the landscape with his mouth twisted.

Preheat the oven to 375°F. Turn the fish on its side and remove the head. Wash the fish and clean thoroughly. With a knife, cut through the skin right round the fish, just where the 'fringe' meets the flesh.

Sprinkle the fish with salt and pepper and lay in ¼ inch of water in a shallow baking pan. Bake in a moderately hot oven for 15 to 20 minutes. The water should have just evaporated as the fish is cooked. Check to see whether the fish is cooked by lifting the flesh from the bone at the head; it should lift off the bone easily and be quite white.

Meanwhile, melt the butter and stir in the freshly chopped herbs. Just before serving catch the skin down near the tail and pull it off gently (the skin will tear badly if not properly cut). Lift the fish onto hot plates and spoon the herb butter over them. Serve immediately.

Ray

Ray (skate) used to be landed in vast quantities in the old Dublin fishing port at Ringsend—so much so that it was known as Raytown. Ray and chips are still much sought after in Dublin chip shops. This was not so everywhere. In 1790 the French scholar and consul in Dublin, Charles Etienne Coquebert de Montbret made a visit to Kinsale, Co. Cork, where he noted 'so abundant are the catches that ray salted by the people of Skerries are thrown out by the fisherman here'.

Skate with Black Butter

Serves 2 as a main course

1 medium skate, weighing 1¼ to 1½lb
1 onion, sliced
2 tablespoons white wine vinegar
a few sprigs of parsley
a little salt

Black Butter
4 tablespoons butter
2 tablespoons white wine vinegar

Garnish
parsley, chopped

This classic recipe was a favorite in Anglo-Irish houses and is one of the most delicious ways of serving a piece of skate.

Choose a pan wide enough for the skate to lie flat while cooking. Put in the fish, cover completely with cold water, add the onion, parsley, salt and the wine vinegar. Bring to the boil gently, cover and barely simmer for 15 to 20 minutes. If the flesh lifts easily from the cartilage, the skate is cooked. Turn off the heat and transfer the fish onto a large serving plate. Skin and lift the flesh on to hot plates, first from one side of the cartilage, then the other, scraping off the white skin. Cover and keep hot.

Next make the black butter. Melt the butter immediately on a hot pan, allow it to foam and just as it turns a good rich brown color, add the wine vinegar. Allow it to bubble up again and then pour sizzling over the fish. Sprinkle with chopped parsley and serve immediately.

Eels

My father and grandfather occasionally cooked eels, and as children we giggled in horror as the eels continued to squirm while they cooked in the frying pan. Needless to say we couldn't be persuaded to try them and it wasn't until my late teens that I realized what I'd been missing.

Eels were far more widely available in ancient times than nowadays. Eel weirs, which have a long history, appear to have been the closely guarded property of individual families, In *The Farm by Lough Gur*, which describes life on a farm in Co. Limerick in the nineteenth century, Cissie O'Brien describes how the eels were caught and either sent to the Limerick market or sold to the Meggy the Eel, an itinerant fish woman from Bruff, who used to peddle them from house to house. Eels are still caught around Lough Neagh, Nun's Island Weir in Galway, in parts of Wexford and in many other parts of the country.

Marian Sisk showed me how to prepare eels. Wash and rub with a green scratchy pad to remove the slime. Just below the neck cut from the underside through the spine, but not through the skin at the back. Holding the eel firmly, pull off the skin, then gut from vent to head end. Cut a little further down below the vent and carefully remove the sac and all the blood, which is poisonous. Wash well under cold running water.

Fried Eel

Cut the eels into pieces about 2 inches long. Roll in seasoned flour and fry in butter in a pan. Eat with bread and butter and a little lemon. Simple and exquisite. Allow 8 oz eel per person.

The Loughsiders around Lough Neagh often deep-fried the eels rather than shallow-frying them in a pan.

Eels
with Scallion & Parsley Sauce

Serves 4

In Never no More, *Maura Laverty gives us a glimpse of life on the edge of the Bog of Allen in the 1920s:*

> Living so far inland our fish dishes were mostly ling or red herrings. Occasionally, however, Mike Brophy took his fishing rod and went down to the mill pond, returning with a few eels or perch. Judy Ryan (the servant girl) would never touch an eel, saying that they were cousins to the serpents. Eels could be fried…A favourite method of cooking eels was to skin the fish, cut them in slices, set them to parboil to take out the grease, then stew them in a creamy white sauce with chopped parsley and scallions.

Skin the eels, wash well to remove any trace of blood inside, cut into 3 inch lengths. Put into a pot, cover with cold water and bring to a boil. Simmer for a few minutes to remove some of the oil; drain.

Bring the milk to a boil with the scallions and parsley. Whisk in the roux and cook until the sauce has a light coating consistency. Season with salt and freshly ground pepper. Add the eels, cover and continue to simmer in the sauce until the eels are fully cooked. Taste and correct the seasoning. Serve with boiled potatoes.

1lb fresh eels
2¹/2 cups milk
roux (see page 40)
2 tablespoons chopped scallions or chives
2 tablespoons chopped fresh parsley
salt and freshly ground pepper

Trout

In the late twelfth century the writer and historian Giraldus Cambrensis wrote in his *Topographia Hibernica*:

> This Ireland is also specially remarkable for a great number of beautiful lakes, abounding in fish and surpassing in size those of other countries I have visited. The rivers and lakes are also plentifully stored with the sorts of fish peculiar to these waters and especially three species—salmon, trout and muddy eels.

When I was a child a local man, Eoin O'Neill, lived simply by fishing and hunting. I used to watch out for him in the evenings as he came home from his day in the woods or on the river bank. 'Catch anything, Eoin?' I'd inquire hopefully. He would always have a story for me and occasionally he'd pluck a little speckledy brown trout out of the deep pockets of his tweedy jacket and drop it into my eager hands. I would race home to my mother, who would cook it for my tea.

Serves 4

Trout
with Spinach Butter Sauce

In the diaries of Amhlaoibh Uí Shúileabháin from Callan in Co. Kilkenny, Amhlaoibh visits the home of Arthur James Hennebry on 20 June 1828, where he sits down to a dinner of 'two fine fat sweet substantial trout, one of them as big as a small salmon'. I like to think he would have enjoyed this rich and delicious sauce, which is also exquisite with salmon, trout, plaice or monkfish.

We sometimes get large rainbow trout which are about two years old and have a wonderful flavor—very much more delectable than the smaller ones.

2 whole rainbow trout (approx. 2lb each)
salt and freshly ground pepper
2 to 4 tablespoons butter
4 sprigs of fennel

Spinach Butter Sauce
3oz spinach leaves
2/3 cup cream
6 tablespoons butter
water if necessary

aluminum foil

Gut the trout and wash well, making sure to remove the line of blood from the inside near the back bone. Dry with kitchen paper, season inside and out with salt and freshly ground pepper. Put a blob of butter and a sprig of fennel into the center of each trout.

Take a large sheet of foil and smear a little butter on the center. Put one trout onto the foil and fold over to make a parcel. Crimp the edges; seal well to make sure that none of the juices escape. Repeat with another sheet of foil and the other trout. Preheat the oven to 375°F. Put the two foil parcels on a baking tray, but make sure that they are not touching. Bake for about 30 minutes.

Meanwhile make the spinach butter sauce. Remove stalks from the spinach, wash and cook in 2½ cups boiling water with a pinch of salt. Cook for 4 or 5 minutes or until soft. Drain, pressing out all the water, and chop finely. Put the cream into a saucepan and simmer on a gentle heat until reduced to about 3 tablespoons, or until it is in danger of burning. Then, on a very low heat, whisk in the butter bit by bit as though you were making a Hollandaise sauce. Stir in the spinach.

When the fish is cooked, open the parcels. There will be lots of delicious juices; use some of these to thin out the sauce. Put the two parcels onto a hot serving dish and bring to the table. Skin the fish and lift the juicy pink flesh on to hot plates. Spoon the spinach butter sauce over the fish and serve immediately.

Salmon

Salmon is mentioned frequently in early Irish literature and in the heroic tales of ancient Ireland.

There is archaeological evidence that salmon was eaten in 7,000 B.C. by Ireland's earliest inhabitants from the Mesolithic (Middle Stone Age) site of Mount Sandel, near Coleraine in Co. Derry.

The most famous salmon in Irish mythology, which is mentioned in *Macgnímartha Find*, was the one that gave boundless knowledge to the young hero, Fionn Mac Cumhaill. He was carefully cooking the magical fish over an applewood fire for his master Finnéigeas when he burst a rising blister on the salmon's skin. He burnt his thumb and spontaneously sucked it to relieve the pain. This meant that, inadvertently, he had the first taste of the salmon of knowledge and so became the wisest of men.

There is a specific season for wild salmon which varies from one part of the country to another. Farmed salmon, now widely produced around the west and south coast of Ireland, is available all the year round.

Serves 8

Poached Salmon

with Irish Butter Sauce

Salmon

2¹/₂lb centre cut of fresh salmon
water
salt

Irish Butter Sauce

2 egg yolks
1 tablespoon cold water
8 tablespoons (1 stick) butter, diced
1 teaspoon lemon juice
¹/₂ tablespoon butter
salt and freshly ground pepper

Garnish

Sprigs of watercress or flat parsley

For maximum flavor, we cook the salmon in the time-honored way, by placing it in boiling salted water.

The proportion of salt to water is very important. We use one heaping tablespoon of salt to every 5 cups of water. Although the fish or piece of fish should be just covered with water, the aim is to use the minimum amount of water to preserve the maximum flavor, so therefore one should use a saucepan that will fit the fish exactly. An oval cast- iron saucepan is usually perfect.

Half fill the pan with measured salted water and bring to a boil. Put in the piece of fish, just covering with water,. and bring back to a boil. Simmer gently for 20 minutes. Turn off the heat, allow the fish to sit in the water. Serve within 15 to 20 minutes.

Meanwhile make the Irish Butter Sauce. Put the egg yolks into a heavy bottomed stainless steel saucepan on a very low heat. Add the cold water and beat thoroughly. Add the butter bit by bit, beating all the time. As soon as one piece melts, add the next. The mixture will gradually thicken, but if it shows signs of becoming too thick or 'scrambling' slightly, remove from the heat immediately and add a little cold water if necessary. Do not leave the pan or stop beating until the sauce is made. Finally add the lemon juice to taste. Pour into a bowl and keep warm over hot, but not boiling, water.

To serve, lift the cooked salmon carefully from the poaching liquid. Peel off the skin gently. Garnish with sprigs of parsley or watercress. Serve with Irish Butter Sauce.

This is the traditional second course on wedding menus all over Ireland. It is sometimes a disappointment, but if you cook fresh wild Irish salmon in well salted water and serve it while it is still slightly warm with some freshly made salads and a good homemade mayonnaise, it's absolutely magical.

Poach the salmon; leave to cool. Meanwhile, make a tomato and mint salad. Remove the cores from six tomatoes and quarter. Sprinkle with a little salt, sugar and black pepper. Toss immediately in a little French dressing; sprinkle with 1 or 2 teaspoons of chopped mint and basil.

Cut a medium cucumber into thin slices and sprinkle with salt, 1 tablespoon of wine vinegar and plenty of sugar. Stir in 2 teaspoons of finely chopped fennel.

To assemble the salmon mayonnaise, put a portion of salmon on each plate when it is just cold. Garnish with a little lettuce, pipe some potato salad onto the lettuce and put a little of the tomato and cucumber salads on each plate as well as one spoonful of egg mayonnaise. Garnish with chopped scallions and watercress and a lemon wedge. Additional mayonnaise can be served separately or put into a bowl on each plate.

Add French dressing, finely chopped parsley, chives and mayonnaise to 4$^{1}/_{2}$ cups stiff, freshly mashed potato to taste. Pipe on to individual leaves of lettuce.

Lower the eggs gently into boiling salted water, bring the water back to a boil and hard-boil the eggs for 10 minutes in boiling water. Drain and put immediately into a bowl of cold water. (Eggs with a black ring around the yolk have been overcooked.) When cold, shell and slice in half lengthways. Sieve the yolks and mix the sieved egg yolk with mayonnaise. Add chopped chives and salt and pepper to taste. Fill into a piping bag and pipe into the whites. Garnish with a sprig of parsley or chervil and serve on a bed of lettuce.

Most people don't seem to be aware that mayonnaise can be made, even with a hand whisk, in under five minutes. The great secret is to have all your ingredients at room temperature and to drip the oil very slowly into the egg yolks at the beginning. Good quality ingredients are essential to a successful mayonnaise.

Put the egg yolks into a bowl with the mustard, salt and the white wine vinegar. Put the oil into a measuring cup. Take a whisk in one hand and the oil in the other and drip the oil on to the egg yolks, drop by drop, whisking at the same time. Within a minute you will notice that the mixture is beginning to thicken. When this happens you can add the oil a little faster, but not too quickly or it will suddenly curdle. Taste and add a little more seasoning and vinegar if necessary.

If the mayonnaise curdles, it will suddenly become quite thin, and if left standing the oil will start to float to the top. You can easily rectify the situation by whisking another egg yolk or 1 or 2 tablespoons of boiling water into the mayonnaise, half a teaspoon at a time, until it emulsifies again.

Serves 8 as a main course

Salmon Mayonnaise

2 or 2$^{1}/_{2}$lb freshly poached salmon (see page 50)
Tomato and mint salad
Cucumber and fennel salad
Piped potato salad (see below)
Egg mayonnaise (see below)

Garnish
chopped scallions
lettuce
watercress
lemon wedges

Piped Potato Salad

Egg Mayonnaise

4 eggs
3 or 4 tablespoons home-made mayonnaise
$^{1}/_{2}$ teaspoons finely chopped chives
salt and freshly ground pepper to taste

Mayonnaise

2 egg yolks, free-range
$^{1}/_{4}$ teaspoon salt
pinch of English mustard or $^{1}/_{4}$ teaspoon French mustard
2 teaspoons white wine vinegar
1 cup oil (sunflower or olive oil or a mixture)

Pickled Salmon

Salted salmon was exported in large quantities to Italy and France during the eighteenth century. In Ireland itself, salmon was consumed fresh near rivers and coastal regions and when the fish were spawning and plentiful. However, in the regions distant from the salmon habitats and during the winter and spring months, pickled salmon had to suffice. This was served as a breakfast dish in the late nineteenth century as described in the 1897 publication *The Sportsman* in Ireland:

> A Sportsman's Breakfast: First, a large bowl of new milk which instantly disappeared; then a liberal allowance of cold salmon soaked in vinegar—…and a bottle of port wine.

To Pickle Salmon: Lismore

From the Receipt Book *of Mrs Dot Drew of Mocollop Castle, Ballyduff, Co. Waterford, dated 1801.*

> Cut up a salmon across into any sized pieces when well wash'd let it be boiled in a strong pickle of salt and water till the fish parts from the bone when quite cold pack it up in a crock […] throwing a little salt petre finely powdered between every layer of fish, when packed close keep it always covered with the following pickle, take one quart of vinegar and one quart of water, 3oz of lump sugar and 12 drops of the best oyle of cloves, twill be fit for use in 3 or 4 weeks, twill look black at first till the oil and fat comes out.

Bream

One of my most valued sources of traditional recipes is John F. Guerin who has lived all his life beside the sea in Ballyheigue, Co. Kerry.

> The traditional Ballyheigue fish dish is boiled bream. The bream is caught with a line off the high rocks; a local knowledge is important to find the right places.

The bream is usually boiled and eaten when cold. It was a favorite dinner for a day in the bog; cold bream, with slices of cornmeal bread and a bottle of cold tea.

Salt Cod or Ling

Salted fish has been a prominent feature of the Irish diet since medieval times, when huge quantities of salted fish (cod and ling) were exported to England. Fresh fish was an expensive luxury for inland Irish communities and salted fish became a necessary and important addition to the diet on Fridays and during the Lenten period, when the consumption of meat was forbidden by the church. John Guerin from Ballyheigue remembers:

> Ling was a favourite fish for Lent in my father's time. The average ling was about $2\frac{1}{2}$ feet long, it was salted and cured and usually hung at the back of the kitchen door. A large slice was cut off when needed and boiled for dinner. The first boil of water was usually thrown away as it was too salty.

A pinch of flour was added to the soup, and it was then served hot with boiled potatoes.

Salt cod and ling (also known as stockfish or hardfish) are still on sale in Cork Market all the year round and form the traditional Cork supper on Christmas Eve.

Serves 4-6

Salt Cod
with White Sauce

Cut the salt cod into medium-sized pieces. Cover with cold water and soak overnight. Next day discard the water, cover with milk and stew until tender (for about 30 minutes).

Meanwhile, melt the butter in a saucepan. Add the chopped onion, cover and cook on a gentle heat until soft. Stir in flour and cook for 2 or 3 minutes, then whisk in the milk, bit by bit. Season, bring to a boil and simmer for a few minutes. A little chopped parsley wouldn't do any harm.

Drain the cod. Serve with the sauce and some freshly boiled potatoes.

1 lb salt cod
milk

White sauce
2 tablespoons butter
1 onion, chopped
1 tablespoon flour
2¹/2 cups milk
salt and freshly ground pepper
chopped parsley (optional)

In many places in Ireland salted ling was called *battleboard* because the drying and salting process rendered the fish rock hard.

Sometimes the cooked salt ling was deboned and flaked and then mixed into some mashed potato with enough of the cooking liquor to make it soft and juicy. Serve hot , with butter melting in the center.

Whiting, ling and rock cod were dried and hung from the rafters, not only in small cabins but also in prosperous farmhouses alongside flitches of bacon. Salted, dried and smoked fish were also widely sold in small village shops all round the country.

The celebrated playwright and novelist John B. Keane, from Listowel in Co. Kerry, writes of salted ling with a deep respect in *Strong Tea*:

> The rafters in the thatched houses of your grandfather's were never without a flitch of it and when your Aunty Mary came back from America, 'twas the first thing she asked for. Bishops and Monsignors were reared on it and it was responsible for the pointing of more fifties than sirloin steak and raw eggs put together.

Salted Ling & Mashed Potatoes

Limpets (Bairneachs)

Limpets (*bairneach* in Irish) are rarely eaten nowadays, but formerly they were part of the Irish diet, not only on the islands but also on the mainland. In *An tOileánach* (*The Islandman*), his famous account of life on the Blasket Island, Tomás O'Criomhthain writes 'and the food I got was hen's eggs, lumps of butter and bits of fish, limpets and winkles—a bit of everything going from sea or land.' There follows an evocative passage where he describes his mother roasting the limpets on an open fire. 'throwing them to us one by one like a hen with chickens.'

Limpets were also often cooked in an ingenious way in the rock pools along the shore. A fire was lit to heat the stones, which were then transferred to the rock pool where they heated the water in the same manner as described in the *Fulachta Fiadh*. The limpets were then cooked in the hot sea water.

There was a tradition in Co. Galway of placing a live limpet or periwinkle at each corner of the house at the spring tide closest to St. Brigid's Day. This ensured good luck and a plentiful catch.

Bairneachs with Bacon

Fry a few strips of bacon in a pan until crisp on both sides. Remove to a plate. Fry the bairneachs in the bacon fat for a few seconds. Serve with bread and butter.

Razor fish

Razorfish (*Ensis ensis*) can be harvested all the year round. Along with many other types of shellfish, razorfish would have formed part of the diet in coastal regions, particularly in the springtime when the low tides made it easy to collect shellfish.

The razorfish is a burrowing bivalve. It holds its ground at the bottom of its burrow with a single foot which protrudes from the end of the shell. Razorfish normally live on sandy ground on the extreme lower shore and in shallow water. The speed with which they can withdraw to the bottom of their burrows makes them difficult to harvest by hand. A pinch of salt dropped into the burrow is supposed to encourage the razorfish to emerge. They are delicious either cooked in a pan like mussels or opened on a griddle over an open fire. Dip in melted butter and eat immediately.

Cockles

Shellfish have certainly formed part of the diet of Irish coastal people since earliest times. In excavations at the historic sites of Oughtymore, Co. Kerry, Park Cave, Co. Antrim and Potters Cave, Co. Antrim, archaeological remains of cockle shells attest that they were very popular in antiquity and also in the Viking period. Traders like the legendary Mollie Malone, the famous Dublin fishwoman celebrated in song and verse, were a common sight, measuring out cockles, mussels and periwinkles from their tin basins on the stalls around old Dublin.

There are many beautiful cockle strands around our Irish coasts. Years ago it was a common sight during the summer months to see hordes of women and children digging cockles with old spoons, gathering them up in their aprons or into tin cans. Sale of the cockles and 'perries' often provided a little extra money to supplement a meagre income. Experienced cocklers know exactly where to dig on the sandy strands at low tide.

The Donegan family showed me the secret of how to collect cockles on the spectacular Barrow Strand in Co. Kerry. We used a rake rather than a spoon or trowel. A little air hole gives a clue as to where the cockle hides deep in the sand. Any cockles lying on the surface are invariably dead, so you should avoid these.

Cockles can be eaten both raw and cooked. They should be washed several times in cold water to remove the sand from the shells. Years ago they were cooked, in a pot over the turf fire. They are every bit as delicious nowadays even when cooked on a stove.

Cockles with Melted Butter

cockles
melted butter

Wash the cockles in several changes of cold water to remove the sand and grit from the shells. Put into a saucepan or frying pan, cover and cook over a medium heat. They open in just a few minutes and are best eaten straight from the shells, just dipped in melted butter. Eat with lots of crusty brown bread. The cockle liquid is also delicious. Cockles are also delectable with a bowl of homemade mayonnaise (see page 51).

Periwinkles

There is evidence from the early historic sites of Oughtymore, Co. Derry, Park Cave, Co. Antrim and Potter's cave Co. Antrim, that winkles were exploited as a foodstuff. In general spring was the season for gathering shellfish, but Easter and Good Friday in particular were special occasions for visiting the seashore. Winkles were a favorite dish on these days, but there was folk belief that after St. Patrick's Day (17 March) limpets were better for eating than periwinkles.

Periwinkles are still gathered around the Irish coasts when the tide is out. When I take my children down to Shanagarry strand to pick the shiny black winkles from between the rocks, I tell them how these little shellfish have nourished Irish people since prehistoric times and helped save fisherfolk from starvation on the south-west coast during the famine times.

Not everybody finds the idea of eating wiggly little sea snails appetizing. I well remember sitting on the pier at Lahinch, as a child, and screwing up my face as my father heartily enjoyed eating periwinkles out of a newspaper cornet. Years later I picked up the courage to taste them and discovered that they are indeed delicious.

fresh live periwinkles
boiling salted water (1/2 cup salt to
every 10 cups water)
homemade mayonnaise (see page 51)
or vinegar (optional)

Bring the water to a boil, add the salt and the periwinkles. Bring the water back to a boil, drain the periwinkles and allow them to get cold. Pick the periwinkles out of the shells with a large pin. Eat on their own or with mayonnaise. Some people like to dip them in vinegar or oatmeal.

Estyn Evans points out that in Ireland winkles were boiled in milk, as a foodstuff for children or to give extra nourishment to calves.

Mussels

Street cries of 'Cockles and Mussels, alive, alive-o' resounded around the streets of Dublin in former times. In some parts of the country, including Bere Island, mussels as well as other shellfish are still shunned as 'famine food'. Despite the fact that the Great Famine was nearly 150 years ago, the horror of it is still very strong in folk memory. Now very much in demand both at home and abroad, plump juicy mussels are being farmed very successfully all around Irish coasts. Following the popularity of the Galway International Oyster Festival, held in September every year and-sponsored by Guinness, the makers of Cork's famous stout, Murphy's, have teamed up with the Bantry Mussel Fair held in May.

Mussels with Melted Butter

fresh mussels, all tightly shut
butter

Wash the mussels in several changes of water, but don't soak them or you'll lose some of the sweet juices.

Put them into a saucepan or frying pan, not too many at a time, cover with a lid or folded tea towel and put on a medium heat. Just as soon as the shells open, take out the mussels and serve warm dipped in melted butter. The mussel broth can be drunk or used for fish soup.

Native Irish Oysters

Native Irish oysters, famous the world over, are in season from September to March when there is an 'R' in the month. The best way to eat them is raw, just like our earliest ancestors who gathered around the mouths of estuaries to feast on shellfish thousands of years ago. There are numerous substantial mounds of oyster shells or shell middens throughout the country; they date from the prehistoric to the medieval periods. A particularly impressive site which probably dates from the late thirteenth/early fourteenth century was discovered during the construction of the 'new school' at Carrigtwohill. Coincidentally the famous Rossmore oysters now come from the oyster beds on the shoreline close by.

Although oysters are now very much a luxury, they were cheap and abundant for centuries. The Irish writer Jonathan Swift sang their praises and celebrated the aphrodisiac qualities of plump Irish oysters.

Irish Oysters

6 to 12 native Irish oysters per person

Garnish
seaweed
1 lemon
a little crushed ice

Oysters must be tightly shut: if a shell is even slightly open, discard it.

Not long before serving, open the oysters. You will need an oyster knife for this operation, unless you are one of the champion oyster openers! Place the oyster on the worktop, deep shell down. Cover your hand with a folded teatowel and hold the oyster firmly. Put the tip of the oyster knife into the crevice at the hinge of the oyster, push hard and then quickly twist the knife. You need to exert quite a bit of pressure (hence it is essential that the hand holding the oyster is protected, in case the knife slips!) When you feel that the oyster is opening, change the angle of the knife and, keeping the blade close to the shell, slice the oyster off the top shell in one movement. Then run the knife underneath the oyster in the deep shell and flip it over: be careful not to lose any of the delicious juices.

Put a bed of seaweed on two chilled plates; place the oysters on the seaweed and add a few lemon wedges.

Serve with fresh brown soda bread and butter and a glass of Guinness or Murphy stout.

Scallops

Up until the early part of this century, scallops were very plentiful around the Irish coast. Then the invention of the steam dredge led to overfishing in many places, so the numbers have decreased. Many older people who live on the islands or around the coast still eat scallops raw, although there seems to be a stigma attached to this—perhaps a relic of famine times.

Traditionally they were cooked in the shell, either in sea water or in fresh water. They were boiled for about four or five minutes and then removed from the water. The 'white bit and the tongue' were set aside and the rest discarded. Ted O'Súilleabháin from Bere Island explained 'You'd have a hot pan with butter melting in it and you'd just fry the scallops on both sides in butter, turn them out onto a plate and eat them. They were very sweet and tasty. When sea water was used as the cooking liquid it was used and often saved and drunk. It was considered to be a tremendous tonic.'

Cluasín or Bay Scallops were cooked in the same way. They are small, but absolutely delicious.

Scallops with Cream & Mushrooms

Serves 12 as a starter, 6 or 7 as a main course

A friend who grew up on the shores of Mulroy Bay in Co. Donegal used to go out in a rowing boat with family and friends on scallop expeditions. They would peer down through the clear water and raise the scallops one by one from the stony bottom with their very effective homemade scalloping hook. The scallops were brought home and cooked at once.

In his work The Rosses *in 1753, the Most Reverend A.B. recounts the unorthodox method of scallop collection:*

Their shellfish they got in the following manner…for scallops and oysters, when the tide was out, the younger women waded into the sea where they knew beds of such fish lay; some of them naked, others having stripped off their petticoats, went with their gowns tucked up about their waists and by armfuls brought ashore whatever number of scallops and oysters they thought requisite. The scallops weighed from two to four pounds each.

Scallop shells were also used after the fish was eaten. The more traditional uses included the production of scallop shell lamps; the shells were also burnt to make lime for whitewashing the house.

12 sea scallops
dry white wine and water to cover
$^3/_4$ cup chopped shallots or onion
2 tablespoons butter
2 to 2$^1/_2$ cups mushrooms, sliced
3 tablespoons flour
half and half
salt and freshly ground pepper
$^1/_2$ to $^3/_4$ cup cheddar cheese, grated
2 tablespoons chopped parsley
fluffy mashed potato (see page 38)

Put the scallops in a medium-sized stainless steel saucepan and cover with a mixture of half white wine and half water. Poach for 3 to 5 minutes (be careful to simmer and not to overcook). Remove the scallops and reduce the cooking liquid to approximately 1$^1/_2$-1$^1/_4$ cups.

Sweat the chopped onions gently in butter until soft (about 5 or 6 minutes). Add the sliced mushrooms and cook for 3 or 4 minutes more. Stir in the flour and cook for a further 1 minute. Add the half and half to the scallop cooking liquid to make up to 2$^1/_2$ cups and pour, stirring continuously, onto the flour in the saucepan. Cook gently to reduce the sauce until the flavor is really good. Season.

Cut the scallops into three or four pieces and add to the sauce with some of the cheese and the parsley. Decorate the scallop shells or serving dish by piping fluffy mashed potato round the edge. Fill the center with the scallop mixture and sprinkle the top with the remaining cheese.

Just before serving, reheat in a moderate oven 350°F until just bubbling (about 20 minutes).

Lobster

Up to relatively recently lobsters were still a modest luxury in Ireland, but nowadays, with the dwindling numbers and large demand for Irish shellfish from European restaurants, particularly in France, Germany and Belgium, the price has gone through the roof. Lobsters were traditionally caught in handmade wicker lobster pots. Most are now plastic, but the system remains the same.

Lobster is best bought straight from the fisherman who has hauled in the lobster pots that he set that morning. If lobsters are kept in a tank for any length of time they waste inside the shells, the flesh becomes stringy and they lose flavor.

Live lobsters should be heavy for their size. The only inedible parts of a lobster are the stomach sac, the gills and the long intestine that runs down the center of the tail. Every other scrap, including the creamy meat in the waistcoat, is edible and if properly cooked, delicious and tender. Lobster is one of Ireland's finest gastronomic treats so save your money for the best!

Serves 4 as a main course

Ballymaloe Hot Buttered Lobster

This simple but exquisite way of serving lobster outsells any other dish at Ballymaloe.

2 live lobsters (approx. 2lb each)

Court bouillon
1 carrot
1 onion
2¹/₂ cups dry white wine
2¹/₂ cups water
bouquet garni
a few peppercorns

8 tablespoons (1 stick) butter
squeeze of lemon juice

Garnish
lemon wedges
sprigs of watercress, flat parsley or fennel

Cover the lobsters with lukewarm salted water in a saucepan. Put the saucepan on a low heat and bring slowly to simmering point; lobster dies at about 112°F. By this stage the lobsters will be changing color, so remove them and discard all the cooking water.

Slice the carrot and onion and put with the wine, fresh water, *bouquet garni* and peppercorns into a stainless steel saucepan. Bring to a boil. Put in the lobsters and cover with a tight-fitting lid. Steam them until the shells have turned red, then remove them from the pot. Strain the cooking liquid and reserve for a sauce.

As soon as they are cool enough to handle, split them in half from head to tail, remove the 'sac' which is just in the top of the head and crack the large claws. Extract all the meat from the body, tail and large and small claws. Scrape out all the soft, greenish tomalley (liver) from the part of the shell nearest the head, and put it with the firmer meat into a warm bowl wrapped in a tea towel.

Heat the lobster shells. Cut the meat into chunks and melt half the butter. When it is foaming toss the meat and tomalley in it until the meat is hot through and the juices turn pink.

Spoon the meat back into the hot shells. Put the remaining butter into the pan, heat and scrape up any bits. Add a squeeze of lemon juice. Pour the buttery juices into small heated ramekins and serve beside the lobster on hot plates. Garnish with sprigs of watercress, flat parsley or fennel, and lemon. Hot buttered lobster should be eaten immediately.

Ballymaloe Hot Buttered Lobster

Scampi or Deep-Fried Prawns
with Tartar Sauce

Scampi, the 'must have' starter of the 1960s and '70s, has remained very popular and is utterly delicious when made with fresh Dublin Bay prawns. Dublin Bay Prawns are neither shrimp nor prawns but miniature lobsters. They are called Langoustines *by the French, but are rarely available in the United States, where jumbo shrimp can be used as a substitute.*

In North Atlantic Seafood, *Alan Davidson explains how these crustaceans first were given their name:*

> It is not, in fact, an inhabitant of Dublin Bay. The name was bestowed because the fishing boats coming into Dublin often had these prawns on board, having caught them incidentally. Since they were not fish, the fishermen could dispose of them on the side to the Dublin street-vendors, of whom Molly Malone of the well-known song, became the archetype. So the prawns were called Dublin Bay prawns because out in the bay was where the vendors got them.

Preheat the oil in the deep fryer to 350°F. Just before serving, dip the very fresh prawns or shrimp in batter and deep fry in the hot oil until crisp and golden. Drain on paper towels. Serve immediately with a little bowl of tartar sauce and lemon.

very fresh Dublin Bay prawns, (jumbo shrimp) peeled
batter (see recipe for Fish and Chips, page 68)
oil for deep frying
lemon wedges

Shrimp

When my husband Tim and his brothers and sisters were little, they used to make regular excursions to Ring Strand with their fishing nets to catch shrimp to bring home for supper. It was either a feast or a famine. When there was an abundance, there were huge plates of shrimp with home-made mayonnaise and freshly baked bread for supper. Afterwards little fingers helped to shell the surplus shrimp, while their mother Myrtle Allen infused fresh butter with thyme leaves and a scrap of garlic. Packed into little pots in the fridge, they kept for several days and are delicious served with hot thin toast. Nowadays the fishermen around the coast catch shrimp in large quantities in special shrimp pots, but one can still go shrimping as in times gone by.

Serves 4 as a first course

Potted Ballycotton Shrimp

¹/₂ clove garlic
salt and freshly ground pepper
4 to 6 tablespoons clarified butter
(see page 69)
1 teaspoon fresh thyme leaves
2¹/₂lb cooked shelled shrimp
1 or 2 teaspoons lemon juice
extra clarified butter for top of pot

How to cook shrimp

Bring 10 cups of water to a boil, add 2 tablespoons of salt and toss in the live or very fresh shrimp. They will change color from grey to pink almost instantly. Bring the water back to a boil and cook for just 2 or 3 minutes. The shrimps are cooked when there is no trace of black at the back of the head. Drain immediately, and spread out on a large baking tray to cool.

When cold, serve with homemade mayonnaise (see page 51) and freshly baked brown bread, garnished perhaps with a lemon wedge. Alternatively, peel first and then serve or use for another recipe.

To peel, first remove the head, pinch the end of the tail and tug it. This will pull off half the shell. Remove the remainder of the shell with your fingers. Shrimp are much easier on the fingers than Dublin Bay prawns!

Crush the garlic to a paste with a little salt. Bring clarified butter to a boil with the thyme leaves and garlic. Add the shelled shrimps and simmer together for 3 to 5 minutes. Season carefully with 1 or 2 teaspoons of lemon juice. Pack into pots and run more clarified butter over the top. Put into the fridge and allow to set. Serve with Melba toast or crusty bread.

Note: *potted shrimp will keep in the refrigerator for 3 or 4 days.*

Serves 4

Melba Toast

2 thin slices of white bread

Toast the bread on both sides. Cut the crusts off immediately and then split the slice in half. Scrape off any soft crumbs, cut into triangles and put the bread back under the broiler, untoasted side up. Leave it for a few seconds until the edges curl up.

Freshwater Crayfish

Cullohill, the little village in Co. Laois where I spent a happy and carefree childhood, was about as far as it could be from the sea. An occasional day trip to the beach in Tramore, Co. Waterford, was the highlight of our holidays. Apart from that rare treat, the River Goul to the west of the village was the place to cool off on hot days. As we paddled and splashed in the shallow pools, older and wiser people would lean over the bridge, watch bemused and warn us to be careful in case the crayfish bit our toes. We giggled and squirmed, but didn't quite believe them. However, I now know that there were—and still are—crayfish in those streams.

Traditionally, Lough Derg, Co. Donegal, the lake which surrounds the well known place of pilgrimage, was noted for its abundant population of crayfish. Similarly, most of the lakes in the limestone regions of the country, such as Lough Sheelin, Lough Leen and Derravaragh Lake, had a plentiful supply.

The crayfish were lifted in old style pots and creels which were circular in shape, with a flat weighted bottom, in much the same style as the lobster and crab creels.

If you are fortunate enough to catch some of these delectable crustaceans (which are now a protected species in many parts of the world), cook them quickly in boiling salted water, using 1 tablespoon of salt to every 4 cups water. Peel them and eat them simply with melted butter or with a homemade mayonnaise (see page 51).

Serves 6 to 8

Ballycotton Fish Pie

2¹/₂lb fillets of cod, haddock, whiting,
salmon or flounder or a mixture
1 medium sized onion, peeled and diced
3 or 4 slices of carrot
1 small bay leaf
a sprig of thyme
3 peppercorns
2¹/₂ cups milk
4 eggs
2¹/₄ cups sliced mushrooms
butter
salt and freshly ground pepper
roux made with 2 tablespoons butter and
2 tablespoons flour (see page 40)
a very little cream (optional)
2 tablespoons chopped parsley
18 cooked mussels (optional)
2lb champ (see page 143) or fluffy
mashed potato (see page 38)

Accompaniment
Parsley Butter or Garlic Butter (optional)
(see pages 45 and 69)

Many different types of fish may be used for a fish pie, so feel free to adapt this recipe a little to suit your needs. Clams would be a good and cheap addition and a little smoked haddock is tasty also.

Put the onions, carrot, bay leaf, thyme, and peppercorns into the milk, bring to a boil and simmer for 3 or 4 minutes. Remove from the heat and leave to infuse for 10 to 15 minutes. Strain.

Meanwhile, hard-boil the eggs for 10 minutes in boiling water, cool and shell. Sauté the sliced mushrooms in a little butter in a hot pan, season with salt and freshly ground pepper and set aside.

Put the fish into a wide pan or frying pan and cover with the flavored milk. Season with salt and ground pepper. Cover and simmer gently until the fish is cooked. Take out the fish, carefully removing any bones or skin. Bring the liquid to a boil and thicken with roux. Add a little cream (optional) and the chopped parsley, roughly chopped hard-boiled eggs, mushrooms, pieces of fish and the mussels. Stir gently, taste and correct the seasoning. Spoon into 1 large or 6 to 8 small dishes and pipe potato or champ on top. The pie may be prepared ahead to this point.

Put into a moderate oven 350°F to reheat and slightly brown the potato on top. This will take about 10 to 15 minutes if the filling and potato are warm, or about 30 minutes if you are reheating the dish from cold.

Serve with garlic butter or parsley butter.

Where shellfish are concerned, Ireland has always had an embarrassment of riches which we have taken for granted, indeed undervalued, for centuries. At Ballymaloe House this selection of delicious Irish shellfish delights guests from all over the world, and is not difficult to prepare. Note that rohans and palourdes are types of clam.

Cook the sea urchins in boiling salted water (allow 1 tablespoon salt to 4 cups water) for 4 or 5 minutes. Remove and allow to get cold.

If using prawns, bring the water to a boil and add the salt. Remove the heads of the prawns and, with the underside of the prawn uppermost, tug the little fan-shaped tail at either side and carefully draw out the trail. (The trail is the intestine, so it is very important to remove it before cooking regardless of whether the prawns are to be shelled or not.)

Put the prawns into the boiling salted water and as soon as the water returns to a boil, test a prawn to see if it is cooked. When it is, remove the prawns immediately. Very large ones may take $1/2$ or 1 minute more. Allow the prawns to cool in a single layer and then remove the shells. Do not cook too many prawns together, or they may overcook before the water even comes back to a boil.

Cook the periwinkles as on page 56.

If using live jumbo shrimp, cook them in boiling salted water also for 2 or 3 minutes, or until the shells have changed color from grey to bright orangey pink. If there is any trace of black on the heads, cook them for a little longer. Drain and allow to cool in a single layer.

Wash the clams or the mussels, palourdes, roghans and cockles and check that all the shells are tightly closed. They can then all be opened in the same manner. Spread the shells in a single layer in a heavy bottomed saucepan. Cover with a folded tea towel or a lid and put the pan on a low heat for a few minutes. Remove the shellfish as soon a they open (if any refuse to open, discard them). Keep the liquid which will exude from the shellfish as they open: it's wonderful for fish soup or a sauce to be served with shellfish.

Remove the beards from the mussels and discard one shell and loosen the mussel from the remaining shell so that the guests won't have to tussle with their forks. Remove the outer round and 'exhaust pipes' (siphons) from the clams or palourdes and roghans and discard one shell. Nothing needs to be removed from the cockles, but discard one shell also.

When the sea urchins are cold, scrape the prickles off the top with a spoon or brush, then tap the centre with the bowl of a teaspoon; the shell usually cracks like an egg, so the center can be lifted out. Be careful not to lose any of the precious juices and make sure to remove any splinters of shell from the center. It will be necessary to provide a teaspoon for eating the sea urchins and a fingerbowl should also be provided if the guests are to peel the shrimps or prawns themselves.

Not long before serving, open the oysters (see page 58). Arrange the shellfish on a large white plate. Place a tiny bowl of homemade mayonnaise in the center and garnish with the lemon and herbs. If you wish to use seaweed, e.g bladderwrack, for garnish you should plunge the sprigs into boiling water for a few seconds, then remove them immediately and refresh in a bowl of iced water. The seaweed will turn bright green and should be used fairly soon, because it begins to get slimy quite quickly.

Serves 6 as a substantial starter

A Plate of Irish Shellfish

All or most of these (not all are available outside Ireland, use substitutes given):

6 sea urchins
18 Dublin Bay prawns or 24 jumbo
    shrimps
18 mussels
18 cockles
18 roghans and 12 palourdes or 30 little
    neck or cherry stone clams
6 native Irish oysters
periwinkles

Garnish
home-made mayonnaise
6 segments of lemon
sprigs of wild watercress or fennel
seaweed, optional

Crabs

The popularity of crab has waxed and waned in Ireland throughout the years. In some cases it was despised as a foodstuff and up to relatively recently, most Irish fishermen had no meas on (or regard for) crabs. However, in recent years a large export market and a smaller but nonetheless significant home market has opened up, so crabs are being landed all around the coast. Might I put in a plea here: resist the temptation to buy crab claws alone. It encourages the inhumane practice of pulling the claws off the live crabs and dumping the bodies, so the crab is left to die unable to feed itself. Quite apart from that, the delicious creamy brown meat in the shells shouldn't be missed.

Crabs are also best straight from the sea and should, like lobsters, feel heavy for their size. The female with the large 'flap' underneath is more delicate than the male and often gives a greater return.

Ivan Allen's Dressed Crab

Many years ago we dropped in to see our friends the Mosses in Bennettsbridge, Co. Kilkenny—well inland. They had just cooked the box of crabs they had brought fresh up from the boats at Dunmore East.

> *We were given a great welcome: another pair of hands to extract the juicy white and brown meat. Stanley Mosse then made up lots of this potted crab which we ate gluttonously on hot buttered toast.*

Mix all ingredients together in a bowl or, better still, purée them in a food processor. Taste carefully and continue to season until you are happy with the flavor; it may need a little more lemon juice. Press the mixture into a pottery bowl, cover and refrigerate.

Serves 8 to 10 as a starter

Stanley Mosse's Potted Crab

5oz (1¼ cups) mixed brown and white cooked crab meat.
8 tablespoons (1 stick) softened butter
2 teaspoons finely chopped parsley
lemon juice to taste

When I first came to Shanagarry crabs were considered to be a nuisance by most fishermen because they found their way into the lobster pots and were much less lucrative to sell. Tommy Sliney, the legendary Ballycotton man who sold his fish from a donkey and cart on the pier occasionally brought us a few, and it was always a cause for celebration. We'd prepare all the other ingredients and then my father-in-law, Ivan Allen, would mix and taste the Dressed Crab. Ballymaloe Tomato Relish is now sold countrywide.

First make the buttered crumbs for the topping. Melt the butter in a pan and stir in the breadcrumbs. Remove from the heat immediately and allow the mixture to cool.

Scrub the crab shells, mix all the ingredients except the topping together, taste carefully and correct the seasoning. The texture should be soft, so add a little more white sauce if necessary. Fill into the shells.

Bake in a moderate oven 350°F, until heated through and brown on top (about 15 to 20 minutes). Flash under the broiler if necessary to crisp the crumbs.

Note: *1lb cooked crab in the shell yields about 6 to 8oz crab meat depending on the time of the year.*

Serves 5 or 6 as a main course

Ivan Allen's Dressed Crab

15oz (3¾ cups) crab meat, brown and white mixed (2 or 3 crabs should yield this)
¾ to 1 cup soft white breadcrumbs
2 teaspoons white wine vinegar
2 tablespoons tomato chutney
2 tablespoons butter
generous pinch of dry mustard or 1 teaspoon French mustard
salt and freshly ground pepper
¾ cup white sauce

Topping
2 tablespoons butter
⅔ cup soft white breadcrumbs

This is a marvellous way of making white sauce if you already have roux made. Put the cold milk into a saucepan with the carrot, onion, peppercorns, thyme and parsley. Bring to a boil and simmer for 4 or 5 minutes. Remove from the heat and leave to infuse for ten minutes. Strain out the vegetables, bring the milk back to a boil and thicken with roux to a light coating consistency. Season with salt and freshly ground pepper, taste and correct the seasoning if necessary.

White Sauce

1¼ cup milk
a few slices of carrot
a few slices of onion
a small sprig of thyme
a small sprig of parsley
3 peppercorns
1½oz roux, (see page 40)
salt and freshly ground pepper

Boiled Fish

with Parsley Sauce

Boiled fish, the least appetizing-sounding dish in the world, is still a very common way of cooking fish in Ireland. John Guerin of Ballyheigue in Co. Kerry told me very recently that cold boiled ling is still one of the favorite meals among fisherfolk in that area. This recipe is taken directly from Annie Kiely's manuscript cookbook, dated 1908, Cork. For today's cooks, the fish should be simmered until it flakes easily.

Take any kind of fish, wash and clean thoroughly. Place in boiling water with a handful of salt, and a little vinegar if liked. Allow it to simmer for half an hour. Place gently in a dish and serve with parsley or butter sauce.

Fish & Chips

I keep wondering if fish and chips qualify as traditional food! Certainly they have been around for longer than the other street pots that are now becoming popular in Ireland. Huge quantities are wolfed down every year all over the country, and there's one fish and chip shop in every village and town—not to speak of countless portable ones at the races, matches and on roadsides everywhere.

Eamonn MacThomáis, the Dublin folklorist, gave me an evocative description of running down to the chipper with his sixpence for a single and chips and racing home with them under his gansey close to his chest to keep them warm for the dinner.

portions of fresh fish, e.g. cod, haddock, skate or plaice
old potatoes, peeled and freshly cut into chips
oil for deep frying

Batter
1 cup plain flour
1³/4 tablespoons olive oil
1 or 1¹/2 egg whites
sea salt

First make the batter. Sieve the flour into a bowl and make a well in the center. Pour in the olive oil, stir, and add enough water to make a batter about the consistency of heavy cream. Allow to stand for at least 1 hour. Just before frying, whisk the egg whites to a stiff peak and fold into the batter, adding a good pinch of sea salt.

Heat the oil to 350°F (not higher, otherwise thicker fillets in particular may be undercooked in the center).

Dip the fish pieces into the batter, one piece at a time, and fry until crispy and golden. Dip the chips in hot oil for a few seconds. Drain both fish and chips well on paper towels. Serve on hot plates (or in wax paper) with a wedge of lemon and a dash of malt vinegar to season.

Serves 4 to 6

Twice Laid

This recipe for a large fish cake came from a little frayed booklet without a cover sent to me by Mrs. Teresa Murray from Clontuskert near Ballinasloe in Co. Galway. I couldn't find a date or name, but each recipe stated the price of the dish. This cost fourpence—old ones at that! Perhaps the name Twice Laid is a reference to the fact that both the potatoes and the fish have been around once before.

1lb cooked potatoes
8oz cooked fish, e.g. cod, flounder, hake or haddock
salt and freshly ground pepper
1 beaten egg, free-range if possible
freshly chopped parsley and chives
2 tablespoons fat dripping or butter

Mash the potatoes with a fork. Remove the skin and bone from the fish and break it up into flakes. Mix the fish with the potatoes and add seasonings. (I took the liberty of adding a beaten egg and some chopped parsley and chives.) Shape into a flat cake and fry it in butter until golden on both sides. It tastes quite delicious.

*Originally an economical dish, using up leftover scraps of boiled fish, fish cakes are now featured on trendy menus. They are absolutely delicious when they are carefully made and served hot with a small blob of garlic butter melting on top. Garlic may sound an unlikely inclusion in a book on traditional Irish food, but in fact the wild forms (*Alliaria petiolata *and* Allium triquetrum*) are very prolific in Ireland. Garlic has been used in salads and as a flavoring, particularly for butter, since early times and is mentioned in the Brehon Laws. Firkins of butter are regularly dug up in Irish bogs, and many are found to have been flavored with garlic.*

First make the garlic butter. Cream the butter, stir in the parsley and a few drops of lemon juice at a time. Add the crushed garlic. Roll into butter pats or form into a roll and wrap in wax paper or foil, screwing each end so that it looks like a cracker. Refrigerate to harden.

To make the fish cakes, melt the butter in a saucepan and toss in the chopped onion. Cover and sweat on a gentle heat for 4 or 5 minutes until soft but not colored.

Scrape the contents of the pan into a bowl. Add the mashed potato and the flaked cooked fish, egg yolk and chopped parsley, or a mixture of fresh herbs. Season well with salt and freshly ground pepper and taste. Form the mixture into fish cakes about 2oz each. Coat them first in seasoned flour, then in beaten egg and finally in crumbs and refrigerate until needed. Fry the fishcakes on a medium heat in clarified butter (see below) until golden on both sides. Serve piping hot with pats or slices of garlic butter and a good green salad

To make clarified butter, melt the butter gently in a saucepan or in the oven. Allow it to stand for a few minutes, the spoon off the crusty white layer of salt particles from the top of the melted butter. Underneath this crust there is clear liquid butter, which is called clarified butter. It is excellent for cooking because it will keep in the refrigerator for several weeks.

Makes 8, serves 4

Fish Cakes
with Garlic Butter

8oz cold leftover fish, e.g. salmon, cod, haddock, whiting (a proportion of smoked fish such as haddock or mackerel is good)
2 tablespoons butter
1 large onion, finely chopped
1 cup mashed potato
1 egg yolk
1 tablespoon chopped parsley or mixed fresh herbs
salt and freshly ground pepper
seasoned flour
1 beaten egg
fresh white breadcrumbs
clarified butter or a mixture of butter and oil for frying

Garlic butter
4 tablespoons butter
4 teaspoons parsley, finely chopped
1 or 2 teaspoons freshly squeezed lemon juice
2 or 3 cloves garlic, crushed

Kedgeree immediately conjures up images of country house breakfasts which were often a veritable feast. It would usually have been served on a silver dish on the polished sideboard, so that guests could help themselves. This recipe was, of course, of Anglo-Indian origin and would have been brought back to Ireland by the many Irishmen who fought in India in the British Army during the Raj.

Cook the rice in boiling salted water for about 8 to 10 minutes. Hard-boil the eggs, also in boiling salted water, for 10 minutes. Drain off the water. Place under a cold tap to cool and stop cooking. Peel and chop roughly.

Remove the skin and bones from the fish and flake into small pieces.

Heat the cream and butter in a saucepan. Add the parsley and chives. As soon as it bubbles, add the rice, flaked fish and the hard-boiled eggs. Season well with salt and freshly ground pepper and a pinch of cayenne. Mix very gently. Taste, correct seasoning if necessary, pile into a hot dish and serve with freshly baked bread or with hot buttered toast.

Serves 6-8

Kedgeree

1lb salmon, freshly cooked, (see page 50) or 8oz cooked salmon and 8oz of cooked smoked haddock
1 cup white long grain rice
3 eggs
2/3 cup cream
3 tablespoons butter
3 tablespoons freshly chopped parsley
1 1/2 tablespoons chopped chives
salt and freshly ground pepper
cayenne pepper

Game

In the past, Ireland's heavily wooded landscape and extensive inland waterways provided the ideal habitat for a variety of wild fowl and other game. Evidence found at the Mesolithic site of Mount Sandel in Co. Derry, dating from 7,000 B.C., suggests that Ireland's earliest inhabitants enjoyed a diet which included duck, pigeon, grouse, goshawk, and capercallie.

Ireland's landscape is dotted with archaeological evidence to illustrate the popularity of venison: specialised sites known as *Fulachta Fiadh*, which means cooking place or boiling place of deer, indicate the importance of deer in the diet, as far back as the Bronze Age (2,000 B.C.).

In more recent times, Arthur Young's observation in Co. Fermanagh, from his *A Tour of Ireland 1776-1779,* also highlights the prevalence of fowl and game in the eighteenth century. He states:

> …living is exceedingly cheap here; besides common provisions which I have everywhere registered, wild ducks are only 3d, snipes 1½d, teal 2d and widgeon the same…

Huge game shoots, complete with beaters, were also held on the large country estates of Ireland well into the twentieth century.

Puffins

Puffins are to be found on several islands off the north and west of Ireland. It is therefore probable that puffins were eaten by the earliest settlers in Ireland, who would have learned to trap them on the rocky ledges around the coast. There are many references to eating puffins, particularly during times of famine. In Robin Flower's account of life on the Blaskets there is a fine description of how some fishermen who were returning home downhearted without a catch during the Great Famine, suddenly spotted a 'company of fine fat birds, puffins and guillemots on a high cliff on Inishvicillane'. They would provide an abundance of food for the hungry islanders, but were almost impossible to reach. Nonetheless, driven by desperation, one of the islanders attempted to scale the sheer cliff face while his companions held their breath in terror. He bravely reached the mouth of the hole in the cliff, lured the birds out and throttled them. He threw down about ten dozen birds to his companions, who eagerly picked up the floating birds off the water and put them in their currachs. When they called to him to join them, he was unable to get down so he bid them goodbye saying 'Home with you now in God's name, for I think these are the last birds I shall ever catch'.

However, the story has a happy ending because next day the fisherman's son managed to rescue his father, who received a hero's welcome from the grateful islanders.

Wild Duck

Duck has been eaten in Ireland since the Mesolithic periods, as evidence from Mount Sandel, in Co. Derry, shows. This site dates to 7,000 B.C. and provides the earliest evidence of human habitation in Ireland

Birds in general, and ducks in particular, also had a particular significance in Celtic and early Irish mythology. A classic example of their use as an artistic motif comes from a bronze trumpet found at Loughnashade, Co. Antrim and dating from c. 200 B.C. A bronze cup with a duck-shaped handle made between c. 100 B.C. and 100 A.D. was found in the River Shannon at Keshcarrigan, Co. Leitrim.

While travelling through Ireland in the eighteenth century, Charles Etienne Coquebert de Montbret stayed in a thatched cottage in Buttevant, Co. Cork, where he received a meal of wild duck, along with snipe and teal. He comments: 'this was not the first time when, expecting nothing, I was better served than elsewhere'.

The most common species of wild duck in Ireland are mallard, teal and widgeon. Other duck which may be legally shot and eaten include gadwell, shoveler, goldeneye, pintail, pochard and tufted duck. However, some of these birds are becoming rare and the laws are changing, so it might be wise to check with the Wildlife Department of the Office of Public Works if you plan to shoot any duck.

Serves 2

Roast Wild Duck

1 duck
3 or 4 juniper berries
1 sprig of thyme
1 sprig of marjoram
butter or 4 or 5 bacon strips
salt and freshly ground pepper
¹/₃ cup game or chicken stock
a splash of wine or juice of 1 orange

Trim the end off the wing tips at the first joint. Chop the ends off the legs just above the 'knee'. Remove the wing bone. Make sure that the crop has been removed.

Season the cavity with salt and freshly ground pepper; pop in a few crushed juniper berries. Smear the breast with butter or wrap it with the bacon and truss with cotton string.

Preheat the oven to 450°F. Roast for about 20 minutes if you like it fairly rare or for 30 minutes if you prefer it better done. Be careful not to overcook or it will be dry. Duck which has been barded with bacon will take up to 10 minutes longer to cook. Just as soon as the duck is cooked, remove to a warm serving dish. Pour the fat from the roasting pan. Add some stock and a splash of red or white wine or the juice of an orange. Boil well, taste, correct the seasoning and strain. Carve the duck and serve the hot gravy with it.

Barnacle Goose

The barnacle goose is referred to as early as the ninth century, when it appears in the poem *Marbán agus Gúaire (King and Hermit)*:

Notes of gleaming-breasted pigeons
The song of the pleasant constant thrush above my house
Bees, chafers, barnacle geese, brent geese
Shortly before Samhain.

Right up to the early part of this century it was common folk belief that the wild Barnacle goose *(Branta Leucopsis)* was actually fish, not fowl, and so could be eaten on days of fast and abstinence.

There was a theory that the barnacle goose first grew out of a worm in the sea, although Giraldus Cambrensis, in his twelfth century *Topographia Hibernica*, believed that it was hatched from an egg. 'They were in shells and already formed. No eggs are laid as is usual as a result of mating. No bird ever sits upon eggs to hatch them…Accordingly, in some parts of Ireland, bishops and religious men eat them without sin during a fasting time, regarding them as not being flesh, since they are not born of flesh.'

This folk belief persisted right up to the present century—a hotel in Dingle, Co. Kerry, is reported to have had barnacle goose on the menu it served to the clergy until the abstinence laws were relaxed in 1966.

Serves 2 or 3

Roast Pheasant
with Game Chips

The pheasant is a relatively latecomer to Ireland, being introduced only in Elizabethan times. However, the introduction was successful. Fynes Moryson, who was secretary to the Lord Deputy, Lord Mountjoy, until Mountjoy's death in 1606, records in his Itinerary *(published in parts between 1617 and 1626) that 'Ireland hath plenty of pheasants, as I have known sixtie served at one feast'.*

Nowadays large sporting estates are stocked annually with game for the shooting season, so the price of the hand-reared pheasant is within everyone's reach. For those of us who enjoy a rich gamey flavor, wild pheasant are unquestionably superior. Corn-fed birds from large shoots have a covering of yellowish orange fat and their flavor is less pronounced. Birds reared in captivity are at the bottom of the flavor league as they have never foraged in the wild, but are totally corn-fed. Pheasant can be hung by the neck for anything from 5 days to 3 weeks, depending on the weather and your taste—a week to 10 days suits me. The pheasant season in Ireland is from 1 November to 31 January.

1 young, plump pheasant
3 tablespoons butter
3/4 cup chopped onions
2/3 cup soft white breadcrumbs
1 tablespoon freshly chopped herbs
e.g. parsley, thyme,
chives, marjoram
salt and freshly ground pepper

Gravy
1 cup game or chicken stock

Game Chips
(see opposite)

Cranberry Sauce
(see below)

Gut the pheasant if necessary and remove the 'crop' which is at the neck end; wash and dry well.

To make the stuffing, melt the butter and sweat the onions until soft but not colored, then remove from the heat. Stir in the breadcrumbs and herbs, season with salt and freshly ground pepper and taste. Unless you are about to cook the bird right away, allow the stuffing to get quite cold before putting it into the bird.

Season the cavity with salt and freshly ground pepper, then stuff the pheasant loosely. Smear the breast and legs generously with butter. Season with salt and freshly ground pepper.

Roast in a preheated moderate oven at 375°F for about 1¼ hours. Test by pricking the leg at the thickest point; the juices should just run clear. If the pheasant is cooked too long it will be dry and tough, but it ought not to be served rare.

Spoon off any surplus fat from the roasting pan (keep it for roasting or sautéeing potatoes). Pour in the game or chicken stock. Bring to a boil, using a whisk to dislodge the crusty caramelized juices so they can dissolve into the gravy. Season with salt and freshly ground pepper, taste and boil until you are happy with the flavor. Pour into a hot gravy boat.

Carve the pheasant and serve with all the trimmings—stuffing, gravy, game chips and cranberry sauce. Watch out for lead shot while you are eating the pheasant.

Serves 6 (approximately)

Cranberry Sauce

6oz fresh cranberries
4 tablespoons water
1/2 cup granulated sugar

Put the fresh cranberries into a heavy-based stainless steel or castiron saucepan with the water (don't add the sugar yet as it tends to toughen the skins). Bring them to a boil, cover and simmer until the cranberries 'pop' and soften—for about 7 minutes. Remove from the heat and stir in the sugar until dissolved. Serve warm or cold.

Note: *cranberry sauce will keep in your refrigerator for a week to ten days.*

Serves 2 or 3
Game Chips

2 large, even-sized potatoes
olive oil for deep frying
salt

Wash and peel the potatoes. For even-sized chips, trim each potato with a swivel-top peeler until smooth. Slice them very finely, preferably on a mandolin. Soak in cold water to remove the excess starch (this will prevent them from discolouring or sticking together). Drain off the water and dry well.

Heat the olive oil to 350°F. Drop in the dry potato slices a few at a time and fry until golden and completely crisp. Drain on paper towels and sprinkle lightly with salt. Repeat until they are all cooked.

If they are not to be served immediately, they may be stored in a tin box and reheated in a low oven just before serving.

per person
Roast Plover

1 plover
bacon
salt and freshly ground pepper
butter
slice of white bread
watercress or parsley sprigs

There are two kinds of plover in Ireland; golden plover, which are wonderful to eat, and green plover, which are less good but more plentiful. (Plover is unavailable in the United States.)

Pluck and gut the plover. Season the cavity with salt and freshly ground pepper. Smear with butter, wrap in bacon and secure with a toothpick.

Preheat the oven to 425°F. Roast the plover for about 15 minutes. Fry the bread in butter and serve the plover on it. Make a little gravy from the pan juices if desired, and pour over the roast bird. Garnish with watercress or parsley.

Roast Pheasant

Pigeon

Pigeon houses were common on Irish country estates from medieval times. I recently visited the well preserved dovecote at Downhill on the North Antrim coast; it was built on top of an existing ice-house and could accommodate two hundred pairs. The pigeons were valued not only for their meat, but also for their eggs. Each pair would have had about sixteen chicks a year. The squabs were culled at about four weeks of age, when the meat was fat and juicy. The pigeon manure was valued as fertilizer for the walled garden nearby. Other pigeon houses that have survived include those at Parke's Castle in Co. Leitrim, Annesbrook in Co. Meath and (a particularly fine example) beside the thirteenth century Augustinian Friary at Ballybeg, near Buttevant, in Co. Cork.

Pigeon Pie

Serves 10 to 12

Wood pigeons have always been very prolific in Ireland. In the country young boys were taught how to shoot by their fathers. Before a big dance or party in Ballymaloe House in the 1950s, my husband Tim and his brother Rory would 'bag' enough to make large quantities of pigeon pie—a relatively inexpensive and absolutely delicious way to feed a large number of people for a winter house party.

breasts from 4 to 6 pigeons
half their weight in bacon
their weight in lean beef
bacon fat or olive oil for frying
8 baby carrots or sticks of carrot
10 to 12 button onions
1 clove garlic, crushed
2 teaspoons flour
1¼ cups red wine
1¼ cups homemade beef stock
½ cup homemade tomato purée
or smaller quantity of canned purée
or tomato paste: use according to
concentration and make up
with extra stock
roux (optional; see page 40)
salt and freshly ground pepper
2 teaspoons chopped thyme and parsley
8oz puff pastry (see page 195)

Remove the rind from the bacon (if there is one) and cut into cubes about 1 inch wide. Cut the beef and pigeon into similar size pieces.

Heat some bacon fat or olive oil in a frying pan and fry the bacon until crisp and golden. Remove to a 2 quart casserole. Add the beef and pigeon pieces, a few at a time, to the frying pan and toss until they change color. Add them to the casserole. Then turn the carrots, onions and crushed garlic in the fat and add them to the meat in the casserole. Stir in the flour into the fat in the pan, cook for a minute or so and then stir or whisk in the wine, stock and tomato purée. Bring to a boil and thicken with roux if necessary. Pour over the meat and vegetables in the casserole. Season with salt and freshly ground pepper, add thyme and parsley and return to the boil. Cover and cook for 1 to 2 hours or until tender (this will depend on the age of the pigeons) in a low oven, 300°F. When cooked, add the mushrooms in cream (see below).

Mushrooms in cream

8 oz sliced mushrooms or portobello
mushrooms
1 to 2 tablespoons butter
¾ cup finely chopped onion
salt and freshly ground pepper
a squeeze of lemon juice
½ tablespoon chopped chives (optional)
½ tablespoon parsley
½ cup cream

Melt the butter in a heavy saucepan until it foams. Add the chopped onions, cover and sweat on a gentle heat for 5 to 10 minutes, or until quite soft but not colored. Remove the onions to a bowl. Increase the heat and cook the sliced mushrooms, in batches if necessary. Season each batch with salt, freshly ground black pepper and a tiny squeeze of lemon juice. Add the onions, parsley and chives to the mushrooms in the saucepan, then add the cream and allow to bubble for a few minutes. Taste and correct the seasoning.

When the pigeon stew is cold, pour it into a deep pie dish. Roll out the puff pastry to cover the dish and bake for 10 minutes at 450°F, then reduce the heat to 375°F and cook for another 20 minutes. Serve with a green salad.

Roast Squab

4 young squabs
salt and freshly ground pepper
butter
8 slices of bacon
1¹/₄ cup game or chicken stock
salt and freshly ground pepper

Preheat the oven to 425°F. Season the cavity of each bird with salt and freshly ground pepper. Smear the breasts and legs with butter, and wrap in a couple of pieces of bacon.

Roast for 30 to 40 minutes depending on size. Transfer to a serving dish. Spoon off the pan juices. Put the roasting pan back on the stove, add the stock and allow to bubble, whisking all the while to dissolve the caramelized meat juices. Boil for a few minutes, taste and season if necessary. Strain and serve with the tender juicy little squabs.

Medlar Jelly (see page 182) would be a delicious accompaniment.

Woodcock & Snipe

Historically game has always been popular with all classes of society in Ireland. In times of scarcity particularly, hunted wild fowl made a welcome addition to the diet.

Unlike most other countries in Europe, Ireland still has expanses of uncleared woodland which provide the perfect natural habitat for game birds such as woodcock. At Temple House in Co. Sligo, the woods have been deliberately managed since the 1800s to yield some of the best snipe and woodcock shooting in Europe. Ireland also has plenty of bogs and marshes favoured by snipe.

Amhlaoibh Uí Shúileabháin from Callan, Co. Kilkenny, comments on the availability of snipe in his diary of 1829. On 22 January 1829 he states: 'It is easy to find out the snipe now, for the frost has driven it from the hill to the running water or the water without ice.'

Both birds are highly regarded, not only for their delicious flesh but also for their innards, with the exception of the gizzard which is removed before the birds are roasted. The brains of woodcock are considered to be a great delicacy. Pluck them carefully, head and all, because woodcock or snipe are traditionally served trussed with their own long beak. They are best hung for 4 to 5 days.

Roast Snipe

Serves 4

4 snipe
4 slices of white bread
4 slices of bacon

George Gossip's game dinners at Tullanisk House, near Birr, in Co. Offaly, are legendary. This is his recipe for roast snipe. Serve one per person, unaccompanied, on its toast, as a starter or light luncheon dish. In Victorian and Edwardian times it was served as a savory to finish a meal!

Hang the snipe for two to three days in warm weather, a week in cold weather. Pluck the bird, including the head and neck. You may have to skin these, but on no account remove the skin from the body of the bird. For convenience you may cut off the wings at the first joint. Do not draw (remove the entrails), as these provide an essential part of the flavor, and are not at all unpleasant. Move the legs forward and pass the beak through the body as a skewer.

Toast a piece of bread on one side only. Butter the toasted side and place, buttered side down, on a baking sheet. Place the snipe on top, cover with a slice of bacon and place in a hot oven, 475°F. When the bacon is crisp and the upper surface of the bread is well browned (after about 5 to 7 minutes), remove from the oven and serve immediately. This cooking time means that the snipe will be quite rare.

If you prefer your game less rare, allow extra time, even up to five minutes more, depending on your taste. In this case, unless you cover it with foil, you will have to trim the burnt edges from the toast and the bacon will be overcooked!

Snipe are in season from 1 September until 31 January, but are usually only available from November.

Woodcock Potted Pie

Serves 4 to 6

This recipe comes from the Kitchen Book of Clonbrock:

Take 2lb of fat bacon, cut it up small and fry it for a few minutes in a stewpan, then add 2½ lb of lean veal or rabbit, cut small and without bone.

4 or 5 goose or rabbit livers—2 bay leaves—1 sprig of thyme and a very little parsley tied in a bundle and 3 large onions.

Stew the whole lot for about 1 hour, take out the herbs, let the rest get cold, then pound it well in a mortar, pass it through a wire sieve, put it back in the mortar, add and mix well with it some pepper, salt and a very little cayenne, 3 fresh eggs, 1oz of shallot chopped very fine, and sweated in butter, a few mushrooms and truffles cut in small squares. Then take a pie dish and line it with some thin slices of fat bacon, put in some of the potted meat, then put in the centre, which has been nicely boned and cut, fill up with potted meat, tie it down with dough. Bake it in a dish with water for 4 hours in a moderately hot oven, take it out, remove the pastry and press it with some heavy weight till cold, then pour on some melted butter and serve—Snipe, Woodcock, Partridges or Pheasant can be equally used.

Roast Thrush

There is a wonderfully evocative description of hunting thrushes on the Great Blaskets on Hallowe'en night in *Twenty Years A Growing* by Muiris O Súilleabhán:

'Now,' said he, 'this is Hallowe'en, and it is not known who will be living when it comes again, so I am going to propose another plan to make a night till morning of it. We will all go in twos and threes with lanterns through the island hunting thrushes, and when we have made our round let everyone come back here. See you have a good fire down for us, Máire, and there is no fear but we'll have a roast for the night.'…Off we went, the three of us with our lanterns, west to the Strand. It was a frosty night, the stars twinkling, the Milky Way stretched across the sky to the south and the Plough to the north, a light easterly breeze coming straight from Slea Head, gíog-gíog-gíog from peewits in the glen, a light here and a light there on the hill-side from the others, and we on our way west to the Great Glen, for many thrushes do be sleeping in the bushes there…We made no stop or stay till we reached the house. As soon as we went in, 'How many have you?' they all cried with one voice.

'Who of yourselves has the most?' said I. 'I have twenty,' said Tomás an Phuncháin. 'Faith,' said Pádraig, 'we have twenty-eight.' With that there was a great outburst, everyone clapping with us.

They were thrown out on the table, and when everyone had added his share there were a hundred. 'Let all begin the plucking now,' said Séamus O Duinnlévy. We began plucking the feathers, all except my sisters Máire and Eileen, Kate O'Shea and Kate Peg, who were busy roasting and washing plates. The house was a pleasant sight now, everyone full of bright laughter, Seán O Criomhthain seated by the fire playing his melodium, four out on the floor dancing a reel, others cooking, others eating; and as soon as each four would finish their meal another four would take their places at the table until all were satisfied.

George Gossip hunting at Birr, Co. Offaly

Hare & Rabbit

The hare is thought to be native to Ireland, while the rabbit was introduced by the Anglo-Normans in the twelfth century. Both have augmented the Irish diet, particularly that of the poorer people, throughout the ages. John Dunton, an English visitor to Ireland in the 17th century, describes a meal at an inn:

> Then enters landlady's daughter…in her hand she brought the hare swimming in a wodden bowl full of oyl of butter. I told my guide that they were verie generous in affording me so much sauce to the drye meate, but he answer'd me that was but the broath for they had boyld it in butter and in another cabin.

There was a common belief that hares (and hedgehogs) sucked the milk from the cows as they lay in the field at night. It was said that malicious women would go abroad at night in the form of a hare, to take the neighbor's dairy profit.

One folktale tells how a farmer lay in wait for the milk-stealing hare. His dog draws blood from the hare. The farmer sets off in pursuit and meets an old woman. He asks her if she has seen the hare, then notices that she is bleeding and realises that she was the hare.

Nowadays rabbits and hares run wild all over Ireland. Rabbits particularly are very prolific and, despite their sweet and cuddly image, are considered to be a pest by farmers. Rabbits are now rarely eaten, partly because they are still associated in many people's folk memory with famine, poverty and hard times, and partly because of the myxomatosis epidemic. Nonetheless I love rabbit, and will miss no opportunity to eat it.

Roast Rabbit in Milk

Serves 4

This recipe was given to me by Anne Kennedy from Rostrevor, in Co. Down. It seems to me to be a good one, because rabbit can be on the dry side, particularly when it is not in the first flush of youth. The milk helps to keep it moist and tender. A young rabbit was called a grazier.

1 young rabbit, cleaned
2 medium onions
³/4 cup fresh white breadcrumbs
1 tablespoon chopped sage
salt and pepper
2 tablespoons butter, melted
2 tablespoons fat drippings
1 tablespoon flour
2¹/2 cups milk

Soak the rabbit in salted water for 2 hours. Boil the onions until tender, then chop and mix with the breadcrumbs, sage, seasoning and butter. Stuff the rabbit with this mixture and sew up the opening.

Place the rabbit in a roasting pan. Dot it with fat drippings and sprinkle with flour, salt and pepper. Pour the milk around the rabbit and bake in preheated oven at 325°F for 2 hours, basting often during the cooking period with milk.

Serve with mashed potatoes and a green vegetable.

To make Hare Soup

From the Receipt Book of Mrs. Dot Drew, Mocollop Castle, Ballyduff, Co. Waterford, dated 1801. It serves about 8 to 10 people.

Take a hare, cut it in pieces, get 3 quarts of water and one of cyder, a bit of lean bacon cellery onions pepper salt and a little sweet herbs stew it on a slow fire if the soup be not thick enough mix a little flour and water. Fry some toasts in butter and now stir in your soup.

This recipe comes from the Kitchen Book of Clonbrock:

Rabbit & Hare Pie

Serves 6 to 8

Make a forcemeat with the hare, beef and bacon, bone the rabbits, put a layer of the forcemeat and a layer of rabbit into the pie dish until it is full, season well. Put on a flour and water crust and bake in a moderate oven for 2 hours—baking with pie dish in a pan of water. Boil the bones of the rabbit and hare with a carrot, onion and bunch of herbs to a good stock. Clear it with the white of an egg, add the gelatin, when cold cut it into neat shapes and garnish the top of the pie. Remove the crust while hot, and if baked too dry pour a little of the stock into it.

1 hare
3 rabbits
¹/₂lb lean beef
¹/₄lb fat bacon
the yolks of 3 eggs and the white of 1 egg
1 cup breadcrumbs
pepper and salt
a little pounded mace and ¹/₂ oz (2 packets)
*   of gelatin*

Venison

Red deer is native to Ireland and important to its myths and early literature. There is evidence that red deer was eaten in Ireland in Mesolithic times—from 7,000 B.C.—at the site of Mount Sandel, near Coleraine in Co. Derry. Deer hunting near the royal site of Rath Cruachain, the ancient capital of the province of Connaught, is alluded to in the early Irish medieval tale: *Táin Bó Fraích (The Cattle Raid of Fraoch)*. Venison from the area around Naas is demanded as tribute for the King of Ireland in the early medieval tale *Lebor na gCert (The Book of Rights)*.

Red deer were hunted and cooked over an open fire by the earliest inhabitants of Ireland. They are mentioned in the legends of the warrior hero, Fionn Mac Cumhaill, and his troupe of young warriors, the 'Fianna', who roamed the landscape hunting and waging war. There are many stories which tell of their deer-hunting exploits. Fionn's name is etymologically related to the Irish word for deer, *fian,* while his son Oisín's name means 'little fawn'. These colourful stories appear in Ireland from the early medieval period onward.

The smaller fallow deer, a relatively recent addition to Irish fauna, were introduced by the Anglo-Normans in the twelfth and thirteenth centuries. They became a common sight in deer parks beside castles and country houses. Bunratty Castle had a deer park in the mid-seventeenth century. In 1646, the Papal Nuncio, Cardinal Rinuccini, wrote 'In Italy there is nothing like its ponds and parks with its three thousand head of deer'.

Lord Powerscourt introduced sika deer to his demesne in Co. Wicklow in the nineteenth century. Venison stew still warms and cheers many a ravenous hunter after a day's shooting on some of Ireland's large estates.

A haunch of venison makes a splendid dish for a country house party. The delicious sauce was created by Queen Victoria's chef, Charles Elmé Francatelli.

Roast Haunch of Venison
with Francatelli Sauce

Serves 20 people (approximately)

1 haunch of venison—approx. 6 to 7lb
8oz salt pork

Marinade
1 tablespoon mixed fresh herbs, thyme,
*   savory, marjoram and sage*
5 tablespoons olive oil
2/3 cup dry white wine

Gravy
2 1/2 cups beef stock
roux (optional, see page 40)
salt and freshly ground pepper

Francatelli Sauce
(see below)

First lard the venison. Cut the pork back fat into ¼ inch wide strips. Insert a strip into a larding needle and draw a lardon through the meat to make a stitch; trim the end. Repeat the stitches at 1 inch intervals to make horizontal rows, positioning each row about ½ inch away from the previous row.

Put the venison into a shallow dish made of stainless steel or cast iron, but not aluminum. Sprinkle the venison with the freshly chopped herbs. Pour the olive oil and wine over the meat. Cover the dish or tray and marinate the meat for about 4 hours at room temperature or in the refrigerator overnight, turning the meat occasionally. The liquid from this marinade will be used to baste the meat during cooking.

Preheat the oven to 350°F. Weigh the venison and calculate 10 minutes to the pound. We like our venison slightly pink and still very juicy, so I usually turn off the oven then and leave the meat to relax for 20 to 30 minutes. While it is cooking, baste the venison every 10 minutes with the oil and wine marinade and turn the meat over half way through. When the venison is cooked, remove to a serving dish while you make the gravy.

Skim the fat from the roasting pan and add about 2½ cups beef or venison stock and perhaps a dash of wine. Bring to the boil, scraping and dissolving the sediment and crusty bits from the pan. Thicken slightly, if you wish, with a little roux, taste and correct the seasoning, pour into a warm gravy boat.

Serve the haunch of venison on a large serving dish surrounded by roast potatoes. Red cabbage, celeriac purée or brussels sprouts would be delicious accompaniments. Carve and serve on very hot plates.

Note: *It is very easy to overcook venison mainly because it goes on cooking after the oven has been turned off.*

Francatelli Sauce

4 tablespoons port wine
1lb redcurrant jelly
stick of cinnamon, bruised
thinly pared rind of 2 lemons

Simmer all the ingredients together for 5 minutes, stirring all the time. Strain into a hot sauceboat.

George Gossip's Game Pie

Serves 8

Venison Stew

*3lb boned shoulder of venison, trimmed
and cut into 1¹/₂ inch cubes
seasoned flour*

Marinade

*1¹/₄-1¹/₂ cups red wine
1 medium onion, sliced
4 tablespoons brandy
4 tablespoons olive oil
salt, lightly crushed black pepper
bouquet garni*

Sauce

*8oz fat bacon, diced
2 tablespoons olive oil
2 large onions, chopped
1 large carrot, diced
1 large clove garlic, crushed
1¹/₂ cups beef or venison stock
bouquet garni
24 small mushrooms, sliced
a little butter
salt and freshly ground pepper
lemon juice or redcurrant jelly
salt, freshly ground pepper and sugar*

Mix the ingredients for the marinade. Add the venison and marinate for 24 to 48 hours. Next day, drain the meat well, pat it dry on paper towels and toss in seasoned flour.

Heat the olive oil in a frying pan and add the bacon. Cook it slowly at first to persuade the fat to run, then raise the heat so it crisps on the outside. Transfer to a casserole.

Brown the venison pieces in the bacon fat and add to the bacon in the casserole. Then toss the onions, carrot and garlic in the remaining bacon fat and add to the casserole. Be careful not to overheat the pan or the fat will burn. Pour off any surplus fat, and strain in the marinade. Stir to dissolve the caramalized juices, bring to a boil and pour over the venison. Add enough stock to almost cover the meat and vegetables. Put in the *bouquet garni* and bring to a boil. Cover and simmer gently, either on top of the stove or in the oven, preheated to 300°F.

Test the venison after an hour, but be aware that it can take up to 2½ hours' cooking time. For best results, it is wise to cook this kind of dish one day and then reheat it the next. This improves the flavor and gives you a chance to make sure that the venison is tender.

Sauté the sliced mushrooms in a little butter. Season with salt and freshly ground pepper and add to the stew.

Finally taste the sauce. It will need seasoning and perhaps also a little lemon juice. It sometimes benefits from a pinch of sugar or some redcurrant jelly (be careful not to use too much).

Venison Pie

Fill a pie dish with the stew mixture, cover with puff or flaky pastry (see page 195) and bake in a medium-hot oven (400°F) until the pastry is golden and fully cooked.

This is an ideal way to use up old or damaged pheasants and the odd pigeon or the like that you cannot think up a good use for. It is really delicious and none the worse for being made from leftovers. Do try to use a number of different types of game for this, as it dramatically improves the flavor. Hare is especially good, but do not use duck.

Fry onions lightly in butter until golden. Add chopped garlic and fry for a further minute. Sprinkle the meats with seasoned flour and brown them gently in a little oil.

Stew slowly in a heavy saucepan (covered) with onions, garlic, bay leaf, stock and wine. Just before the meat is done, add the mushrooms and continue cooking until everything is tender. If there is too much sauce strain and return the sauce to the heat and boil down rapidly until sufficiently reduced. Allow to cool.

This stage is best completed a day or so in advance for the flavors to intensify. It may also be made up in larger amounts and then frozen in the required portions.

Line a small pie dish with puff pastry. Fill with the mixture (having first checked the seasoning), cover, decorate and glaze with an egg wash.

Bake in a hot oven until golden brown. Serve with baked or mashed potatoes, red cabbage, celery and redcurrant jelly.

George also sent me this entertaining account of a typical breakfast before a day's shoot:

Shooting trips are often an all-male affair, with a distinct lowering of standards. Personal memories involve enormous fried breakfasts, making full use of any leftover potatoes from the previous night; vast numbers of under-done kidneys; fried eggs either runny, or very over-cooked and leathery; a dozen eggs poaching all-together in a saucepan, lots of fried bread, wonderful black puddings, made by the local butcher in a roasting tin and cut in thick slices, like cake, and far, far too many rashers and sausages. Thick slices of bread, thickly buttered. Comparisons between each others wives' marmalade. To drink, strong tea or even stronger coffee, made in a jug and filtered through a sieve with too wide a mesh. Beware the question 'Would you like a starter?' It probably means a glass of Paddy! Usually the dogs are allowed to lick the frying pans, before they are washed.

Serves 6

George Gossip's Game Pie

1¹/₂ lb game meat, off the bone and sliced or diced, pheasant, pigeon, rabbit, venison or the like.
8oz bacon diced
²/₃ cup game stock made from the bones of a hare for preference
²/₃ cup red wine
2¹/₂ cups button mushrooms
2¹/₂ cups pickling onions (or sliced large onions)
2 cloves garlic
salt and pepper
bay leaf
flour, butter and oil
12oz homemade puff pastry
1 egg
milk

Poultry

Domestic fowl were bred in Ireland from the early Christian era; the texts and borders of many medieval Irish manuscripts feature the motif of an entwined cock and hen. *The Book of Kells*, now on view in Trinity College, Dublin, is the most famous example.

Our choice of poultry now seems meager in comparison to that of earlier times. Brid Mahon writes, in *Land of Milk and Honey*, that 'Giraldus Cambrensis, writing in the twelfth century, mentions flocks of cranes, geese with prodigious croakings, falcons, wild peacocks, wild hens, snipe, woodcock, pheasants and nightingale as well as "clouds of larks singing the praises of God".'

Poultry has always been associated with festive meals—whether it was the goose for Michaelmas, the turkey for Christmas or the roast chicken for Sunday. The gourmet diarist Amhlaoibh Uí Shúileabháin noted, with great satisfaction, in his entry for Easter Sunday, 6 April 1828:

> Easter Sunday and Christmas Day are the two best days for eating. Today I had chicken and smoked ham for my dinner.

Modern intensive rearing means that chicken and even turkey are no longer eaten solely on religious festivals or holidays. However, the flavor and texture are infinitely better in naturally raised, free-range birds. At Kinoith we have a huge flock of hens to provide us with wonderful fresh eggs for the cookery school.

Traditional Roast Stuffed Chicken

with Bacon & Parsley Sauce

1 chicken, free range if possible, 3¹/2-5lb
a little soft butter
2 to 2¹/2lb piece bacon
toasted breadcrumbs
roux (optional; see page 40)

Stock

giblets and wish bone (keep the liver for a
chicken liver pâté)
1 sliced carrot
1 sliced onion
1 stick celery
a few parsley stalks and a sprig of thyme

Stuffing

3 tablespoons butter
³/4 cup chopped onion
1 cup soft white breadcrumbs
2 tablespoons finely chopped fresh herbs
e.g. parsley, lemon thyme, chives
and marjoram
salt and freshly ground pepper
a little soft butter

Garnish

sprigs of flat parsley

Roast chicken is everyday food nowadays, but it was a rare treat up to the late 1950s when the intensive rearing of chickens began to bring down the price. Our hens hatched out several clutches of chicken in the ditches every year, so the cocks were fattened up for the table and the pullets kept for laying. Roast chicken was a longed-for treat when I was at boarding school in Wicklow. I shall never forget the ripple of excitement that ran around the refectory when roast chicken was served for Mother Prioress's feast day—and that was in the sixties. Search for a really free-range chicken if you want to recapture the forgotten flavor.

First remove the wishbone from the neck end of the chicken. This isn't at all essential, but it does make carving much easier later on. Tuck the wing tips underneath the chicken for a neat shape. To make the stock, put the wishbone, giblets, carrot, onion, celery and herbs into a saucepan. Cover with cold water, bring to a boil, skim and simmer gently while the chicken is roasting. Strain and skim any fat from the surface before using.

Next make the stuffing. Sweat the onions gently in the butter until soft, for about 10 minutes, then stir in the crumbs, herbs and a little salt and pepper to taste. Allow it to get quite cold.

If necessary wash and dry the cavity of the bird, then season and half fill with cold stuffing. Season the breast and legs, and smear with a little soft butter. Preheat the oven to 350°F. Weigh the chicken and allow about 20 minutes to the pound and 20 minutes over. Halfway through the cooking, turn the chicken upside down to allow the juices to run into the breast. Baste a couple of times during the cooking with the buttery juices.

Put the bacon piece into a pan of cold water, bring to a boil, cover the saucepan and simmer until the bacon is tender (about 1 hour). Change the water several times, particularly if the bacon is salty. A skewer should go through the bacon easily when it is cooked and the skin should peel off without resistance. I then sprinkle the fat with a few toasted and sieved dry breadcrumbs.

To test the chicken prick the thickest part at the base of the thigh and examine the juices: they should be clear. Remove the chicken to a carving dish, keep it warm and allow to rest while you make the gravy.

To make the gravy, spoon off the surplus fat from the roasting pan. Pour in the stock from the giblets and bones (you will need 2 to 2¹/2 cups depending on the size of the chicken). Using a whisk, stir and scrape well to dissolve the caramelized meat juices from the roasting pan. Boil it up well, season and thicken with a little roux if you like. Taste and correct seasoning. Serve in a hot gravy boat.

If possible serve the chicken on a nice carving dish surrounded by crispy roast potatoes and some sprigs of flat parsley. Serve each person a slice of bacon, some brown and white meat, gravy and parsley sauce.

Parsley Sauce

2 tablespoons finely chopped
fresh parsley
2¹/2 cups fresh milk
1 to 1¹/2oz roux (see page 40)
salt and freshly ground pepper

Remove the stalks from the parsley, put the stalks into a saucepan with the cold milk, bring slowly to a boil, then remove the stalks. Whisk the roux into the boiling milk until thickened; add the chopped parsley. Season with salt and freshly ground pepper. Simmer for 5 to 10 minutes on a very low heat, then taste and correct the seasoning before serving.

Traditional Roast Stuffed Chicken

Most farmers' wives kept at least a few hens and sold the eggs for 'pin money'. The broody hens hatched out a clutch or two of chicks hidden in the hay rick or the back of the haggard in the summer. Birds no longer in the first flush of youth were often poached gently and served with a cream and parsley sauce.

Season the chicken with salt and freshly ground black pepper and place in a heavy casserole with the carrot, celery, onion, *bouquet garni* and peppercorns. Pour in water, water and wine, or stock. Cover and bring to a boil, then simmer either on top of the stove or in the oven for 1½ to 3 hours, depending on the age of the bird. When cooked, remove the chicken from the casserole.

Strain the cooking liquid and skim the fat from the surface. Return to the casserole. Discard the vegetables; they have already given their flavor to the cooking liquid. If it tastes a little weak, reduce the liquid by boiling it uncovered for a few minutes. Add cream and reduce again. Thicken to a light coating consistency with roux. Taste, add salt and correct the seasoning. Skin the chicken and carve the flesh into 2 inch pieces, then add the meat and the chopped parsley to the sauce and allow it to heat through and bubble up.

Finally, just before serving, mix the egg yolk with the ¼ cup heavy cream. Add some of the hot sauce to this mixture and then carefully stir into the chicken. Taste, correct the seasoning and stir well, but do not allow to boil further or the sauce will curdle.

Serves 8

Poached Chicken

with Cream & Parsley Sauce

a 4 to 4½lb chicken, free-range if possible
salt and freshly ground black pepper
1 large carrot, sliced
1 stick celery
1 large onion, sliced
bouquet garni made up of a sprig of thyme,
  parsley stalks, a tiny bay leaf
5 peppercorns
2½ cups approx. water or water
  and white wine or light homemade
  chicken stock
1 cup cream
1oz approx. roux (see page 40)
2 or 3 tablespoons chopped parsley

Enrichment

1 egg yolk
¼ cup heavy cream

Chicken & Bacon Press

Serves 8 to 10

1 large chicken
2lb bacon in one piece
2 onions
2 carrots
1 stalk celery
a few parsley stalks
a few sprigs of thyme and maybe
a sprig of marjoram
5 peppercorns
2 tablespoons chopped parsley

This recipe was handed down through Myrtle Allen's family, and is still in frequent use. Originally it was a handy way of using up a boiling fowl past its prime, but nowadays it is almost impossible to find a boiling fowl, either before or after its prime!

Put the chicken and bacon into a saucepan with the onions, carrot, celery, herbs, salt and a few peppercorns.

Add about 2 inch of water. Bring to a boil, cover, and cook in a moderate oven 350°F for 1½ to 2 hours, depending on the size and age of the chicken. Discard the vegetables.

When the chicken and bacon are cooked, skin and chop the meat into ¾ inch dice while it is still hot. Add the parsley, taste and correct the seasoning, then press into a bowl. Pour a little of the cooking liquid over the top, cover with a plate and weight it down. Leave the mixture overnight in the fridge. Cut into slices and serve with a salad.

A more elaborate version can be made by layering the chicken, bacon and chopped parsley.

Goose

Years ago, most farms in Ireland would have reared geese. The fowl were the responsibility of the farmer's wife and there was a tradition of making presents of geese to friends or to poor families.

In many parts of the country the first corn of the year was ground into flour and baked into bread for the Michaelmas feast in September. The last sheaf of corn was the centerpiece for the table. There were many traditions associated with the last sheaf: in some places, the girl who tied it had the honor of opening the first dance of the evening with the farmer's son. Until recently, 'a set of ware' was the most common present given to young Irish couples when they married. The big serving platter from the set would be given pride of place on the dresser, reserved for the rare occasion when a goose or turkey was cooked.

There's an old saying in Ireland that if you eat goose on Michaelmas Day, 29 September, you will not be 'in want' for the rest of the year. By this time, the geese which hatched out in spring will be plump and wonderfully juicy and tender.

I have vivid childhood memories of the preparations for the Michaelmas feast in a neighbor's house. The bird was smothered several days ahead and hung by the neck in the larder. It was then plucked. The wings were kept (and much sought after for brushing out dusty corners). The large feathers were sometimes made into quills or fishing floats, and the smaller ones and the precious down were collected for stuffing pillows and feather beds. From time to time, as the goose cooked, the fat was poured off. Some of it was used to roast potatoes, but the rest was stored for myriad purposes. It was rubbed into chests to stop wheezing. It was used to shine the kitchen stove even to polish leather shoes. Nothing was wasted.

A goose looks enormous, but it has a large carcass and so looks as if it will serve more people than it does. Allow at least 1lb uncooked weight per person.

Traditionally goose is stuffed with a potato stuffing. There are many variations; this is one I particularly like.

First make the stuffing. Boil the potatoes 'in their jackets' in boiling salted water until cooked. Peel and mash.

Melt the butter and sweat the onions in a covered saucepan on a gentle heat for about 5 minutes. Add the apples and cook until they break down into a fluff, then stir in the mashed potatoes and herbs. Season with salt and pepper. Allow to get quite cold before stuffing the goose.

To prepare the goose, remove the wishbone for ease of carving. Put it into a saucepan with the giblets, onion, carrot, *bouquet garni* and peppercorns. Cover with cold water, bring to a boil and simmer for about 2 hours. (Add the wing tips to the stock if desired.)

Season the cavity of the goose with salt and freshly ground pepper and fill with the cold stuffing. Sprinkle some sea salt over the breast and rub it into the goose skin. Roast for 2 to 2½ hours in a preheated moderate oven, 350°F.

Take the roasting pan from the oven three or four times during the cooking and pour off the excess fat. (Store this fat in your refrigerator—it keeps for months and is wonderful for roasting or sautéeing potatoes.) To test whether the goose is cooked, prick the thigh at the thickest part. The juices which run out should be clear; if they are pink the goose needs a little longer. When cooked, remove the goose to a large serving dish and put it into a low oven while you make the gravy.

To make the gravy, pour or spoon off the remainder of the fat and save. Add about 2 cups of the strained giblet stock to the roasting pan and bring to a boil. Using a small whisk, scrape the pan well to dissolve the meaty deposits which are full of flavor.

Taste for seasoning and thicken with a little roux if you like a thickened gravy. If the gravy is weak, boil for a few minutes to concentrate the flavor; if too strong add a little water or stock. Strain and serve in a hot gravy boat.

Carve the goose. Serve with apple sauce (see page 92) and the gravy.

Serves 8-10

Michaelmas Goose

with Traditional Potato & Apple Stuffing

1 goose, 10lb approx.
sea salt and freshly ground pepper

Stock
giblets—neck, heart and gizzard
1 small onion
1 carrot
bouquet garni consisting of 1 sprig thyme, 3 or 4 parsley stalks, a small piece of celery, 6 or 7 peppercorns
cold water to cover

Stuffing
2lb potatoes
4 tablespoons butter
1lb onions, chopped
1lb cooking apples, peeled and chopped
1 tablespoon chopped parsley
1 tablespoon chopped lemon balm
salt and freshly ground pepper

Gravy
2½ cups goose stock made from the giblets
roux (optional; see page 40)

Serves 4

Papie's Roast Duck

with Sage & Onion Stuffing

1 duck, approx. 4 lb
(allow 1 lb duck per serving)
salt and pepper

Stuffing
3 tablespoons butter
³/4 cup chopped onion
1 cup soft white breadcrumbs
1 tablespoon finely chopped sage
salt and freshly ground pepper

Stock
neck and giblets
1 carrot, sliced
1 onion, sliced
bouquet garni or parsley stalks, thyme
sprig, small celery stalk
2 or 3 peppercorns

My maternal grandfather, whom we called Papie Tynan, was very fond of his food. He reared ducks, geese, chicken and guinea fowl for the table. The ducks and geese had a happy life, puddling about in the pond and pecking at the windfall apples in the orchard, and they tasted exquisite. Every scrap of the ducks and geese was used, including the blood which was made into a soft pudding and eaten on bread. The feathers were kept for pillows, and the down for quilts.

Put the neck, gizzard, heart and feet into a saucepan with a sliced carrot and onion. Add the bouquet garni. Cover with cold water and add peppercorns, but no salt.

Bring slowly to a boil, skim and simmer for 2 to 3 hours. This will make a delicious broth which will be the basis of the gravy. Meanwhile, singe the duck and make the stuffing.

To make the stuffing melt the butter on a gentle heat, add the onion and sweat for 5 to 10 minutes until soft but not colored. Remove from the heat and add the breadcrumbs and freshly chopped sage. Season with salt and freshly ground pepper to taste. Unless you are cooking the duck immediately, allow to cool.

When the stuffing is quite cold, season the cavity of the duck and stuff. Roast in a moderate oven 350°F for about 1½ hours. When the duck is cooked, remove to a serving dish and allow to rest while you make the gravy.

Skim the fat from the cooking juices (keep the duck fat for roast or fried potatoes). Strain the stock and add to the juices in the roasting pan, bring to a boil, taste and season if necessary. Strain the gravy into a sauceboat and serve with the duck.

Serves 4

Apple Sauce

1 lb cooking apples
1 tablespoon water
approx. ¹/4 cup sugar (depending on
tartness of apples)

Peel, quarter and core the apples, cut the pieces into two and put in a stainless steel or cast iron saucepan, with sugar and water. Cover and put over a low heat. As soon as the apples have broken down, stir and taste for sweetness. Serve warm as an accompaniment to the duck.

The turkey did not make its appearance in Europe until Elizabethan times. In Ireland, for most of this century it has been associated almost exclusively with Christmas feasting. However, like many other festive foods, it has now become commonplace and it is not at all unusual to find a turkey on the table for an Easter, midsummer or bank holiday lunch.

To recapture the rich sweet flavor of the roast turkey of our childhood, search for a free-range bird that has been reared naturally.

Remove the wishbone from the neck end of the turkey, for ease of carving later. Make a turkey stock by covering with cold water the neck, gizzard, heart, wishbone, wingtips, vegetables and *bouquet garni*. (Keep the liver for pâté.) Bring to a boil and simmer while the turkey is being prepared and cooked, approximately 3 hours.

To make the stuffing bring about 4 cups water to a boil in a saucepan. Throw in the chestnuts and boil for 5 to 10 minutes, until the shell and inside skin peel off easily. Pick them out one at a time. The flesh should be soft. Chop them finely. Melt the butter, sweat the onions and chestnuts in it until soft. Add the breadcrumbs and herbs, taste and season carefully. Mix well.

Weigh the turkey and calculate the cooking time. Allow approximately 15 minutes per lb and 15 minutes over. Brush the turkey with melted butter, alternatively, smear well the breast, legs and crop with soft butter, and season with salt and freshly ground pepper, cover loosely with parchment paper and roast in a preheated moderate oven (350°F) for 1 to 1½ hours.

To test the turkey, prick the thickest part at the base of the thigh and examine the juices. When they run clear the turkey is done. Remove the turkey to a carving dish, keep it warm and allow it to rest for a few minutes while you make the gravy.

To make the gravy, spoon off the surplus fat from the roasting pan. Deglaze the pan juices with fat-free stock from the giblets and bones. Using a whisk, stir and scrape well to dissolve the caramelized meat juices from the roasting pan. Boil it up well, season and thicken with a little roux if you like. Taste and correct the seasoning. Serve in a hot gravy boat.

If possible, present the turkey on your largest serving dish, surrounded by golden crispy roast potatoes. Garnish with large sprigs of parsley or watercress and maybe a sprig of holly. Make sure no one eats the berries.

Serve with bread sauce and cranberry sauce (see page 74).

Bread sauce sounds so dull, if I hadn't been reared on it I might never have tried it. It is another ingenious way of using up stale bread. I even love it cold!

Bring all the ingredients except the cream to a boil in a small, deep saucepan. Season with salt and freshly ground pepper. Cover and simmer gently on a very low heat or cook in a low oven at 325°F for 30 minutes. Remove the onions and add the cream to the sauce just before serving. Correct the seasoning. Add a little more milk if the sauce is too thick.

Serve hot, from a warm sauceboat.

Serves 10 to 12

Old-Fashioned Roast Turkey

with Chestnut Stuffing & Bread Sauce

1 10 to 12lb fresh turkey with neck and
    giblets, preferably free-range
butter
salt and freshly ground black pepper
roux (optional; see page 40)

Stock
neck, gizzard, heart, wishbone and
    wingtips of turkey
2 carrots, sliced
2 onions, sliced
1 stick celery
bouquet garni
3 or 4 peppercorns

Chestnut Stuffing
12 tablespoons (1½ sticks) butter
3 cups chopped onions
1lb chestnuts, shelled and skinned
3¾ cup approx. soft breadcrumbs
½ cup chopped fresh herbs, e.g. parsley,
    thyme, chives, marjoram, savory,
    lemon balm
salt and freshly ground pepper

Garnish
large sprigs of fresh parsley or watercress

Serves 12

Bread Sauce

2 cups milk
1 cup breadcrumbs
2 onions, each stuck with 6 cloves
4 tablespoons butter
salt and freshly ground pepper
¾ cup heavy cream

Lamb

Irish lamb is for the most part naturally reared on lush green pastures. Connemara and Kerry lambs have a flavor all their own and are much sought after. No lamb I've tasted from any high-quality restaurants in Europe could equal the flavor of the lamb I buy from my local butcher, Michael Cuddigan, who rears his animals on rich old pastures full of wild flowers and herbs. There are still many conscientious butchers around the country who haven't forgotten the old ways.

Roast Stuffed Loin of Lamb

with Onion Sauce & Mint Sauce

*1 whole boned loin of lamb (6¹/₂lb
approximately—allow 6 to 8oz
of boned loin per person)*
1 carrot
1 onion
1 stick of celery
bouquet garni
roux (see page 40)
*1 tablespoon freshly chopped parsley,
chives and thyme (optional)*

Fresh herb stuffing

3 cups chopped onion
12 tablespoons (1¹/₂ sticks) butter
5 cups approx. soft breadcrumbs
*¹/₂ cup freshly chopped herbs e.g. parsley,
thyme, chives, marjoram,
savory, lemon balm*
salt and freshly ground pepper

First make the stuffing. Sweat the onions gently in the butter until soft, for approximately 10 minutes, then stir in the crumbs, herbs and a little salt and pepper to taste. Allow to get quite cold.

Put the lamb bones into a saucepan with a carrot, onion and celery and a *bouquet garni*. Cover with water, bring to a boil and simmer for a few hours to make a little stock for the gravy.

Lightly score the fat side of the lamb. Turn over and trim off 3 or 4 inches of the excess flap end, which will be extra to what you need when you roll up the lamb. Sprinkle the joint with salt and freshly ground pepper. Spread the stuffing on the boned side, roll it up like a swiss roll and tie with cotton string.

Roast in a moderate oven at 350°F for about 1¹/₂ hours. When the loin is cooked, remove it from the roasting pan, place it on a serving dish and keep it warm.

To make the gravy, skim the fat from the juices in the roasting pan and pour in about 2 cups of lamb stock. Scrape the sides of the pan with a spoon or whisk to dissolve the caramelized juices. Allow the stock to boil for a few minutes. Whisk in a little roux for a slightly thicker gravy if preferred. Season with salt and freshly ground pepper and, if you have them, add perhaps a sprinkling of freshly chopped herbs.

Serve with mint sauce and onion sauce.

Mint Sauce

*2 tablespoons finely chopped
fresh mint*
2 teaspoons sugar
¹/₃ cup boiling water
*1 tablespoon white wine vinegar
or lemon juice*

Put the sugar and freshly chopped mint into a sauce boat. Add the boiling water and vinegar or lemon juice. Allow to infuse for 5 to 10 minutes before serving the sauce.

Onion Sauce

6 onions, thinly sliced or finely chopped
8 tablespoons (1 stick) butter
1 teaspoon salt
¹/₂ teaspoon freshly ground pepper
1 tablespoon flour
*2¹/₂ cups milk or 2 cups milk
and ¹/₂ cup cream*

Sweat the onions in the butter until really soft. Season with salt, a pinch of sugar (if needed) and freshly ground pepper. Do not allow to brown. Blend in the flour and milk and bring to a boil, stirring frequently. Simmer gently for a further 5 minutes.

In former times sheep were kept primarily for their wool. The meat was eaten only when the animal was old or died by accident.

In The Farm by Lough Gur, *which describes rural life in Ireland in the late 19th century, Mary O'Brien recalls that 'except when a sheep or lamb fell and had to be killed, we never had mutton'.*

…'The crayther! fallin' from the rocks, the way it did to break its neck, and it neither a lamb or a sheep.' 'With mint sauce, it is lamb,' I said firmly, 'make a good fire and have it on the spit in plenty of time!'

Spring lamb served with a fresh mint sauce made from the first of the new season's mint is our traditional Easter dinner.

Choose a nice leg of spring lamb with a thin layer of fat. Trim the shank end. Season with a little salt and pepper. Preheat the oven to 350°F. Roast the lamb for about 1 hour for rare, 1$\frac{1}{4}$ hours for medium and 1$\frac{1}{2}$ hours for well done. When the lamb is cooked, remove the joint to a carving dish. Rest the lamb in a low oven for 10 minutes before carving.

Meanwhile make the gravy. Pour off the fat from the roasting pan and add the stock. Bring to a boil, whisking to dissolve the caramelized deposits in the pan. Thicken with a little roux if desired. Serve with gravy and mint sauce and lots of crusty roast potatoes.

Serves 6-8

Roast Leg of Lamb
with Mint Sauce

1 leg of spring lamb, 6lb approx.
salt and freshly ground pepper

Gravy
1 cup homemade lamb or chicken stock
roux (optional; see page 40)

Mint Sauce
(see opposite)

Preheat the oven to 350°F. Trim the excess fat from the lamb and cut into square pieces. Pull off the skin and remove the central core from the kidneys. Cut each half into large chunks.

Heat the chopped lamb fat in a large heavy pan over a low heat until the lamb fat liquefies. Remove and discard the rendered fat pieces. Cut the lamb chops in half if very large. Add the lamb and cook in batches over a high heat for 2–3 minutes until golden on both sides. Remove to a plate, add the kidneys, and toss to seal them on both sides. Add to the lamb.

Put the onions into the pan and fry for 4–5 minutes until golden. Put a layer of lamb chop on top, sprinkle with thyme leaves, then add the kidneys. Season with salt and pepper. Arrange the potato slices on top in a pretty circular pattern (see front cover photograph). Pour in the hot stock so that the potatoes are almost covered and dot the top of the potatoes with the butter, and sprinkle over a little more thyme. Cover the pot, transfer to the oven, and bake for 30 minutes or until the potatoes are crisp and golden.

Irish Lamb and Potato Hotpot

8 lamb shoulder or neck chops (bone in),
    1 inch thick
4 lamb kidneys
2 tablespoons lamb fat or vegetable oil
2 large onions, thinly sliced
1 tablespoon fresh thyme leaves
1$\frac{1}{2}$ lb baking potatoes, peeled and
    thinly sliced
3$\frac{1}{4}$ cups hot lamb or chicken stock
2 tablespoons butter
Salt and freshly ground pepper

Irish Stew

Irish Stew. A nourishing and economical dish, if a little indigestible. All honour to the land that has brought it before the world.

Molloy, Samuel Beckett

There is a certain amount of argument about what constitutes an authentic Irish stew—and who really knows, anyway? It seems reasonable to assume that Irish stew was the inevitable result of combining simple, available ingredients in the big, black, three-legged pot and cooking them over the fire. After all, this dish originated in Irish cabins where utensils were scarce. A griddle, a kettle, a frying pan, a three-legged pot and a bastible or pot oven would have constituted the entire *batterie de cuisine*.

Florence Irwin, a Northen Irish cookery instructor and cookery writer of fifty years ago, tells us how in the 'big house', when a pig or sheep was killed, the griskins, spare ribs or scrag end of the neck of mutton were shared among the farm laborers and neighbors. The meat was put straight into the big pot with onions and peeled potatoes and then covered with water. (The potatoes were peeled for stew, otherwise they were boiled in their jackets.)

Stew would sometimes have provided soup first, because the bones from the neck would have given tremendous flavor to the liquid. In my grandaunt's house in Tipperary this was often the case.

Purists maintain that carrots would not have been added to an original Irish stew, but they were certainly part of Irish stew in many parts of the Midlands and also in Cork and Kerry. They are also included in the much-loved version we serve nowadays at Ballymaloe. Pearl barley was also added in a version I tasted in Youghal, Co. Cork.

Ballymaloe Irish Stew

Preheat the oven to 350°F.

Cut the chops in half and trim off some of the excess fat. Place the trimmed-off fatty pieces in a heavy pan and cook over gentle heat so that the fat runs out. Discard the solid bits that remain.

Peel the onions and scrape or thinly peel the carrots. Cut the carrots into large chunks, or, if they are young, leave them whole. If the onions are large, cut them small; if small, they are best left whole.

Toss the meat in the hot fat on the pan until it is slightly brown. Transfer the meat into a casserole, then quickly toss the onions and carrots in the fat. Build the meat, carrots and onions up in layers in the casserole, carefully seasoning each layer with freshly ground pepper and salt. Pour the stock into the pan, stir to dissolve the caramelized scrapings and pour into the casserole. Peel the potatoes and lay them on top of the casserole, so they will steam while the stew cooks. Season the potatoes. Add a sprig of thyme and bring to a boil on top of the stove. Cover and transfer to a moderate oven or allow to simmer on top of the stove until the stew is cooked. This will take about 1 to 1½ hours, depending on whether the stew is being made with lamb or mutton.

When the stew is cooked, pour off the cooking liquid and skim off the fat. Reheat the liquid in another saucepan. Slightly thicken it with a little roux if you like. Check seasoning, then add chopped parsley and chives and pour it back over the stew. Bring it back up to boiling point and serve directly from the pot or in a large pottery dish.

Serves 4 to 6

Ballymaloe Irish Stew

2½ to 3lb shoulder lamb chops not less than 1 inch thick
5 medium or 12 baby onions
5 medium or 12 baby carrots
salt and freshly ground pepper
2½ cups stock (lamb stock if possible) or water
8 potatoes or more if you like
1 sprig of thyme
1 tablespoon roux (optional; see page 40)
1 tablespoon chopped fresh parsley
1 tablespoon chopped fresh chives

Peel the potatoes and cut into slices about ⅓ inch thick. Quarter or thickly slice the onions, or leave whole if they are little. Layer the meat, potatoes and onions, season each layer well with salt and freshly ground pepper, and cover the top with whole peeled potatoes. Fill to about two-thirds full with water or lamb stock. Add the thyme, put a butter wrapper on top and cover with the lid of the saucepan. Bring to a boil and simmer for 1 to 2 hours, or until the meat is meltingly tender and the potatoes are steamed and fluffy. Sprinkle with lots of chopped parsley and serve from the pot on to very hot plates.

Serves 4

Ulster Irish Stew

2lb neck of lamb
2lb potatoes
1lb onions
salt and freshly ground pepper
water or lamb stock
1 sprig of thyme
chopped parsley

Irish Stew Pie

Serves 6 to 8

2lb neck end of leg of mutton or lamb
2lb old potatoes, peeled
salt and freshly ground pepper
4 cups sliced onion
2½ cups lamb or chicken stock or water

Pastry

1⅔ cups plain white flour
pinch of salt
5 tablespoons butter
1½oz suet, grated
⅔ cup water
beaten egg to glaze

I have spent many fascinating hours poring over the manuscript cookbook of Annie Kiely of Blackpool in Cork. This little gem, which has yielded many fascinating recipes, was lent to me by Marjorie French. In it was the first and only reference I came across for Irish Stew Pie. We tried the recipe with these measurements and found it delicious.

First make the pastry. Put the flour into a bowl with a pinch of salt and add enough water to mix to a firm dough. Cover and refrigerate. Cream the butter lightly with the suet. Roll out the pastry to the thickness of ¼ inch. I try to keep it in a rectangle. Cover two-thirds of the pastry with flakes of half the suet and butter mixture. Fold into three like a business letter, so that there is a layer of fat between each layer of pastry. Seal the ends with the rolling pin. (If you have time, cover and chill for 10 to 15 minutes at this stage.) Turn the pastry so that the folds are at the sides, and roll it out in the direction of the open ends. Again, try to keep it in a rectangle. Cover two-thirds of the pastry with the remainder of the flakes of butter and suet. Fold the pastry into three again, cover and chill while you prepare the pie.

Cut the neck end into small pieces, about 1 inch square. Put a layer into a pie dish. Slice the potato into ¼-inch slices and put a layer on top of the meat. Season with salt and freshly ground pepper, and add some sliced onion, then another layer of meat and so on, up to the top of the pie dish. Add the stock or water. Cover with a pastry lid. Brush the pastry with a little egg wash. Bake in a moderate oven at 350°F for 1 hour.

Mutton Pie à l'Irlandaise

Lamb & Oyster Pie

6 lamb chops
4 onions
8 potatoes
1 to 2 dozen oysters

Pastry

6 large potatoes
salt, pepper and nutmeg
2 egg yolks
2 tablespoons butter
egg wash

Charles Elmé Francatelli, chef to Queen Victoria, gave a recipe for Mutton Pie à L'Irlandaise in The Cook's Guide, *published in 1871.*

Cut the meat into pieces about 2 inches square. Season well with salt and freshly ground pepper, peel the onions and cut into quarters. Peel the potatoes and keep whole. Mix the meat with the onions and add water to almost cover. Lay the potatoes on top, bring to a boil, then cover and cook until the meat is tender. This will take approximately 1 to 1½ hours, depending on the quality of the meat.

Meanwhile make the potato pastry. Scrub the potatoes and cook in boiling salted water. As soon as they are cooked, peel and mash. Season with salt, freshly ground pepper and nutmeg. Mix with the egg yolks and butter, taste and correct seasoning.

As soon as the lamb and vegetables are almost cooked, open the oysters and add to the pie.

Roll out the potato paste on a floured board and cover the pie. As you can imagine, the potato mixture is quite soft, so this is easier said than done! You may have to patch it a little. Brush with egg wash and bake in a moderate oven at 350°F for a further 30 to 40 minutes.

My local butcher, Michael Cuddigan, explained to me that lamb is 'spring lamb' from Easter until June, then until Christmas it is 'lamb', and strictly speaking it is 'hogget' from Christmas until Easter. Mutton is virtually impossible to find nowadays, but a nice leg of hogget cooked in the same way is very flavorsome—a wonderful dish for a cold winter's evening. Ballymaloe House is one of the few places where hogget is served on the menu—often braised with winter vegetables or wild garlic.

The gourmet writer Amhlaoibh Uí Shúileabháin, who kept a record of many of the meals he ate in his diaries, tells us that on 14 September 1828 'four of us dined with Father James Hennebry: we had boiled leg of mutton with carrots and turnips'.

Ask your butcher to cut the leg at the shank end. Weigh the meat and work out the cooking time: for every 1lb allow 30 minutes, then add another 25 minutes to the time. Put the meat into a saucepan just large enough to fit it nicely. Cover with water, add a good sprinkle of salt and bring to a boil. Remove any scum that rises to the surface. Add the vegetables and bay leaf. Cover the pan; simmer very gently until cooked.

Meanwhile make the sauce. Melt the butter in a saucepan, stir in the flour and cook for a minute or two. Gradually whisk in the milk, bring to a boil and simmer for 4 or 5 minutes. Season with salt and freshly ground pepper and put aside until you are ready to serve the meat. Just before serving add $2/3$ cup of degreased broth from cooking the meat. Bring back to a boil, add the roughly chopped capers and a tablespoon of chopped parsley, if you like. Taste and correct the seasoning. Carve the meat into slices at the table and serve with the caper sauce.

Serves 6 to 8

Boiled Mutton or Hogget

with Caper Sauce

1 6^{1}/2lb leg of mutton or hogget
salt
3 onions, halved
4 or 5 carrots, halved if large
2 sticks of celery halved
6 peppercorns
1 sprig of thyme
1 bay leaf

Caper Sauce
2 tablespoons butter
1 tablespoon plain white flour
2^{1}/2 cups milk
salt and freshly ground pepper
2 tablespoons chopped capers
1 tablespoon chopped parsley (optional)

When a sheep or a pig was killed, the meat would traditionally have been shared with neighbors and friends and as much as possible eaten fresh. The remainder was 'corned' for leaner times. I was delighted to discover only quite recently that Mr Coughlan in the Old English Market in Cork still does corned mutton to order. He said that it is not so popular now, but there was a time when he would sell about 100lbs a week, all the year round. It was cooked with cabbage and swede turnips in the same water.

Put the corned mutton into a saucepan and cover with cold water. Add the onions and carrots and bring to a boil. Cover and simmer. Meanwhile peel the rutabaga and cut into 1 inch cubes. Add these to the pot after the corned mutton has been cooking for 2^{1}/2 hours. Cut the cabbage into thick chunks and add to the pot. Continue to cook until the mutton is meltingly tender and the vegetables fully cooked.

Serve the meat on a hot dish surrounded by rutabaga and cabbage, well seasoned with freshly ground pepper and butter. Taste for seasoning. It may need a little salt, but usually doesn't. Eat hot with lots of boiled potatoes and parsley sauce.

Corned Mutton

with Parsley Sauce

1 leg of corned mutton, 6^{1}/2lbs approx.
2 onions, quartered
2 or 3 carrots, cut in chunks
1 rutabaga
1 cabbage
freshly ground pepper, butter and salt if needed.
parsley sauce (see page 88)

Kerry Pies

Years ago when my mother-in-law, Myrtle Allen, began to collect old Irish recipes, this was one of the first to arouse her curiosity. Mutton pies, made in Kerry, were served at the famous Puck Fair in Killorglin in August, and taken up the hills when men were herding all day. Traditionally they were cooked in the bastible and reheated in mutton broth, then served in a deep plate with some of the broth over the top. It sounds strange, but the old people who remember it are adamant that it was delicious.

This is our version. The original hot-water crust pastry was made with mutton fat, but we have substituted butter for a really rich crust.

1 lb boneless lamb or mutton
(from shoulder or leg—keep bones for stock)
2 1/2 cups chopped onions
2 1/2 cups chopped carrots
2 tablespoons flour
1 cup mutton or lamb stock
1 teaspoon chopped parsley
1 teaspoon thyme leaves
salt and freshly ground pepper

Pastry
3 cups white flour
pinch of salt
12 tablespoons (1 1/2 sticks) butter, diced
1/2 cup (100ml) water
1 egg beaten with a pinch of salt to glaze

Cut all surplus fat off the meat, then cut the meat into small neat pieces about the size of small sugar lumps. Cook the scraps of fat in a hot, wide saucepan until the fat runs. Discard the pieces. Cut the vegetables into slightly smaller dice and toss them in the fat, leaving them to cook for 3 to 4 minutes. Remove the vegetables and toss the meat in the remaining fat over a high heat until the color turns. Stir the flour into the meat. Cook gently for 2 minutes and blend in the stock gradually. Bring to a boil, stirring occasionally. Return the vegetables to the pan with the parsley and thyme leaves. Season with salt and freshly ground pepper and leave to simmer. If using young lamb, 30 minutes will be sufficient; an older animal may take up to 1 hour. When the lamb is cooked, allow it to cool slightly.

Meanwhile make the pastry. Sieve the flour and salt into a mixing bowl and make a well in the center. Put the butter cubes into a saucepan with the water and bring to a boil. Pour the liquid all at once into the flour and mix together quickly; beat until smooth. At first the pastry will be too soft to handle, but it will become more workable as it cools. Roll out 1/8 to 1/4 inch thick and line two pie pans, 6 inches in diameter and 1 1/4 inches deep, or one 9-inch diameter pan.

Fill the pastry-lined pans with the slightly cooled meat mixture. Cut lids from the remaining pastry, brush the edges of the base with water and egg wash and put on the pastry lids, pinching them tightly together. Roll out the trimmings to make pastry leaves or twirls to decorate the pie tops. Make a hole in the center and brush the pastry carefully with egg wash.

Bake the pie or pies at 400°F for about 40 minutes. Serve hot or cold.

Potted Meats

Tasty potted meats were another way of using up little scraps of the leftover Sunday joint. In the days of the pestle and mortar this was a labor-intensive business, but nowadays delicious potted meats and fish can be made in seconds using a food processor. Spices were traditionally used for potted meat but I also find some fresh herbs, for example parsley, chives and thyme leaves, can be a delicious addition. Chicken, ham, beef and venison all make successful potted meats.

4 oz cooked meat
1 oz jellied meat juices if available
2 to 4 tablespoons butter, cut into cubes
spices e.g. freshly ground nutmeg, mace, allspice or juniper berries, depending on the meat
salt and freshly ground pepper
clarified butter (see page 69)

Remove any fat and gristle from the meat. Chop the meat finely and pound to a paste. Alternatively, put into a food processor and process for a few seconds. Add the cubed butter, salt, freshly ground pepper and spice. Process for a further few seconds, taste and add seasoning until you are happy with the flavor. Pack the meat into little pots or ramekins and pour a layer of clarified butter over the top to exclude the air. These will keep for a week to 10 days in the refrigerator. Serve with hot buttered toast.

Kerry Pie

Many Irish men served in the British Army in India in the days of the Raj and developed a taste for curries; the memory of the tantalizingly spiced food remained with them after their return. Many came home armed with little boxes of spice mixtures lovingly blended by their Indian cooks, which they hoped would enable Irish cooks to reproduce the flavours of the Indian curry they had grown to love. This is one of the most delicious curries I've tasted.

Blanch, peel and chop up the almonds (they should be the texture of nibbed almonds). Put them in a saucepan with the cream and simmer for 5 minutes. Turn off the heat and leave to infuse for 15 minutes.

Peel the ginger thinly with a vegetable peeler, then pound it into a paste in a pestle and mortar or chop finely with a knife. (You need about 2 teaspoons of pounded ginger.) Cut the meat into 1½ inch cubes and mix it with the ginger and a sprinkling of salt. Melt the butter and cook the onion rings and crushed garlic in it for 5 minutes. Grind the coriander, pepper, cardamom and cloves in a clean spice or coffee grinder. Add the spices to the onions and cook over a medium heat for 5 minutes. Remove the onions and add the meat to the saucepan. Stir over a high heat until the meat browns, then return the onion and spices to the pot. Add the almond cream, turmeric and sugar. Stir well. Cover and simmer gently on top of the stove, or in a low oven at 325°F, until the meat is cooked (for about 1 hour). Finish by adding lemon or lime juice to taste.

Serve with boiled rice and other curry accompaniments such as mango or tomato chutney, mint chutney, rayta, Indian breads and poppadums.

Note: *1 sizeable leg of lamb or mutton will yield approx. 3lb of meat. You may as well make three times the recipe as curry keeps well and also freezes perfectly.*

Serves 4

Captain Donovan's Mild Madras Curry

2oz almonds
1¼ cups light cream
1-inch piece fresh ginger
1 lb boneless lamb or mutton (leg or shoulder is perfect)
salt
2 tablespoons ghee or clarified butter (see page 69)
2 onions, sliced in rings
2 cloves garlic, crushed
1 teaspoon coriander
1 teaspoon black peppercorns
½ teaspoon green cardamom seeds
¼ teaspoon cloves or 4 whole cloves
2 teaspoons turmeric powder
1 teaspoon sugar
juice of 1 lime or lemon

Beef

The cattle of early Ireland were generally smaller than the modern improved breeds. According to Finbar McCormick, in his unpublished thesis in Universtiy College Cork, they were usually short, with horns which curved forwards and inwards, a high forehead and a pronounced protruberance between the horns.

In early Ireland cattle were rarely slaughtered for their meat. The size of your herd of cattle was an indication of your wealth and status. Only for special occasions would a cow or bullock be killed and eaten. In the ninth century tale, *Bricriu's Feast*, guests are enticed to the banquet with the promise of 'a lordly cow that…since it was a calf…has eaten nothing but meadow grass and corn'.

In his *Letters from Ireland, 1698*, John Dunton describes a meal of beef in the home of one O'Flaghertie, in the west of Ireland:

> We return'd before the heate of the day to our greate cabbin, where we had at dinner, no less than a whole beef, boyl'd and roasted.

And, on September 29, 1831, the gourmet writer Amhlaoibh Uí Shúileabháin recorded in his diary that he had 'a dinner of beef and potatoes for four pence halfpenny' in one of Dublin's eating houses.

Up to recent times roast beef was standard Sunday fare in many prosperous Irish households. The leftovers were often turned into shepherd's pie on Monday or Tuesday.

Serves 10 to 15

Roast Beef

with Batter Pudding & Gravy

prime rib of beef on the bone, with a
nice covering of fat (well hung)
salt and freshly ground pepper

Gravy

2¹/₂ cups stock (preferably
homemade beef stock)
roux (optional; see page 40)

Roasting times

15 minutes per lb for rare
20 minutes per lb for medium
25 minutes per lb for well done

The old Irish breeds of cattle were Kerry, Maoile and Dexter. However, my butcher, Michael Cuddigan, says that the best roast beef comes from Pole Angus cattle.

Ask your butcher to saw through the upper chine bone of the beef, so that the 'feather bones' will be easy to remove before carving. Weigh the roast and calculate the cooking time (see below). Preheat the oven to 475°F.

Score the fat and season with salt and freshly ground pepper. Place the meat in a roasting pan with the fat side uppermost. As the fat renders down in the heat of the oven, it will baste the meat. The bones provide a natural rack to hold the meat clear of the fat in the roasting pan.

Put the meat into the fully preheated oven. After 15 minutes turn down the heat to a moderate oven (350°F) until the meat is cooked to your taste.

There are various ways of checking if the beef is cooked. I usually put a skewer into the thickest part of the roast, leave it there for about 30 to 45 seconds and then put it against my wrist. If it still feels cool, the meat is rare; if it is warm, it is medium rare; if it is hotter, it's medium; and if you can't keep the skewer against your wrist for more than a second, then you know the meat is well done. Also, if you check the color of the juices you will find they are clear, as opposed to red for rare or pink for medium.

When the meat is cooked it should be allowed to rest on a plate in a warm oven for 15 to 30 minutes before carving, depending on the size of the roast. The internal temperature of the meat will continue to rise by as much as 5°F, so remove the roast from the oven while it is still slightly underdone.

Meanwhile make the gravy. Spoon the fat off the roasting pan. Pour the stock into the cooking juices remaining in the pan. Boil for a few minutes, stirring and scraping the pan well to dissolve the caramelized meat juices (I find a small whisk ideal for this). Thicken very slightly with a little roux if you like (years ago flour would have been sprinkled over the fat in the pan, but I prefer to use roux). Taste and add salt and freshly ground pepper if necessary. Strain and serve in a warm gravy boat.

Carve the beef at the table and serve with horseradish sauce and batter pudding (see opposite). Add gravy and lots of crusty roast potatoes.

Sieve the flour into a bowl and make a well in the center of the flour. Drop in the eggs. Using a small whisk or wooden spoon, stir continuously, gradually drawing in flour from the sides and adding the milk in a steady stream at the same time. When all the flour has been mixed in, whisk in the remainder of the milk and the cool melted butter. Allow the batter to stand at rest for 1 hour.

Grease hot muffin pans with oil or beef fat drippings and fill them half to three-quarters full with batter. Bake in a hot oven (450°F) for about 20 minutes.

Serves 8 to 10
Batter Pudding

1 cup flour
2 eggs, preferably free-range
1¼ cups milk
1 tablespoon butter, melted and cooled
oil or beef fat drippings for greasing the pans

Horseradish grows wild in many parts of Ireland and looks like giant dock leaves. It has been used for many years, particularly by Anglo-Irish families, to make a punchy sauce to accompany roast beef. If you can't find any near you, plant some in your own garden. It is very prolific and the root can be dug up at any time of the year. Scrub it well and peel it before grating.

Put the grated horseradish into a bowl with the wine vinegar, lemon juice, mustard, salt, freshly ground pepper and sugar. Fold in the softly whipped cream, but do not overmix or the sauce will curdle. It keeps for 2 to 3 days; cover so that it doesn't pick up flavors in the refrigerator.

This is a fairly mild horseradish sauce. If you want to really clear your sinuses, you can increase the amount of horseradish!

Serves 8 to 10
Horseradish Sauce

1½ to 2 tablespoons grated horseradish
2 teaspoons wine vinegar
1 teaspoon lemon juice
¼ teaspoon mustard
¼ teaspoon salt
pinch of freshly ground pepper
1 teaspoon sugar
1¼ cups softly whipped cream

It was only gradually, from the early part of this century, that ranges and cookers (or stoves, as they were frequently called) came into general use. I remember in the 1950's the excitement generated when a new range arrived in a friend's house in my village in Co. Laois. Before that, food was cooked over or beside the open fire.
Pot roasting was a common method, particularly for a rich, flavorsome Sunday roast. A flat-bottomed pot oven was used, but nowadays a good heavy casserole gives a similar result. This dish can be cooked on top of the stove or in the oven.

Heat a little beef fat dripping in a heavy casserole, brown the meat on all sides and season with salt and freshly ground pepper. (I can't resist adding a sprinkling of thyme leaves at this point, or perhaps smearing the beef with grainy mustard.) Cover with a lid and cook on the lowest heat possible for 2½ to 3 hours. The beef can also be transferred to a preheated low oven, at 275°F.

When the roast is cooked, remove to a serving plate and make a little gravy in the casserole dish. Skim off the fat from the meat juices, add the stock, bring to a boil and simmer for a few minutes. Taste and add seasoning if necessary; thicken lightly with a little roux if you like.

Serve the pot-roasted beef with the gravy. The traditional accompanying vegetables would have been carrots and potatoes, but in the autumn I love zucchini in cheese sauce, buttered mashed rutabagas or carrot and parsnips.

Serves 6 to 8
Pot-roasted Beef

4lb well hung best topside or silverside
1¼ cups beef stock
beef dripping
salt and freshly ground pepper
thyme leaves (optional)
grainy mustard (optional)
roux (optional, see page 40)

Serves 6 to 8

Beef & Guinness Stew

Guinness, Ireland's famous black stout, has been brewed in Dublin since 1759. It has a very special place in Irish life. In Dublin Tenement Life: An Oral History, *publican John O'Dwyer recalls the importance of stout in the lives of the poorest tenement dwellers in Dublin:*

> They had *nothing*. They *lived for pints*. Drink was the main diet. It was food…they used to call the pint the 'liquid food'.

Nowadays the 'liquid food' is used increasingly in cooking. It is a tasty addition to stews and casseroles, helping to tenderize the meat and imparting its distinctive malty flavor to any dish. This recipe makes a wonderful gutsy stew which tastes even better a day or two after it is made.

*2lb lean stewing beef
3 tablespoons oil
2 tablespoons flour
salt and freshly ground pepper and a pinch of cayenne
2 large onions , coarsely chopped
1 large clove garlic, crushed (optional)
2 tablespoons tomato purée, dissolved in 4 tablespoons water
1 1/4 cups Guinness
2 cups carrots, cut into chunks
sprig of thyme*

Trim the meat of any fat or gristle, cut into cubes of 2 inches (5cm) and toss them in a bowl with 1 tablespoon oil. Season the flour with salt, freshly ground pepper and a pinch or two of cayenne. Toss the meat in this mixture.

Heat the remaining oil in a wide frying pan over a high heat. Brown the meat on all sides. Add the onions, crushed garlic and tomato purée to the pan, cover and cook gently for about 5 minutes. Transfer the contents of the pan to a casserole, and pour some of the Guinness into the frying pan. Bring to a boil and stir to dissolve the caramelized meat juices on the pan. Pour onto the meat with the remaining Guinness; add the carrots and the thyme. Stir, taste, and add a little more salt if necessary. Cover with the lid of the casserole and simmer very gently until the meat is tender—2 to 3 hours. The stew may be cooked on top of the stove or in a low oven at 300°F. Taste and correct the seasoning.

Scatter with lots of chopped parsley and serve with champ (see page 143), colcannon (see page 147) or plain boiled potatoes.

Corned Beef

Corned beef has a long history in the Irish diet. It is listed as a 'delicious prodigious viand' in the eleventh century text *Aislinge Meic Con Glinne*:

> Many wonderful provisions,
> Pieces of every palatable food
> full without fault,
> perpetual joints of corned beef.

Traditionally the most effective means of preserving beef after the slaughter was to corn beef pieces in a simple wet pickle of salt, sugar, saltpeter and water. Salted beef appeared frequently on menus of the aristocratic classes, and also of those not so well off, if they were fortunate enough to procure beef at all. Fresh beef was a rare and luxurious treat for all classes.

Corned beef has always been associated with Cork City. Between the late 1680s and 1825 beef-corning was the city's most important industry. In this period, Cork exported corned beef to England and much of Europe, and as far away as Newfoundland and the West Indies.

Serves 6 to 8

Corned Beef with Cabbage

Although this dish is eaten less frequently nowadays in Ireland, for Irish expatriots it conjures up powerful nostalgic images of a rural Irish past. Originally it was a traditional Easter Sunday dinner. The beef, killed before the winter, would have been salted and could now be eaten after the long Lenten fast, with fresh green cabbage and floury potatoes. Our local butcher corns beef in the slow, old-fashioned way which, alas, is nowadays more the exception than the norm.

Put the brisket into a saucepan with the carrots, onions, mustard and the herbs. Cover with cold water, and bring gently to a boil. Simmer, covered, for 2 hours. Discard the outer leaves of the cabbage, cut in quarters and add to the pot. Cook for a further 1 to 2 hours or until the meat and vegetables are soft and tender.

Serve the corned beef in slices, surrounded by the vegetables and cooking liquid. Serve with lots of floury potatoes and freshly made mustard.

4lb corned brisket of beef
3 large carrots, cut into large chunks
6 to 8 small onions
1 teaspoon dry English mustard
large sprig fresh thyme and some parsley
*   stalks, tied together*
1 cabbage
salt and freshly ground pepper

Ballymaloe Spiced Beef

Serves 10 to 15

Traditionally spiced beef was a special and novel treat at Christmastime. Throughout the rest of the year, beef was most frequently eaten salted. The exotic spiced flavors of this Christmas dish, therefore, made a welcome change. Spices were difficult and expensive to procure, which meant that spiced beef was a once-yearly indulgence.

Although spiced beef is associated with Christmas, nowadays in Cork we eat it all year round! It may be served hot or cold and is a marvellous stand-by. If it is properly spiced and cooked it will keep for 3 to 4 weeks. This delicious recipe for spiced beef has been handed down in Myrtle Allen's family, and, although I have tried several others, it is still my favorite.

The spice recipe makes enough to cure five cuts of beef, each cut being approximately 4lb in size.

3 to 4lb boned beef, chuck, round or brisket

Ballymaloe Spice for Beef
1 cup sugar
12oz salt
1/2 cup whole black pepper
1/2 cup whole allspice (Pimento or Jamaican pepper)
3/4 cup whole juniper berries

Grind all the spice ingredients (preferably in a food processor) until fairly fine. Store the mixture in a screw top jar; it will keep for months, so make the full quantity even if it is more than you need at a particular time.

To prepare the beef, trim away any unnecessary fat. Rub the spice well over the beef and into every crevice of the beef. Put into an earthenware dish and leave for 3 to 7 days, turning occasionally. (This is a dry spice, but after a day or two some liquid will come out of the meat.) The longer the meat is left in the spice, the longer it will last and the more spicy the flavor will be.

Just before cooking the meat, roll and tie it neatly with cotton string into a compact shape, cover with cold water and simmer for 2 to 3 hours or until soft and cooked. If it is not to be eaten hot, put it on a baking tray or into an appropriate sized bread pan; cover it with a board and a 4lb weight or whatever comes to hand. Leave for 12 hours.

Cut into thin slices and serve with some freshly made salads and homemade chutneys, or use in sandwiches.

Spiced beef was one of the many dainties served at dinner for 'Little Woman's Christmas' by Aunt Kate in James Joyce's short story The Dead:

> While Gabriel and Miss Daly exchanged plates of goose and plates of ham and spiced beef, Lily went from guest to guest with a dish of hot floury potatoes wrapped in a white napkin…Mary Jane waited on her pupils and saw that they got the best slices, and Aunt Kate and Aunt Julia opened and carried across from the piano bottles of stout and ale for the gentlemen and bottles of minerals for the ladies.

Pound the herbs and spices together and mix well with the salt, sugar and minced onion. Tie the beef up well and place in an earthenware crock. Cover the meat with the spice mixture, rubbing it well in by hand for several minutes. Replace the lid. Turn the meat once a day, every day for two weeks, rubbing the spice mixture in each time.

To boil the spiced beef, dice the vegetables and place in the bottom of a pot. Place the meat on top and cover with cold water. Boil (for about 30 minutes per 1lb and then 30 minutes over). When tender take out and press between two plates with a weight on top. Leave overnight.

Serves 20 to 25

Aunt Lil's Spiced Beef

6lb beef chuck, boned and rolled
thyme, mixed herbs, mace, nutmeg, cloves,
*   allspice, black pepper,*
bay leaf
6 teaspoons mixed spice
1lb salt
1/2 cup moist brown sugar
1 onion, finely minced

to boiling the spiced beef
1 onion
3 carrots
1 small turnip
1 stick celery
parsley
peppercorns

I adore shepherd's pie—so much so that I would almost cook a roast specially to make it! Cooking raw minced beef simply doesn't give the same flavor. Now that the price of beef has gone through the roof, people seldom allow themselves the luxury of buying a roast large enough to yield the necessary leftovers. Despite its name, in Ireland shepherd's pie is almost always made from beef, but you can of course use lamb.

Melt the butter in a frying pan and add the onion. Cover with a butter wrapper and cook over a slow heat for 5 minutes until soft but not colored. Add the flour and cook until brown. Pour in the stock, bring to a boil and skim. Add the tomato purée, chopped parsley, thyme leaves, salt and pepper and simmer for 5 minutes.

Add the meat to the sauce and bring to a boil. Put in a pie dish, cover with the mashed potatoes and score the top with a fork. Reheat in a moderate oven (350°F) for about 30 minutes. Garnish with parsley and serve with garlic butter (see page 69).

Serves 6 to 8

Shepherd's Pie

1lb minced cooked beef
2 tablespoons butter
1 cup chopped onion
2 tablespoons flour
1 2/3 cups stock and leftover gravy
1 teaspoon tomato purée
1 dessertspoon chopped parsley
1 teaspoon thyme leaves
salt and freshly ground pepper
1lb potatoes, cooked and mashed

Pork

The early Irish pig was thin, scrawny and vicious in temperament. It was agile, capable of clearing a fence, or so we are told by the antiquarian visitor, Thomas Carleton, who visited Ireland in the years before the famine.

Until medieval times pigs were fattened on mast, the fruit of beech and oak, which was said to give the flesh a delicious flavor. After the widespread adoption of the potato, virtually every hovel could afford to rear a pig in good years, because the animal could be fed on surplus potatoes, potato skins and sour milk.

Every scrap of the pig was used. The head was salted and boiled with cabbage or turnips or made into brawn. The feet, called 'crubeens' in Ireland, were boiled and eaten on their own or with cabbage, or included in the brawn. The stomach was sometimes stuffed and roasted and was known as mock goose. In the days before soccer balls could be bought in every village shop the bladder or 'padgín' was donated to the children, who pumped it up with air and had endless hours of fun with it.

The pig's liver was fried and the skirts and kidneys cooked together. The pig's blood, various trimmings and bits of lard were mixed with meal and blood to make into puddings. The heart was stuffed and pot roasted in the bastible, or sliced and stewed. The pork steaks and griskins and some loin were eaten fresh; the remainder was salted down for bacon. The lard was rendered and some was made into slim cakes.

Killing a Pig

Killing the pig was a very important social occasion, planned several weeks ahead. Many of the neighbors would come to lend a hand. Each neighbor who came would bring a fist of salt for the curing, and when the work was done everyone would get a share of the fresh pork and the black and white puddings. In some cases the farmer himself killed the pig, but on my relatives' farm in Tipperary, a local man skilled in the killing of pigs would arrive on an ass's cart, bringing all the tools of his trade—a mallet, a knife, a saw, an apron and a galvanized bath. He was highly thought of and had to be booked ahead.

As a child I loved all the excitement and wanted to be in on all the action with my brothers. I was highly indignant when I was barred from watching the actual killing simply because I was a girl—an early taste of male chauvinism!

As soon as the pig was stunned, its throat was cut and the precious blood was collected in a basin underneath for the puddings. Salt was added and the blood was stirred constantly to prevent coagulation. Then two or three fellas would rush off for buckets of almost boiling water from the black pot over the open fire. The pigs would be scalded in the big bath and then hiked up on to a table, or creel, which was balanced on top of the bath. Then three or four helpers would quickly shave off the hairs, being careful not to damage the skin. The intestines were removed and a few buckets of cold spring water from the pump were thrown over the carcass. The pig was then hung up by the back legs from the rafters in a cool, airy, white-washed outhouse, with two or three little pointed sticks propped into the center to keep its inside open.

This accomplished, the laborious business of washing the intestines began, under the running water from the pump in the yard. The women usually did this and I was allowed to help. The large intestines were used for the white puddings and the small for the black. When the washing and scraping was complete, the intestines were put into salted water which was changed regularly until the puddings were made the following day or the day after. The morning after the pig was killed the butcher would come back and divide the pig in two lengthways; he would then extract the pork steaks, liver and kidneys. The pork steaks were the sweetest and most sought-after part of the pig.

Then the carcass was butchered. Spare ribs and loin were kept to be eaten fresh. The bacon curing got underway. Salt and saltpeter were rubbed vigorously into the meat which was then carefully packed between layers of salt in a wooden wine barrel from the distillery. The meat remained in the vat for three weeks, after which it was hung up on hooks from the rafters in the kitchen. Sometimes a ham was hung up inside the huge chimney over the open fire for smoking.

Most farmers killed a pig at certain times of the year (some of the most prosperous killed several pigs on the same day). There was a custom that pigs should be killed only when there was an 'R' in the month i.e. never in the summer—an eminently sensible precaution in the days before refrigeration. In some counties, such as Mayo and Galway, it was believed that the deed should be done under a full moon, but that was not the case in our area in the midlands of Ireland.

Pigs were kept somewhere close to the house where they could be fed easily. They were prized possessions, not only providing several months' supply of meat for the household, but also leaving enough over to share with neighbors, who would share their own meat in turn.

Pork has suffered more than almost any other meat from modern intensive rearing methods. For many years I longed for the taste of the sweet juicy pork we ate as children, so last year, to the great consternation of my husband and family, I bought two darling saddleback pigs from West Cork and a black Berkshire boar from the Comeragh mountains. They live happily and completely naturally in our orchard and have produced several large litters of piglets, which delight us all. My boar would appear to be a descendant of the early Irish pig, as he too can clear a fence with the greatest of ease. I've spent many hours chasing him around the immediate countryside. The pork is sweet and delicious!

For really good crackling, score the skin at ¼-inch intervals running with the grain—let your butcher do this if possible, because the skin can be quite tough. (This will also make it easier to carve later.)

Next make the stuffing: sweat the onions gently in the butter for 5 or 6 minutes. When they are soft, stir in the breadcrumbs, freshly chopped herbs and a little salt and pepper to taste. Cool.

Preheat the oven to 375°F. Put the joint, skin side down, on the work top and sprinkle with salt and freshly ground pepper. Spread the stuffing over the meat, roll up tightly and tie with cotton string. Season the rind with salt. Roast on a rack, allowing 25 to 28 minutes per pound. Baste every now and then.

Just before the end of cooking time remove the pork to another roasting pan, replace it in the oven and turn up the temperature to very hot—450°F, to get crisp crackling. When the joint is cooked the juices should run clear. (You should never eat pork pink.) Put the pork onto a hot serving dish and allow to rest in a very cool oven while you make the gravy in the original roasting pan.

Spoon off the fat from the roasting pan and add the chicken stock. Whisk to dissolve the scrapings on the pan. Bring to a boil. Season and thicken with a little roux, if desired. Freshly chopped herbs may be added to the gravy. Serve with crispy, roast potatoes and apple sauce.

Serves 10 to 12

Traditional Roast Pork

with Crackling & Apple Sauce

1 loin of pork with the skin still on, approx. 5lb

fresh herb stuffing
3 tablespoons butter
¾ cup chopped onion
1 cup soft white breadcrumbs
2 tablespoons chopped herbs (parsley, thyme, chives, marjoram, savory, perhaps very little sage or rosemary)
salt and freshly ground pepper

gravy
2½ cups homemade chicken stock
roux (optional; see page 40)

Apple sauce (see page 117)

A Christmas Feast

For Eamonn Mac Thomáis's childhood Christmas there was no goose or turkey but instead a 'bit of roast', usually pork or a bit of ham or bacon (his father had died when he was fourteen). The pudding and iced cake were a present from the grocer they dealt with, and in a good year he would also include a big red candle and a bottle of sherry or port wine.

After the Christmas dinner the mother would douse herself in sherry and there would be great gas, she'd be half cocked for the afternoon. All the rest of the family were pioneers [total abstainers], so she'd have the bottle to herself.

Pot Roasted Pork Steaks

Serves 6 to 8

What is known in the states as pork fillet (or tenderloin) is called pork steak in Ireland. It was the most highly-prized piece when the pig was killed. This is one of the ways my mother often used to cook it when we were children.

4 slices pork tenderloin
lard or soft butter
flour
1¼ cup chicken stock or water

Stuffing
2 tablespoons butter
1 onion, finely chopped
1lb freshly cooked potatoes
1 tablespoon chopped parsley
thyme (optional)
salt and freshly ground pepper

Garnish
fresh parsley sprigs

First make the stuffing. Melt the butter in a heavy saucepan, add the chopped onion, cover and sweat over a gentle heat for 8 to 10 minutes. Meanwhile peel and mash the potatoes, add the softened onion and chopped parsley, add a little thyme if you like. Season with salt and freshly ground pepper.

Trim the fillets of gristle. Unless they are very fat (which is most unlikely nowadays) leave what little fat there is. Split each fillet down one side and open out flat. Season with salt and freshly ground pepper. Divide the stuffing between two fillets. Lay the other fillets on top and truss or sew all around the edge with cotton thread. Smear each with a little very good lard or soft butter.

Heat a heavy casserole, preferably oval. Brown the fillets on each side. Cover with wax paper and the lid of the saucepan.

Cook on a gentle heat on top of the stove or put into a preheated moderate oven at 350°F for 45 minutes to 1 hour. Baste every now and then.

To serve, remove the stuffed fillets to a serving dish. Skim the fat from the cooking juices, return them to the casserole, add a little flour and stir well. Return to the heat and cook for a minute or two, then add the chicken stock or water, bring to a boil, stirring all the time with a little whisk to dissolve the caramelized sediment. Taste and correct seasoning. Strain into a gravy boat and serve with the pork fillets simply garnished with sprigs of fresh parsley. Cut the fillets into thick slices to serve.

Griskins

It has been suggested that the word griskin comes from the Viking word griss, *meaning young pig. Perhaps the Vikings introduced this cut of meat to the Irish.*

pork tenderloin trimmings
butter
salt and freshly ground pepper

Trim any fat from the pork steak. Cut into ¾-inch thick slices. Melt a little butter in a pan. As it begins to foam, season the pork with salt and freshly ground pepper. Put it into the foaming butter and cook on a pretty high heat until golden on one side, then turn over and cook the other side. Serve immediately with bread and butter or as part of the main meal, accompanied by potatoes and vegetables.

This wholesome, rib-sticking dish—which is perfect for a winter's day—came to me from North Tipperary.

Slice the kidneys and the vegetables, then place in a pot with the chops. Cover with water and add the herbs and seasonings. Cook over a low heat for about 30 minutes.

Make a pliable dough with the flour, suet, baking powder, salt and enough milk to mix. Roll out on to a floured board, cut to fit inside the pot and place on top of the meat. Cover with a lid, allowing the pastry room to rise. Cook for 1½ hours over a low heat.

Serves 4 to 6

Císte

2 pork kidneys
1 large onion
1 large carrot
6 pork chops
mixed herbs
salt and freshly ground pepper

Pastry
2 cups plain flour
4oz grated beef suet
½ teaspoon baking powder
salt
⅔ cup milk

Salted pork ribs, bought and often cooked in a sheet, are a great Cork speciality, known as 'bodice'. This follows the Cork tradition of naming various bits of offal after items of women's clothing. We also eat skirts (see page 127)!

Cover in cold water, bring to a boil and simmer for an hour or more until soft and juicy. Season with English mustard and eat with your fingers. Mashed potatoes, carrots or turnips are often served with bodice.

Serves 2 to 4

Bide Bodice

1 bodice, about 11 pork ribs

Bought pork sausages are the great standby in the basic Irish diet, available in every corner shop and longed for by many a homesick Irish emigrant. They vary in quality from one supplier to the other.

Homemade sausages are coarser in texture, juicy and delicious. You don't have to bother to fill them into sausage casings, so they only take minutes to put together and make a cheap and comforting meal.

Mince the pork. Chop the herbs finely and mix through the crumbs. Crush the garlic to a paste with a little salt. Whisk the egg, then mix all the ingredients together thoroughly. Season with salt and freshly ground pepper. Fry a little knob of the mixture, taste to check the seasoning, and correct if necessary. Divide into sixteen pieces and roll into lengths. Fry the sausages gently in a barely oiled pan until golden on all sides. They are particularly delicious served with a big bowl of buttery champ (see page 143), colcannon (see page 147) or apple sauce.

Serves 8

Homemade Sausages

with Apple Sauce

1lb fatty pork
1 or 2 teaspoons mixed fresh herbs e.g. parsley, thyme, chives, marjoram, rosemary or sage
⅔ cup soft white breadcrumbs
1 clove garlic
salt and freshly ground pepper
1 egg, preferably free range

Apple Sauce

The trick with this sauce is to cook it on a very low heat with only a tiny drop of water, so that it is nice and thick and not too watery.

Peel, quarter and core the apples. Cut the pieces in two and place them in a stainless steel or castiron saucepan, with sugar and water. Cover and cook on a very low heat until the apples break down in a fluff. Stir and taste for sweetness.

Serve warm or cold.

Serves 8

Apple Sauce

1lb cooking apples
1 tablespoon water
¼ cup approx. sugar (depending on how tart the apples are)

An Irish Breakfast

Serves 4

Bacon and Eggs is of Irish origin, according to a story told by the late Oscar Ashe, quoted by Florence Irwin in Irish Country Recipes*:*

An old Irish peasant woman was frying the morning bacon for her good man in a pan over the peat fire. In the open chimney above roosted the fowls on the cross-beams from which the hams were hung to smoke. She turned to drive out of doors an old sow and her litter and the other domestic animals which shared the cabin at night with the rest of the family. As she was so occupied a hen dropped an egg from its roost. It struck the edge of the pan and its contents spilled into the sizzling fat. And so when the good woman came to take the pan from the fire, lo! for the first time she beheld an egg fried with bacon. She set the dish before her good man who consumed the lot, and he went forth to the monastery where he laboured, marvelling. And so the fame of the dish penetrated the monastery walls, and from monastery to monastery it spread, and from land to land, and from peoples to peoples, and was relished by rich and poor alike, and all by the grace of God and the irregular proclivities of the lazy old hen.

4 pork sausages
2 tomatoes
salt, pepper, sugar
butter
4 ³/4inch thick slices white pudding (see page 132)
4 ³/4inch thick slices black pudding (see page 132)
bacon slices
4 free-range eggs

Prick the sausages and fry on a medium heat until golden all over. Drain and keep hot. Cut the tomatoes in half, put on to a oven-proof plate and season with salt, pepper and sugar. Place a pat of butter on each tomato, cover loosely with parchment paper and cook in a moderate oven at 350°F, for 5 to 10 minutes. Alternatively, fry gently in a frying pan.

Fry the puddings gently on both sides and drain on paper towels. Cut any rinds off the bacon and fry until just crisp on a very hot pan. Finally, heat a little bacon fat or butter in a clean pan, crack the eggs and cook on a gentle heat as desired. When cooked, divide the 'spoils' between four hot plates and serve immediately with lots of fresh soda bread and hot toast.

To Cure Bacon

This recipe for a procedure that would have been common in many households up to the middle of this century is taken from the Receipt Book of Eliza Helena Odell, Odell Ville, Co. Limerick. It is dated 26 August 1851.

2¹/2 cups English salt
²/3 cup of Irish or bay salt
¹/3 cup of saltpetre
²/3 cup of black pepper (ground)
1lb of molasses

These proportions to every cut of bacon. Let the marrow be taken out of the bones of the Hams and Gammons and fill the holes with salt and saltpetre.When the pig is cut up sprinkle it with salt and leave it on a sloping flag or board to drain until next day. Then wipe each piece dry and rub the treacle well in at both sides. Put a layer of salt about an inch deep into the tub, then pack nicely a layer of meat (hams first), the skin side down, and sprinkle well the flesh side with pepper and saltpetre (which have first been mixed) then a layer of salt, then meat and so on to the top, press down the meat with stones and do no more till you hang it in four weeks, if the pickle don't rise in four weeks sprinkle salt over it to form some and also if the compliment of salt run short add more, for each layer must be thick enough to pickle out the meat—hams and bacon are treated the same way, but if heavy meat it is an improvement to give the hams and gammons slight hand rubbing, be sure to exclude all air and have the heads well cleaned from blood and the brains removed. Coarse brown sugar will do as well as treacle.

Traditional Irish Breakfast

From Annie Kiely's manuscript Receipt Book, Cork, 1908:

Take 4 pounds of bacon put down in one gallon of cold water, when it comes to a boil skim it and allow it to simmer for 1½ hours when done remove the skin and grate on some of the deepest colour stale breadcrumbs. Then brown before the fire or in the oven for a few minutes. Cabbage or greens should be previously prepared having washed them well in cold water and leaving them in the water for 1 hour then take another saucepan of boiling water add to it 1 or 2 cups of broth in which the meat is boiled, put in a small lump of washing soda and a pinch of salt, the soda preserves the green colour and softens it, place the cabbage in boiling water and allow it to boil for half an hour. When done put it in a cylinder and place a heavy weight upon it to press out the water. When dishing arrange the cabbage nicely around the dish leaving the centre vacant for the bacon. Serve the rest of the cabbage in a vegetable dish, the remainder of the broth can be added to beef or pea soup.

Bacon & Cabbage

Without question Ireland's national dish—less widely known abroad but much more widely eaten, particularly in rural Ireland, than the legendary Irish stew.

Cover the bacon in cold water and bring slowly to a boil, discarding any white froth. Each time it forms, replace the water and reboil. Cover with hot water and simmer, for one hour or until it is warmed through.

Meanwhile, remove the outer leaves from the cabbage. Cut the cabbage into quarters, remove the center core. Cut each quarter into thin strips across the grain. About 30 minutes before the bacon is cooked, add the cabbage. Continue to cook until the cabbage is soft and tender and the bacon fully cooked through. Remove the bacon to a hot plate and strain the water off the cabbage. Return the cabbage to the pan with a lump of butter; season with white pepper. Serve with the bacon and, traditionally, boiled potatoes and parsley sauce (see page 88).

Serves 12 to 15

Bacon & Cabbage

4 to 5lb ready-to-eat Canadian bacon with a nice covering of fat
1 head cabbage, Savoy, or spring cabbage, depending on the time of year
butter
white pepper

In search of Dublin Coddle

For years I was intrigued by Dublin Coddle. It sounded utterly revolting and when I attempted to make it from the recipes I could find it looked and tasted revolting too. Every time I went to Dublin I would sound out a taxi driver about coddle. Most of them grew instantly nostalgic. Some talked of sneaking home to 'the Mammy's' for a feed of coddle, but, interestingly, just as many talked about 'the wife' or 'herself' making it regularly. So there's no question that traditional Dublin Coddle is alive and well and still being made on a regular basis in Dublin.

As with Irish Stew, feelings run high on what a real coddle should be. One taxi driver had confided to me that his thoroughly modern wife put tomato and peas in to give it a bit of color. When I attempted to share this gem of information with the next taxi driver, however, he was so aghast that he turned right round in the seat to look me straight in the eye—and as a result nearly hit a bus.

'Not at all!' he declared emphatically, proceeding to give me a blow by blow account of how coddle should be made. 'Put the rashers, sausages, potatoes and onions into a pot, cover them up with cold water and boil 'em up for an hour or so. Oh, and a nice bit of pepper,' he added. Should I brown the sausages? I ventured to ask. 'Not at all, amn't I after telling you how to make it?' What would you eat with it? 'Tea and bread and butter, or maybe a bottle of stout if you had it.'

Eventually one chap told me about the essential condiment that no cookery book had mentioned—the bottle of Chef or YR Sauce (in the United States, A1 or brown sauce is the best alternative) to shake over the top. Several other people confirmed this—so there you are now!

Winnie Dunne's Dublin Coddle

Well, it took Kevin Dunne, born and bred in the Liberties, in the heart of Dublin, to take the mystery out of coddle for me. One Sunday morning in my kitchen in Cork, well outside the Pale, he went to the village for the bacon and sausages while I peeled the onions and potatoes. This is Dublin Coddle as his mother made it.

No one ever measures for Dublin Coddle but to feed four people we had—

8 good sized potatoes
4 good sized onions
8 bacon slices (we left the rind on)
8 sausages
pepper

Kevin put the potatoes straight into a medium sized pot, chopped up the onions into chunks and added those, then laid the rashers and sausages on top. He put the pot under the cold tap until the ingredients were almost covered, then put the pot on the Aga and brought it to the boil. Then he added lots of pepper (no salt, as good Irish rashers will ensure that it is salty enough!) We covered the pot and simmered the mixture for an hour or so. I looked into the pot every now and then, and about halfway through left the lid slightly ajar to reduce the liquid somewhat. The potatoes got a little fluffy but still kept their shape. It still looked distinctly unappetizing (lots of chopped parsley scattered over the top would take the harm out of the sausages which still appear to be raw) but surprise, surprise, it tasted absolutely delicious! (I'm not joking; delicious is not too strong a word for this dish.) I didn't have a bottle of YR Sauce to hand, but ate the coddle with lots of butter. Now I understand why this simple, good-humored dish is such a favorite—and why so many Dubs look forward to coming home to a plate of it after a night of liquid entertainment! It's comfort food at its best—although with all those salty rashers in it, it would give you a mighty thirst!

Dublin Coddle

In our restaurant at Ballymaloe House we serve bacon steak with a crispy coating, accompanied by Irish whiskey sauce.

Cover the piece of bacon with cold water. Bring to a boil. If the bacon is salty, discard the water and start again; you may need to do this twice or, in extreme cases, three times. Boil for about 45 minutes or until it is cooked. Remove the rind and trim away any surplus fat. Slice into steaks ¹/₂ to ³/₄ inch thick. Dip the steaks in seasoned flour, then in beaten egg, and finally coat with white breadcrumbs. Heat the clarified butter and oil in a heavy frying pan. Fry the chops gently until they are cooked through and golden on both sides and serve with Irish whiskey sauce.

Put the sugar into a bowl with water, stir over a gentle heat until the sugar dissolves then bring the syrup to a boil. Remove the spoon and do not stir. Continue to boil until it turns a nice chestnut-brown color. Remove from the heat and immediately add the hot water. Allow to dissolve again and then add the Irish whiskey. Boil or a minute or two. Serve the sauce hot or cold.

Serves 4 to 5

Ballymaloe Bacon Chop

2lb ready-to-eat Canadian bacon (boneless and without the fatty end)
1 cup seasoned flour
1 egg beaten with a little milk
fresh white breadcrumbs

For frying
2 tablespoons clarified butter (see page 69)
or 1 tablespoon butter and 1 to 2 tablespoons olive oil

Irish Whiskey Sauce

1¹/₄ cup superfine granulated sugar
¹/₃ cup plus 1 tablespoon cold water
¹/₃ cup hot water
3 tablespoons Irish whiskey

Wakes

Wakes, although primarily to mourn the dead, were important social occasions in Irish tradition, and have remained so until relatively recent times. During a wake, courtships might commence and marriages were sometimes arranged ('twas many a match was made at a wake'). Relatives, neighbors and friends gathered in the house to pay their last respects to the dead. The corpse was laid out in the best bedroom or parlor, or even sometimes in the kitchen.

There was a strong tradition of feeding the mourners and even very poor families would virtually beggar themselves to provide a fine repast of funeral meats, cakes, tea, porter, whiskey and, of course, 'poteen'. John Dunton describes a Dublin wake in his 17th-century work, *Letters from Ireland, 1698*, edited by Edward MacLysaght (Dublin, 1982):

> About midnight, most of the company being then gathered that was expected to come, great platters of boiled flesh were brought into the barn, and an abundance of bread, all made in fine white cakes of wheat flour. I do not here mean small cakes, like our saffron ones or biscuits, but of size as large as a sieve and near three inches thick, portions of which with flesh were distributed to every one of the people and great tubs of drink which was brewed that day followed on hand-barrows…And now came tobacco, pipes and sneezing.

As a child in a country village I remember walking with some neighbors to a local woman's wake. The whole affair had a profound effect on me. When we arrived at the simple white-washed cottage, we were ushered into the bedroom where the corpse was laid out in the bed. Everyone spoke in hushed tones. First we knelt beside the bed and I watched in horror as the older women kissed the corpse (fortunately we were not expected to follow suit), then we joined other mourners who sat on chairs around the walls of the tiny bedroom. Every now and then I gathered up courage and stared in fascination at the corpse, so still and waxen with the rosary beads woven through her fingers. The blessed candles flickered at the four corners of the bed and the little Sacred Heart lamp under the holy picture illuminated the room in an eerie way. Gradually the mourners began to whisper; snuff was passed around for the men and older women and gradually the air thickened as some of the men smoked clay pipes slowly and thoughtfully. After a certain time they were replaced by new arrivals and we were then called into the kitchen. Even though we lived very close by, we were pressed to have tea and cold meats and sweet cake before we walked home in the dark.

At most wakes, as the night wore on, people would reminisce about the life of the deceased; they would go on to tell stories of the imaginary *Bean sí* in hushed tones. This ghostly figure was said to follow some families, and could be heard keening (wailing) and seen combing her long grey hair on the night before the person died. In many cases, wakes games were also played, such as Hunt the Slipper or Forfeits, and other party games, some of pagan origin.

I came across many recipes specifically intended for wakes and funerals in my research for this book. Cold ham was a great traditional standby.

If the ham is salty, soak it in cold water overnight. Next day discard the water. Cover the ham with fresh cold water and bring it slowly to a boil. If the meat is still salty, there will be white froth on top of the water. If so, discard this water, cover the ham with fresh cold water again and repeat the process. Finally, cover the ham with hot water and simmer until it is fully cooked. Allow about 20 minutes to 1lb cooking time. Allow the ham to cool; remove the skin, which should peel off easily, then sprinkle the surface with fine dried breadcrumbs.

People who lived through 'hard times' were very thrifty; not a scrap of food was wasted because they knew what it was like to be 'without'.

Put the crusts, preferably of white bread, into a very cool oven to dry out and allow them to become dry and crisp. They can then be crushed with the aid of a rolling pin and then sieved. Dried crumbs keep almost indefinitely in a sealed jar. Traditionally, they were used for sprinkling on the fat surface of cold ham or bacon, but they also make a perfect coating for croquettes or rissoles.

Serves 12 to 15

Funeral Ham

1 fresh or lightly smoked ham with a nice layer of fat, 10 to 12lb
Raspings (fine dried breadcrumbs)

Raspings

This method of cooking a whole ham was sent to me by Noreen Lehane of Cork City. It was given to her by an old lady from West Cork.

Steep the ham overnight (depending of course on the amount of salt, otherwise a few hours will do). Next day parboil it and leave the ham in the water overnight. Remove the ham from the water and dry it thoroughly. Make up a paste of flour and water, then wrap the ham completely in the paste. Put it into a hot oven for about half an hour and reduce the heat to low. A large ham on the bone would take about six hours, a medium ham about five hours and a boned and rolled ham about four hours.

When cooked, remove from the oven. At this stage the paste will be very hard and you will need a hammer to break it.

Next skin the ham and remove some of the fat, if it needs it. Glaze in the oven until golden brown.

By this method the ham does not reduce and remains deliciously moist throughout the cooking process.

To Cook a Whole Ham

Offal

Cork City has been an important trading port since the later medieval period. The provisioning of the ships involved thousands of people. The best cuts of meat were sold fresh and salted, other cuts were corned and spiced, and a great deal of offal was eaten by the Corkonians themselves. Offal is the generic name for the edible by-products of an animal following butchering. A certain weight of offal was allocated to each slaughterhouse worker as part of his weekly wage, hence the Cork people's great love for offal, which remains right up to the present day. The Cork Market, originally known as the English Market because when it was founded in 1788 the Irish were not allowed to trade inside its walls, still has many stalls which do a lively trade in pigs' heads, tails, offal bones, skirts, kidneys, bodices (salted spare ribs), crubeens, tripe and drisheen.

Pig's Head

My eldest son reckons to be very cool; like many of his generation nothing seems to faze him. However, one day recently when he lifted the lid off a pot on the stove, he shrieked and uttered some quite unprintable expletives when he caught sight of the pig's head bubbling in the pot. My daughters continually count my happy piglets in the orchards to make sure that none of them end up in brawn. They were appalled at the unmentionable bits of this and that they occasionally glimpsed while I tested recipes for this book—pigs' tails, bodice, tripe, drisheen…such a lily-livered lot, this generation. I've become very partial to a bit of pig's head myself!

I buy my pig's heads from Foleys in Castle Street in Cork City—one of the few shops where they are still available.

Pigs Head & Cabbage

Serves 4 to 6

half a pig's head
a head of cabbage
a lump of butter
pepper

Remove the brain and discard. Wash the pig's head well. Put in a large saucepan, cover with cold water and bring to a boil. Discard the water, refill the pan with fresh water and continue to cook, covered, for 3 to 4 hours, or until the meat is soft and tender and almost lifting off the bones.

Meanwhile, remove the outside leaves from the cabbage. Cut the cabbage into quarters and remove the center core. Cut each quarter into thin strips across the grain. About 30 minutes before the pig's head is cooked, add the cabbage and continue to cook until the cabbage is soft and tender and the pig's head is fully cooked through.

Devotees of pig's head would simply surround the pig's head with cabbage on a plate and serve this. However, for a less dramatic presentation and ease of carving, the bones can be removed and the pig's head cut into slices. Don't forget to give each person a piece of tongue and ear. The pig's ear is a particular favorite.

Pig's Tails

Serves 6

with Rutabaga

Paddy McDonnell's stall in the Cork market is just one of several which sells pigs' tails, skirts and kidneys and bodices. He tells me that he still sells about 200 tails a week, but he is concerned because they are becoming more difficult to find nowadays. Most pigs reared in an intensive way have their tails docked.

Pigs' tails are irreverently known in Cork as 'slash farts' or 'pigs' mud-guards'! Mrs. Cullinane cooked these pigs' tails for me in her home in Ballymacoda and very tasty they were too.

6 pigs' tails
1 rutabaga, peeled and cut into
1 inch cubes
a generous knob of butter
salt and freshly ground black pepper

Cover the pigs' tails with cold water, bring to a boil, then discard the water. Cover with fresh water and bring to a boil again.

Add the rutabaga to the pot, cover and continue to cook until the pigs' tails are soft and tender and the turnips fully cooked.

Remove the tails and keep aside. Mash the rutabagas with a generous lump of butter. Season. Put in a hot bowl and serve the pigs' tails on top.

Serves 12 to 15

Collared Head

small pig's head and tongue (unsalted)
2 pig's feet
peppercorns
mace
mixed herbs
cloves
2 onions

Cut the head in two, remove eyes and brains and any gristle. Wash well and scrape where necessary. Scrub the feet well. Just cover the meat with water in a pot, add the herbs, spices and onions. Simmer for 4 hours over a low heat until the meat is very tender. Remove the meat from the bones and return to the pot to reduce the liquid. Remove the skin from the tongue. Cut up meat and tongue into small pieces. Fill a mold or bowl with meat, packing it well. If it is too dry, add a little stock from the pot. Allow to cool with a weighted plate on top. When cold, turn out and slice.

Pig's Tails

Brawn

Serves 16 to 20

There are countless different recipes for brawn. Many of them use pigs' heads as a basis and some will also include a couple of crubeens (trotters), ox or lamb's tongues, or a bit of shin of beef.

Brawn was known by a variety of names in Ireland; it was also called collared head and pig's head cheese. The ingredients vary, with some including only pig's head, as in the 1810 recipe for 'A Pretty Collar' from Mocollop Castle, outside Waterford (see opposite); others press 'pig's cheek' and feet; while other recipes include pig's head, feet and sheep's tongues. Our grandparents would be amused to note that brawn is making a comeback and now appears regularly on the menus of trendier restaurants.

half a salted pig's head
1 chicken
2 carrots, sliced
2 onions, sliced
1 stick celery (optional)
a sprig of thyme and a few parsley stalks
4 or 5 peppercorns
1 tablespoon chopped fresh parsley and thyme
2 pudding bowls, 2¹/₂ cups each

Wash the pig's head, remove the brain and discard. Put the head into a saucepan and cover with cold water. Bring to a boil then discard the water. Bring to a boil in fresh water and cook for 3 or 4 hours or until the meat is soft and tender and parting from the bones.

Meanwhile put the chicken into another saucepan. Add the carrots and onions, celery if you have it to spare, parsley stalks and sprig of thyme. Add about 2¹/₂ inches of cold water and a few peppercorns. Cover, bring to a boil and cook until the bird is tender.

When both meats are cooked, remove them from the cooking liquid and take the meat from the bones. Skin the chicken and chop it and the pig's head into pieces. Mix the meats together and add the chopped parsley and thyme leaves. Taste and correct the seasoning.

Pack the meat into one large or two small pudding bowls and add a little of the cooking liquid from each pot. Press with a weight.

When cold, turn out and serve in slices with a salad. Brawn will keep for several weeks in the refrigerator.

A Pretty Collar

This recipe was taken from the receipt book of Mrs Dot Drew from Ballyduff, Co. Waterford, dated 1810:

The face and feet and ears of a pig put in salt a day or two wash them very clean and have them quite free from hairs and put them to boil in a little water. Slip out the bones and put em back in the water they were boil'd in and let em boil like in a good thick jelly. Cut up the meat in small pieces and season it with pepper salt and allspice. Cut some of gristle of the ear small. Have just warm some of the jelly and stir in some minced meat… Put it in a basin or mug to shape it.

To Prepare Collared Head

The preparation of collared head is also recalled by Mary O'Brien in The Farm by Lough Gur:

From pig's heads she made brawn or collared head…the little girls helped—hindered—her as she went about her preparations. We— and mother—made collared head, boiling part of the meat almost to jelly, then chopped the meat very small and spiced it with pep- per, allspice and finely ground nutmeg. Then we put it in a mold which opened on a hinge and we kept shut with a skewer. Then it was set and turned out of the shape. It made a dish fit for a King.

Serves 15 (approximately)

Collared Head

1 whole pig's head (2 half-heads)
1 ox tongue
2 medium size onions
1 level tablespoon salt
2 teaspoons pepper
1 tablespoon allspice

Sister Bernadette from the Presentation Convent, Crosshaven, Co. Cork, sent me her favourite recipe for collared head:

Soak the heads for 24 hours. Cook until very tender and leave to cool in water. They should be so well cooked that you will need to take them up with both hands. Leave overnight. Next day gather the pig's jelly around them and on the dish. You will need ²/₃ cup, so if not sufficient get the remainder from the pot in which they were cooked. Skin and remove the meat from the bone. Cut into ¼ inch pieces, fat and lean as it comes.

On the same day as the pig's heads, cook the ox tongue until very tender and leave to cool in water. Next day, skin and cut up in small pieces (do not use the fat) and mix with the pig's head meat. Get a large pot and parboil the finely chopped onions in the pig's jelly. Mix the salt, pepper and spice with the meat and add to the pot. Bring to a luke warm heat (do not boil). Stir to prevent burning, but do not overstir.

As collared head containers are no longer sold, I got a handyman to prepare an empty pea or bean can for me. He bored a circular row of holes around the base plus across and two rows of holes lengthways on sides. I kept the cover of the can. Put mixture into can, cover, and press with a half brick or old iron until all the fat has oozed out through the holes. Put on a dry dish and leave refrigerated until next day.

To turn out of the can, place on the side of the burner (low heat) for about 5 minutes and insert a flat knife around sides of can. It will keep in the refrigerator for around 10 days.

Crubeens

'Crubeens are a grand thing, but they'd give you a mighty thirst.'

Salted pigs' feet or trotters, known in many parts of Ireland as crubeens, became widely available with the establishment of the commercial bacon factories in Cork, Waterford, Limerick, Dublin and Belfast in the latter half of the nineteenth century. Cork was a major provisioning port and crubeens were exported in huge quantities to the West Indies. Up to the 1940s it was commonplace to see women selling cooked crubeens from baskets in the city streets. According to the historian Eamonn Mac Thomáis, crubeens in Dublin were known as 'Georges Street mouth organs', after the highly regarded pork butcher's shop located there.

Big pots of crubeens were cooked up and served in pubs, particularly on Saturday nights and fair days. Canny pub owners were not altogether unaware of the fierce thirst that these tasty little morsels provoked! Crubeens were eaten with the fingers—a thoroughly greasy and messy business—and washed down with copious quantities of beer or porter. The grease proved to be difficult to remove from the glasses, which was the primary reason why some of the classier pubs decided to discontinue this original Irish pub grub. Crubeens, though still available, are not now as widespread. However, crubeens can still be bought around Cork City and I was delighted to hear that the stalls of the Old English Market in Cork sold out of crubeens, and were literally incapable of dealing with the demand, during Ireland's exploits in the World Cup in 1994. O'Flynns of Marlboro Street, with true Cork wit, label the crubeens in the window of their butcher's shop 'low mileage pig's trotters'.

Put all the ingredients into a large pot, cover with plenty of cold water, bring to a boil and skim. Boil gently for 2 or 3 hours or until the meat is soft and very tender. Eat the crubeens either warm or cold, smeared with a little mustard if liked.

Crubeens

6 pig's feet
1 large onion
1 large carrot
1 bay leaf
5 or 6 parsley stalks
a good sprig of thyme
a few peppercorns
enough unsalted cold water to cover well

This recipe for crubeens was supplied by Mrs. Margaret Moriarty from Cahiracruttera, Inch, Co. Kerry:

When I see the dry brown objects offered for sale in shops and vans, I realize they bear little resemblance in color, and I am sure in taste, to the crubeens that were dished up to us many years ago.

'Crubeens and cabbage' were 'on the menu' in our house when there was a plentiful supply of hard white cabbage heads in the haggard. Here's how my mother cooked them.

First the crubeens—six or seven were washed and scraped, put into a skillet, and covered with cold water to which a good drop of vinegar was added. The skillet was hung over the fire until the water boiled. Then it was removed—the water poured off—the crubeens taken out- and the nails (loosened then) were removed. They were washed again, put back in the skillet, covered with fresh cold water, and brought to a boil. After a few minutes boiling the cabbage, crisp and washed, was ready to be put in. When the water was boiled up again, the skillet was removed, and put by the side of the fire—sitting on a few live coals where it simmered for at least three hours until dinner time (no fast cooking as we are told to do cabbage now). By dinner time the crubeens were beautifully soft, white pink and juicy and flavored with the cabbage, which in turn was flavored and glazed with the gelatin off the crubeens.

At dinner we each had a crubeen lying on a bed of lovely cabbage (not a dry crubeen on one side of the plate and a heap of dry cabbage on the other), plus a dish of potatoes boiled in their jackets and bursting at the seams.

Serves 3 to 6

Margaret Moriarty's Crubeens

Black & White Puddings

Ireland is still famous for its black and white puddings and sausages. Nowadays many butchers take great pride in producing their own specialities. The standard continues to rise, partly due to the National Competition in Black and White Pudding and Sausage Making, organized by the Irish Master Butchers' Federation every year. Black puddings may be stored in the fridge for 5 or 6 days.

Black and white pudding and sausages are integral to the traditional Irish breakfast of pork sausages, tomatoes, bacon and eggs (see page 118).

White Puddings

liver, lights, heart
about 15 cups breadcrumbs
meat from belly of pig
12 cups wholewheat flour
$^1/_3$ cup ground allspice
1 nutmeg
2 or 3 teaspoons thyme
dash cayenne pepper
pepper to taste
salt
more spices can be used if liked

Traditionally, the liver, lights (lungs) and heart of the pig were used to make white pudding, which did not have any blood in it. This is my Aunt Lil's recipe.

Boil the liver, lights and heart until tender. Boil meat from the belly, and any other scraps left around when pig is cut up, in about 8 cups of water. Take up and keep water (for use in black puddings).

Mince all meat and boil together with other spices. If you think the mixture is not dry enough, add more wholemeal flour and breadcrumbs. Fill into white pudding casings, cover with cold water and boil gently for about 45 minutes. Put a tin plate in the bottom of the pot when boiling and add salt to water.

To prepare the casings for both black and white puddings, first separate the fat from the intestines. Cut the fat off with scissors (first removing the sweetbreads). Wash the intestines thoroughly under cold running water, then put into salt water until needed. Change the brine often, about four times a day. Drain and rinse before filling the casing. Cut up the fat that you remove from the intestines, wash it and put it into salt water until needed. Change the water regularly as for the intestines to remove the blood. This fat is used for the black pudding.

Black Puddings

about 10 cups of pig's blood
5lb well dried coarse wholemeal
$^1/_2$ of liver and $^1/_2$ of heart of pig well cooked
and minced
1lb pork scraps, cooked and minced
$^1/_4$ cup black pepper
$^1/_4$ cup allspice
1 grated nutmeg
$^1/_4$ cup salt

This recipe was sent to me by Birdie Gardiner, Mohober, Mullinahone, Co. Tipperary.

Put the blood, minced meat, liver and heart, into a large basin. Add the salt and spices to the dried wholemeal and mix all into the blood and meat. It has to be a rather soft, batter-like mixture; if it is too thick to pour into the skins through a funnel, add some of the (hot) water in which the meat scraps (not the liver) have been cooked. The pudding skins should be cut into lengths about a yard long and one end tied securely. The mixture should be put into the skins, leaving a little room at the end before tying in the middle like a figure 8. Put into boiling water and simmer gently for an hour, keeping them moving in the pot by stirring with a long handled wooden spoon. A wide-necked funnel is needed to get the mixture into the puddings.

The white puddings were filled with the same mixture, without the blood, of course, and using a bit more fatty scraps and more nutmeg. It did not have to be poured, and was more like a dough or stiff cake mixture. I can barely remember seeing a pig killed, but my mother tells me that it was a twice-yearly operation and gave me the recipe which was used when she was growing up.

May Fitzgerald of Ballycullane, Inch, Co. Kerry also sent us her grandmother's recipe for black pudding, which she made when the pig was killed. May makes it regularly with lamb's blood, which she tells me she gets from her obliging butcher.

Beat up the blood in a bowl with egg beaten, cut onions small and boil with pearl barley. Put bacon scraps (I keep any left over scraps of fat and lean) in a saucepan and render until brown. Sometimes I fry the onion as well, instead of boiling with the barley. Add all, both scraps and fat, to blood. Then add all other ingredients—oatmeal, pearl barley, onions, salt, pepper, other seasonings and enough milk to make a wet mixture.

Put the mixture in a heavy greased saucepan. Bring to a boil, stirring all the time, as it burns easily. Then push to the side of the fire for a few hours. Turn out, leave to cool, and then roll out with the hands into convenient-sized puddings. Serve with bacon for a lovely breakfast or supper dish.

Black Puddings —Co. Kerry

5 cups pig's or lamb's blood
pearl barley
oatmeal
onions
bacon scraps
milk
seasonings (salt, pepper, mace, sage, cinnamon, spice—just a pinch of each)

This recipe came from a very old undated leaflet called Home Grown Food Stuffs —Some Useful Recipes. *It was used in lectures given by domestic economy instructresses in Co. Galway under the auspices of the parish councils, and was sent to me by Mrs. Teresa Murray from near Ballinasloe, Co. Galway.*

Add salt, meal and spices to the blood and leave until the next day. Then add chopped suet and chopped onions and herbs if liked. Mix well and turn into well-greased bowls. Steam for about 1½ hours. Stir occasionally at the beginning to prevent the meal resting at the bottom of the bowl. May be eaten hot or kept till cold. Cut in slices and fried in bacon fat, makes an excellent and very cheap dish. The butchers do not charge anything for the blood.

Note: *nowadays you will need to order the blood a week ahead from your butcher. Making puddings is a gory business and, take it from me, you can't expect the same family support as when you are making fairy cakes!*

Black Pudding —Galway

to ½ gallon freshly drawn sheep's blood add:

1 tablespoon of salt
½ lb oatmeal
2 teasp. pepper
1 teasp. spice
½ lb chopped suet
1 or 2 chopped onions
freshly chopped herbs e.g. parsley, thyme, chives (optional)

This is Aunt Lil's famous black pudding which she always made after the pig was killed (see page 114).

Wash the intestines well in several changes of running water. Turn inside out and carefully scrape off the fat. Boil the fat in 10 cups water or pork broth until cooked. Strain off the fat and mince. Reserve the cooking liquid.

Beat the blood and put it through a sieve. Put the bowl of cooking liquid over a basin of hot water. Add all other ingredients, and stir well. Fill the mixture into casings with the aid of a funnel. (Do not fill too much; allow space for swelling and prick with a sterilized darning needle so the casings don't burst during cooking.) Put into a saucepan of cold water, bring to a boil and simmer very gently for about 1 hour.

Cut into thick slices and cook gently on both sides, either in a little bacon fat or in melted butter.

Black Pudding —Tipperary

approx. 10 to 12 cups blood from pig (as soon as the blood is drawn, stir and add salt)
small intestines
½ cup ground allspice
¼ cup ground white pepper
salt to taste
1 freshly grated nutmeg
2 teaspoons thyme
dash cayenne pepper
1 cup white breadcrumbs
¾ cup wholewheat flour (these two can be increased if not thick enough)

Blood

In many parts of Ireland, Kerry and Donegal in particular, during periods of famine when everything else had failed, the peasants had the habit of bleeding the cattle 'which they had not the courage to steal'. They sometimes mixed sorrel or oatmeal through the blood or boiled it into a broth. 'Kerry cows know Sunday' became a proverb, because it was to provide the Sunday dinner that they were bled.

Duck Blood

Serves 6 to 8

1¾ cups duck or goose blood
salt and freshly ground pepper
¼ cup finely chopped onion
⅔ cup fresh milk
2 tablespoons butter

As soon as ducks were killed, their necks were cut and their blood collected in a bowl. This delicious mixture was made the next day.

Sprinkle the fresh blood with a little salt and leave in a cool place overnight. Next day put it into a heavy-bottomed saucepan with the onion, milk and a lump of butter. Season with salt and freshly ground pepper. Cook on a low heat for about 20 minutes or until the mixture thickens and becomes similar to the texture of a soft scrambled egg.

Eat warm with fresh brown bread and butter. Spoon it up on top of the bread and eat it.

Goose Pudding

Serves 6 to 8

blood from one goose (stir ½ teaspoon of salt into the blood as soon as it is taken from the goose—congealed blood can be refrigerated for a day or two).
skin from the goose neck (optional)
1 cup finely chopped onions
3 tablespoons butter
⅓ cup breadcrumbs
1 cup porridge oats
¾ teaspoon salt
1 flat teaspoon cinnamon
1 teaspoon mixed spice
1 level teaspoon ground nutmeg
1 goose liver, chopped

Traditionally geese were killed around Michaelmas, Christmas and the New Year. Every drop of blood was saved to make goose pudding.

Jack O'Keeffe, whose mother came originally from the Sliabh Lúachra area on the borders of Cork and Kerry, showed me how to make this goose blood pudding which has been passed down in his family for many generations. The Sliabh Lúachra area is noted for traditional Irish music and storytelling and the longevity of its inhabitants. Goose pudding was a common rural dish well into the twentieth century.

Sweat the onions in the butter over a low heat. Put the breadcrumbs and oats into a bowl. Add salt, pepper, mixed spice, cinnamon and nutmeg. Then add onions and blood; mix and break up well. Stir in the chopped liver and mix again. Cook a tiny bit of the mixture and taste for seasoning.

If you are using the goose neck, turn it inside out and fill loosely with the mixture to allow for expansion. Knot the narrow end and sew the wide end to secure it tightly. Alternatively, fill the mixture into a pudding bowl, cover with a tight fitting lid or a double thickness of wax paper and tie as for a steamed pudding.

Bring a saucepan of cold water to a boil and add 1 teaspoon of salt. Prick the goose neck pudding with a darning needle and add to the saucepan of boiling water. Bring back to a boil and then reduce to a simmer. Cook for 1 to 1½ hours on a very low heat with the lid on, pricking during the cooking time also. If using a bowl, steam the pudding for 1½ hours in a covered saucepan.

The goose pudding will keep for a week or so refrigerated or it may be frozen. Cut in thick slices and fry gently in a little butter.

Drisheen in Cork Market

Hidden behind the city's main thoroughfare, Patrick Street, the former English Market in Cork is a bustling colourful hive of activity. Third and fourth generation traders sell vegetables, offal and buttered eggs, side by side with New-Age hippies tempting their customers with a *mélange* of olives, sundried tomatoes and exquisite Irish farmhouse cheeses.

Just inside the huge archway at the Grand Parade end of the market is O'Reilly's stall, which sells tripe and drisheen—the famous Cork black pudding made from sheep's blood.

It is fascinating to observe the mix of customers. On a recent visit I noted not only Leeside natives, but also Chinese and German customers, devotees from Killarney and Macroom, and an elegantly dressed lady home on holidays from the United States after fifty years of absence from Cork. She was nostalgically buying drisheen to relive her childhood memories. In the background, fifteen pounds of tripe and ten pounds of drisheen were being packed for an exiled Cork man living in Dublin! He had sent a friend specially down by train to collect the precious order. There was much merriment around the stall when it was revealed that this man had 'the misfortunate' to be married to a Dublin woman who refused point blank to cook him tripe or drisheen or to be in the house when it was cooked. However, the Corkman had hit on a solution. On 'the wife's' night out, he would have a tripe and drisheen party for all his exiled Cork cronies.

I wonder whether he managed to find a bit of tansy in the Dublin suburbs, to spike the white sauce that is traditionally often served with drisheen? Mr. Bell's stall in the Cork Market sells tansy, which originally was also added to the drisheen itself.

It is possible that drisheen has been available in Cork since the early medieval period, as a pudding called *dressán* is mentioned in the eleventh century tale *Aislinge Meic Con Glinne*. However, as Sexton points out, it is more likely that the popularity of drisheen was established in the late seventeenth century. Between that time and 1825, the City of Cork was the largest centre for the exportation of salted beef in the British Isles. Prior to shipment, the cattle were butchered in the City's slaughter-houses and the large quantities of blood were used in the preparation of puddings.

Drisheen

Our local butcher Michael Cuddigan remembers when virtually every butcher in the Cork area made drisheen. He no longer sells it in his butcher's shop, but was delighted to come with a gallon of blood and a bag of intestines to show how he makes his much sought-after drisheen.

bag of lamb's intestines
20 cups sheep's blood
1¼ cup fresh creamy milk
1½ teaspoons salt
chopped tansy (optional)

First we gave the casings a good rinse under the tap and Michael showed me how to turn them inside out. We then measured out 4 cups of the thin blood from the top and mixed it with the fresh creamy milk and 1½ teaspoons of salt, adding a little chopped tansy. I tied the ends of the casings with cotton string and then, using a funnel, we filled them up and pressed out the air, allowing a little space for expansion during cooking.

The casings were then lowered into a saucepan of warm well-salted water and brought gently to a boil. This process should not be hurried; it is necessary to keep the drisheen down in the water because they have a tendency to rise to the top. As soon as the water reaches boiling point, turn off the heat. The drisheen should feel firm to the touch. Carefully remove them to a large plate, cool then refrigerate and use as required.

To cook drisheen, put a ring of drisheen into warm salted water, and bring gently to almost boiling. Drain and cut into 3 to 4 inch lengths. Slit in half lengthways, serve on very hot plates with melted butter and lots of white bread.

Drisheen with Tansy Sauce

Declan Ryan of Arbutus Lodge in Cork serves this great Cork speciality with a tansy sauce. He says he makes a rich, buttery, peppery, white sauce, by first infusing the milk with a small sprig of tansy. When the milk comes to a boil, he thickens it with buttery roux and seasons well to taste. The drisheen is gently poached, then split in half lengthwise and spread with a little melted butter and served with the tansy sauce.

Declan explained that his father always ate drisheen with buttered white bread underneath. He's not sure whether this was to do with his family's passion for stretching everything with bread and butter or whether it was an authentic Cork tradition!

Tripe

Tripe is mentioned frequently in the eleventh century tale *Aislinge Meic Con Glinne*. It was a common and regularly available commodity in the shops of Cork City in 1649. Tripe also featured as an important item in the diet of the City's Franciscan friars throughout the eighteenth century.

Traditionally the stomach tissue of sheep, pigs and cows was consumed. Today, however, all tripe is invariably beef tripe. The most abundantly available comes from the first stomach or rumen and is termed 'plain' or 'blanket' tripe. More popular, but not always available, is the 'honeycomb' which comes from the second stomach or reticulum. It is given its name because of its characteristic honeycombed texture and it is a decided favorite with Irish housewives.

Tripe is an everyday dinner dish and is also served as a Saturday night tea-time dish. It is a very bland foodstuff and relies almost exclusively on the accompanying sauce for its flavor. Traditionally it was eaten with bread and butter and sherry, followed by tea and sweet cake.

Serves 4

Tripe in Batter

8oz tripe
batter (see page 68)
fat drippings

Wash the tripe in hot water. Put it into boiling water and simmer for 45 minutes to 1 hour, skimming well. When quite tender, remove the tripe, dry it, cut in pieces about 2 inches square, and cool. Heat the drippings in a frying pan. When hot, dip the pieces of tripe into the batter and fry at once. Serve hot with a good mustard.

This recipe was given to me by Michael Ryan of Isaacs Restaurant in Cork. This was how his father cooked tripe and onions.

Serves 2 to 4

Tripe & Onions

1lb tripe
1 small onion, peeled and sliced
cold milk—sufficient to cover
roux (see page 40)
salt and freshly ground pepper

Put the tripe into a saucepan, cover with a lid and place on a gas or electric burner for about 5 to 10 minutes.

Discard the liquid in the pot, add the sliced onion and cover with cold milk. Simmer gently for about 1 hour until the tripe is tender. Strain off the milk into another pan and bring back to a boil, whisk in the roux, season with salt and pepper. Pour back into the saucepan with the tripe, heat through. Check seasoning—it will take quite a bit of pepper.

Serve on a slice of buttered white bread.

Tripe & Drisheen

After adding the thickened liquid back to the saucepan, you could if you wish add some drisheen to the tripe. Simply peel and slice some cooked drisheen, add it to the saucepan and heat through before serving.

Serves 6 (approximately)

Stuffed Beef Heart

1 beef heart
salt and freshly ground pepper
2½ cups beef stock
1 tablespoon mushroom ketchup (optional)
roux (see page 40)

stuffing
6 tablespoons butter
1½ cups finely chopped onions
1 tablespoon chopped chives
1 tablespoon thyme leaves
1 tablespoon marjoram
1 tablespoon chopped parsley
2 cups white breadcrumbs
salt and freshly ground pepper

In Tudor times fanciful names were created to disguise the true nature of the dish and to add a sense of intrigue. One such name for stuffed hearts was 'Love in Disguise', which was sure to confuse the diner.

Trim the heart and cut away the 'plumbing' to make a nice pocket. Wash thoroughly in cold salted water; dry well.

Next make the stuffing. Sweat the onions in the butter for about 10 minutes until soft. Then stir in the breadcrumbs, herbs and a little salt and pepper to taste. Allow to cool.

Season the inside of the heart with salt and freshly ground pepper. Fill with the fresh herb stuffing, piling the extra on the top. Cover with parchment paper and tie with cotton string if necessary. Put into a deep roasting pan or casserole and add the beef stock. Season with salt and freshly ground pepper. Cover and bake in a moderate oven at 350°F for about 3 to 3½ hours or until the meat is cooked and tender.

When the beef heart is fully cooked, remove carefully to a serving dish. Bring the cooking liquid to the boil, thicken with a very little roux and correct the seasoning to taste. Strain into a sauceboat and serve with the sliced stuffed heart.

Sheeps' hearts

Follow the same recipe. The stuffing will be sufficient for four to six sheeps' hearts, but the cooking time should be reduced to about 1 hour. Sheeps' hearts are more tender and juicy than beef heart.

Sheep's Liver

In parts of Ireland the liver of the newly killed sheep was put in one piece on the tongs over the embers of the open fire and roasted. Ellen O' Sullivan from Bantry, Co. Cork, now in her late seventies, told me about this and said they used to fight over it as children. Her family lived about 10 miles from the nearest habitation, so they were virtually self-sufficient. They killed a sheep several times a year and every scrap was eaten.

Lambs' Tails

I had never heard of lambs' tails being eaten until I began work on this book. However, Lil O' Connell from North Tipperary told me of how her husband Bob loved 'a feed' of lambs' tails a few times a year. She remembers dreading it because there were so many lambs tails to be skinned and cooked—none were to be wasted. The lambs would have been about two months old. I mentioned this on a radio program and several other people telephoned to say that they, too, had recollections of lambs' tails being eaten. Everybody assured me they were wonderful to eat.

lambs' tails (allow 2 per person)
butter
salt

Peel the tails, wash, cook in boiling salted water for about 45 minutes or until the meat is soft and tender. Serve with bread and butter.

Lil explained how the tails were traditionally eaten: 'rub butter on both sides, sprinkle with salt and eat like corn on the cob, sweet and delicious'.

Note: *Ann Kennedy, of Rostrevor, tells me that friends of hers in Gloucestershire, who have many sheep, prepare lambs' tails by coating them with crumbs and deep-frying. She writes: 'I've never tasted anything so delicious.'*

Roast kidneys are moist and succulent. This is a traditional method of cooking them; I use our old Aga, but it works as well in a conventional oven.

Serves 4

Roast Lamb Kidneys

4 lamb kidneys in suet
sea salt

Preheat the oven to 450°F. Put the kidneys on to a rack in a roasting pan and cook for 40 to 45 minutes or until much of the fat has rendered out and the outside is crisp and brown. Split in half, serve on hot plates, sprinkled with sea salt. Eat with fresh soda bread or toast.

This recipe for a much-loved Cork dish was given to me by Eileen Aherne, a well known fruit and vegetable stallholder in the Cork Market, who enjoys it every week.

Serves 2 to 4

Skirts & Kidneys

2lb skirts (membrane separating the stomach from a pig's heart and lungs)
2 pigs' kidneys
3 onions
salt and freshly ground pepper
seasoned flour
water

Slice the onions thickly. Remove the membrane from the skirts, cut each into approximately 2-inch pieces. Split the kidneys, remove the 'plumbing', and cut into 1-inch pieces. Wash, dry well and toss both skirts and kidneys in seasoned flour. Put the meat and sliced onions into a saucepan, cover with water and bring to a boil. Simmer for 1 to 1½ hours or until soft. Serve with mashed potatoes and rutabagas.

Amhlaoibh Uí Shúileabháin records in his diary for Shrove Tuesday, 1831, that he bought 'six neats' tongues to preserve for Easter', and every country house sideboard would have featured pickled ox tongue occasionally. There's a great saying around Cork, often applied to someone out of favor (particularly after a night of liquid socializing!): 'Ah, there'll be nothin' but hot tongue and cold shoulder for you for dinner!'

Serves 8 to 10 (approximately)

Pickled Ox Tongue

1 pickled ox tongue
cold water
no salt

Cover the tongue with cold water and bring to a boil. Cover the saucepan and simmer for 3 to 4 hours, or until the skin will easily peel off the tip of the tongue. Remove from the pot and reserve the liquid. As soon as the tongue is cool enough to handle, peel off the skin and remove all the little bones at the neck end. Sometimes I use a skewer to prod the meat to make sure that no bones are left behind. Curl the tongue and press it into a small plastic bowl. Pour a little of the cooking liquid over the tongue, put a side plate or saucer on top and weigh it down. Serve it thinly sliced, with red currant jelly.

Note: *Pickled ox tongue will keep for up to a week in the refrigerator.*

Spiced Ox Tongue

Spiced tongue was a common nineteenth century dish on the tables of the Irish middle classes. It was spiced with cloves and flavored with onion, thyme, parsley, salt and pepper.

In Cork, spiced ox tongue is available just before Christmas, when a few tongues are thrown into the spice barrel. Mr Breslin in Cork Market spices tongues for me occasionally and they have been much enjoyed, not just at Christmas, but on summer picnics also.

Cook as for pickled ox tongue.

Potatoes

There is a long-established belief that Sir Walter Raleigh introduced the potato into Ireland in 1588, planting the first crop in his garden at Myrtle Grove, in Youghal, Co. Cork. However, Redcliffe Salaman, in his authoritative work *The History and Social Influence of the Potato*, suggests that potatoes may have been introduced into Ireland from plundered ships of the Spanish Armada which were wrecked on the west coast. Within a century of its introduction, the potato was a common item in the Irish diet. Commentators such as John Stevens in his *Journal* of 1689-91 noted that it was the staple food of the poorer people:

> The meaner people content themselves with little bread but instead thereof eat potatoes which with sour milk is the chief part of their diet.

The potatoes beloved of the Irish are not the waxy varieties, but the dry ones, whose skins crack towards the end of cooking—referred to as 'balls of flour', or 'smiling spuds'. Damp waxy potatoes are still scorned in Ireland as being 'wet or soapy'. Favourite varieties of potato are Home Guard, British Queens, Kerr's Pink, Golden Wonders, Aran Banners, Records and Champions. One of the finest sights in Ireland around the end of July and the beginning of August, is fields of Golden Wonders and British Queens in full bloom—a sea of pale purple and white blossom. The famous 'Ballycotton potatoes' are much sought after in the former English Market in Cork.

The Potato in Irish Cooking

Potatoes were easily grown in Ireland, and with only an acre or two of land a farmer could grow enough potatoes to support his whole family. A system of cultivation called the 'lazy-bed' system developed—wide raised beds were cultivated by hand or with a distinctive spade known as a 'loy' or 'fack'. They were enriched with manure from the milch cow or pig, and sometimes, in coastal regions, also with seaweed and shells.

The dangers of a whole society's dependence upon a single foodstuff began to emerge in the 1820s and '30s, when several local harvest failures occurred. It was not until 1845–1846, however, that countrywide failure of the potato crop, caused by potato blight *(Phytophthora infestus)*, caused widespread famine. With the poor deprived of their sole foodstuff, starvation and disease were soon apparent.

The wretched famine years of 1847–1848 are recalled in Mary O'Brien's *The Farm by Lough Gur:*

> It was heart-breaking…to see poor people tottering to the door, half-fainting, swaying on their skeleton feet, as they held out little bags for the crust or a spoonful of flour—all we had to give them. One old man was found dead in the turnip garden: too weak to pull it up…little children died on the floor of the cabin where they slipped from the weak arms of their mother…it wasn't only starvation, more died from typhus and other diseased brought about by want, than lack of food. Corn, which came at last, and maize meal, sent from America, saved those who were still alive.

Over one million people died, and the same number emigrated, mainly to the United States, between 1845 and 1851.

In the eighteenth, nineteenth and even into the twentieth century, potatoes were usually boiled, largely due to the scarcity of cooking utensils. Even prosperous farming households would have cooked over the fire, in a big black three-legged pot—a griddle, pot oven, a kettle and frying pan being the only other cooking implements. The potatoes were boiled in their jackets and served heaped up in the center of the table in a wooden frame or more commonly in a round shallow basket made from sally saplings (peeled osiers). Local names for this varied around the country, a *sciob* in Cork, a *sciath* in Kilkenny, a *ciseóg* in Galway, and a scuttle in Clare.

Olive Sharkey, in her book *Old Days, Old Ways*, recounts her father's memories of his potato dinners:

> The potato dinner was always the favourite meal in his home, years ago, with everyone reaching hungrily for the spuds the moment my grandmother placed them in their basket on the table. It was essential that everyone learn to peel their potatoes quickly or they might miss out, the greedy, skilful peelers hoarding up little caches of spuds on their plates before actually tucking in.

In Donnacha O'Drisceoil's memory of life on Cape Clear, potatoes were considered to be the most important part of the meal. Anything served with them was what he called *anlann*, the sauce, used to complement the potato—rather than the other way round!

Champp

Like many other simple peasant dishes champ has stood the test of time. It now features on the menus of more fashionable restaurants in London, Paris and New York. As with Ireland's other great potato dish, colcannon (see page 147), there are many regional variations. Ulster is a particularly rich source of recipes.

A huge quantity of potatoes were boiled for each meal in the big black pot over the open fire. The pounding of the potatoes, using a heavy wooden pounder called a beetle, was usually men's work. Florence Irwin, in *Irish Country Recipes* (1937), gives a wonderfully evocative picture of the laborious procedure:

> The man of the house was summoned when all was ready, and while he pounded this enormous potful of potatoes with a sturdy wooden beetle, his wife added the potful of milk and nettles, or scallions, or chives, or parsley and he beetled it 'till it was as smooth as butter, not a lump anywhere. Everyone got a large bowlful, made a hole in the centre, and into this put a large lump of butter. Then the champ was eaten from the outside with a spoon or fork, dipping it into the melted butter in the centre.

Champ also features in this well-known children's rhyme—an indication of its enduring popularity:

> There was a woman
> Who lived in a lamp
> She had no room to beetle her champ
> She's up with her beetle
> And broke the lamp
> And then she had room
> To beetle her champ.

A common folk custom was to offer a bowl of champ to the fairies at Halloween. This would be left on field posts or under trees, such as hawthorns or whitethorns, which were particularly associated with fairies.

One of the best-loved ways of cooking potatoes was (and is) to mash them with boiling milk, add chopped scallions or chives and serve this creamy, green-flecked mixture with a blob of yellow butter melting in the center. Leeks, nettles, peas and brown crispy onions are all delicious additions.

Scrub the potatoes and boil them in their jackets. Finely chop the scallions. Cover the scallions with cold milk and bring slowly to a boil. Simmer for about 3 to 4 minutes, then turn off the heat and leave to infuse. Peel and mash the freshly boiled potatoes and, while hot, mix with the boiling milk and scallions. Beat in some of the butter. Season to taste with salt and freshly ground pepper. Serve in one large or four individual bowls with a knob of butter melting in the center.

Champ may be put aside and reheated later in a moderate oven at 350°F. Cover with foil while it reheats so that it doesn't get a skin.

Note: *in Maura Laverty's charming book* Kind Cooking, *an identical dish to champ is called thump. Maura Laverty came from Co. Kildare.*

Serves 4

Champ

6 to 8 unpeeled baking potatoes, e.g. Russet or Yukon Gold
1 bunch scallions (use the bulb and green stem)
1¹/2 cups milk
4-8 tablespoons butter
salt and freshly ground pepper

Parsley Champ   Add 2 to 3 tablespoons of freshly chopped parsley to the milk, bring to a boil for 2 or 3 minutes only, to preserve the fresh taste and color. Beat into the mashed potatoes and serve hot.

Chive Champ   Substitute freshly chopped chives for parsley.

Dulse Champ   Soak a couple of fists of seaweed in cold water for an hour or more. Drain and stew in milk until tender, about 3 hours. Add a good knob of butter and some pepper and beat into the mashed potato. Taste and correct the seasoning. Serve hot.

Pea Champ   This special champ could only be made for a few weeks when the fresh green peas were in season. Cook the peas in the boiling salted milk with a pinch of sugar until tender. Add to the mashed potatoes and pound together in the usual way.

I am indebted to Deborah Shorley for this recipe, which she calls Claragh champ after the locality in which she first tasted it. We call it Ulster champ down here.

When we were children, we were always told as we peeled our potatoes that Cork people ate their spuds 'skin and all'. As in this recipe, I prefer to cook the potatoes in their jackets rather then peeling them first.

Cook the potatoes in boiling salted water until tender; drain well and dry over the heat in the pan for a few minutes. Peel and mash with most of the butter while hot. Meanwhile bring the milk to a boil and simmer the peas until just cooked, about 8 to 10 minutes. Add the parsley for the final 2 minutes of cooking. Add the hot milk mixture to the potatoes. Season well and beat until creamy and smooth.

Serve piping hot with a lump of butter melting in the center.

Serves 8

Claragh Champ

*4lb baking potatoes, e.g. Russet or
    Yukon Gold*
4 to 8 tablespoons butter
2¹/₂ cups milk
1lb young peas, shelled weight
12 tablespoons chopped parsley
salt and freshly ground pepper

Nettles have been valued in Ireland since ancient times, not only as a food, but also as a purifier of the blood. The belief is still strong, particularly among older people in the country, that one should have at least three dinners of nettles in April and May to clear the blood and keep away the 'rheumatics' for the coming year.

Scrub the potatoes and cook in boiling salted water until tender. Meanwhile, chop the young nettle tops and cook in the milk for about 20 minutes. As soon as the potatoes are cooked, drain and peel immediately while they are still hot. Mash until soft and free of lumps. Pour in the boiling milk and the nettles and a good lump of butter. Beat the mixture until soft and creamy. Season with salt and freshly ground pepper.

Serve hot with a lump of butter melting into the center.

Serves 4

Nettle Champ

*1¹/₂lb baking potatoes, e.g. Russet or
    Yukon Gold*
1 cup chopped nettles
1¹/₄ cups milk
2 to 4 tablespoons butter
salt and freshly ground pepper

This is another really delicious version of champ—less well known than the others. I came across it in Ulster, but it is now also firmly entrenched in Cork.

Scrub the potatoes and cook in boiling salted water until cooked through. Meanwhile wash and slice the leeks into thin rounds. Melt 2 tablespoons butter in a heavy pot, toss in the leeks and season with salt and freshly ground pepper. Cover with parchment paper and the lid of the saucepan. Cook on a gentle heat until soft and tender.

As soon as the potatoes are cooked, drain them thoroughly. Peel the potatoes and mash immediately. Bring the milk to boiling point. Beat the buttered leeks and their juices into the potatoes with enough boiling milk to make a soft texture. Season with salt and freshly ground pepper.

Serve immediately with a lump of butter melting in the center.

Serves 4

Leek Champ

1lb potatoes
12oz leeks
2 to 4 tablespoons butter
1 to 1¹/₄ cups milk
salt and freshly ground pepper

Serves 4 to 6

Champ & Crispy Onions

champ (see page 143)
fat drippings or butter
2 or 3 large onions cut into ¹/4-inch
wide rings

This was a popular dinner when my mother was a child in Co. Kilkenny, on Fridays when meat was forbidden.

Melt the drippings or butter in a frying pan and cook the onions until nicely browned. Put a good helping of champ on each plate, put some onions around the edge. Make a well in the center and put in a lump of butter. Dip a forkful of champ and onions into the butter, and enjoy.

Poundies

My father-in-law, Ivan Allen, now in his eightieth year, still speaks longingly of the Poundies he had as a child in Co. Tyrone. He remembers the potatoes being mashed with a big pounder (hence the name), after which lots of butter, salt and pepper and gravy were added. The gravy would probably have been left over from the Sunday roast of beef or lamb. He says that the potatoes were always quite soft and brown in color when they were served.

Serves 6

Cally

2lb baking potatoes, e.g. Russet or
Yukon Gold
2 fat scallions or 1 finely chopped
small onion
²/3 cup milk
salt and freshly ground black pepper
4 tablespoons butter

This potato dish from Dublin is very similar to champ.

Cook the potatoes in their jackets in boiling salted water. Meanwhile slice the green and white parts of the scallions finely and put with the cold milk into a saucepan. Season with salt and pepper and bring slowly to a boil. Allow to simmer while the potatoes are cooking. Just as soon as the potatoes are done, peel and mash them, then quickly beat in the milk and scallions. Taste and add more seasoning if necessary. Serve immediately onto hot plates. Make a well in the center of each helping and pour in some melted butter. Dip every forkful of cally into the melted butter and enjoy, as generations of Irish have done before you!

Bruisy

An exiled Leitrim man who is now living in Dublin described to me a potato dish called bruisy from his childhood. The cooked potatoes were mashed together with butter and young nettles.

You could taste the iron—then you criss-crossed it with a knife and cut it into squares and made turf out of it. You would drink milk with it. The game was to eat each sod of turf.

Colcannon

There are many regional variations of colcannon—Ireland's best-known traditional potato dish. In some areas green cabbage was added, in others kale was preferred. In parts of Dublin, Wicklow and Wexford, parsnips were added, and onions or scallions are featured in several of the versions.

Colcannon was one of the festive dishes eaten at Halloween, when a ring and a thimble would be hidden in the fluffy green-flecked mass. The ring denotes marriage, but the person who found the thimble would be a spinster for life.

Poems have been written and songs sung about this much-loved dish:

Did you ever eat colcannon
When 'twas made with yellow cream
And the kale and praties blended
Like a picture in a dream?
Did you ever scoop a hole on top
To hold the melting lake
Of the clover-flavoured butter
Which your mother used to make?

Serves 8 (approximately)

Colcannon

*2¹/₂ to 3lb baking potatoes, e.g. Russet or
    Yukon Gold*
1 small spring or Savoy cabbage
1 cup approx. boiling milk
salt and freshly ground pepper
4 tablespoons approx. butter

Scrub the potatoes. Put them into a saucepan of cold water, add a good pinch of salt and bring to a boil. When the potatoes are about half cooked (about 15 minutes for old potatoes) strain off two-thirds of the water. Replace the lid on the saucepan, put onto a gentle heat and allow the potatoes to steam until they are fully cooked.

Remove the dark outer leaves from the cabbage. Wash the rest and cut into quarters, remove the core and cut each quarter finely across the grain. Boil in a little boiling salted water until soft. Drain, season with salt, freshly ground pepper and a little butter.

When the potatoes are just cooked, put on the milk and bring to a boil. Pull the skin off the potatoes, mash quickly while they are still warm and beat in enough boiling milk to make a fluffy purée. (If you have a large quantity, put the potatoes in the bowl of a food mixer and beat with the paddle). Then stir in about the same volume of cooked cabbage and taste for seasoning. Serve immediately in a hot dish, with a lump of butter melting in the center.

Colcannon may be prepared ahead and reheated later in a moderate oven at 350°F, for about 20 to 25 minutes. Any left over colcannon may be formed into potato cakes or farls and fried in bacon fat until crisp and brown on both sides.

Serves 8 (approximately)

Dublin Parsnip Colcannon

1 lb parsnips
1 lb baking potatoes, e.g. Russet or
Yukon Gold
1 lb curly kale
1 to 1¼ cups creamy milk
2 tablespoons approx. chopped scallions
4 tablespoons approx. butter
salt and freshly ground pepper

Several Dubliners have spoken to me about a parsnip colcannon that 'the Mammy used to make'. Threepenny or sixpenny bits were sometimes hidden in the colcannon at Halloween for the children to find. The proportion of parsnips to potato varied.

Scrub and peel the potatoes and parsnips, put them into a saucepan, cover with cold water, add a good pinch of salt and bring to a boil. When the potatoes and parsnips are cooked, strain off the water, replace the lid on the saucepan, put on a gentle heat and allow to steam for a few minutes, then mash.

While they are cooking, bring a pot of well salted water to the boil, remove the central rib from the kale and cook the leaves until tender. Drain and chop finely.

When the potatoes are almost cooked, put on the milk and bring to a boil with the scallions. While the potatoes and parsnips are still warm, stir in the chopped kale and beat in enough boiling milk to make fluffy purée. (If you have a large quantity, use the bowl of a food mixer and beat with the paddle.) Add the butter and taste for seasoning. Stir over the heat and serve immediately in a hot dish with the butter melting in the center.

Colcannon may be prepared ahead and reheated later in a moderate oven at 350°F for about 20 to 25 minutes.

Serves 4

Pandy

A light fluffy mashed potato dish often made for children or older people if they were feeling unwell. Alice Taylor gives this lyrical description of making pandy in her book Quench the Lamp:

Pandy first required a big, soft, flowery spud with a long smile across its face. Starting at the smile, the skin was eased off gently and the naked spud, almost too hot to handle, was transferred fast by hand into another plate, leaving its clothes in a heap behind it. Next a lump of yellow butter was placed on top, from where it ran in little yellow streams down the sides. A gentle little poke with the fork opened up a cavity into which went a drop of milk or a spoon of cream skimmed off the top of the bucket, followed by a shake of salt. Finally, the entire slushy combination was lightly whipped together and frequently tasted to ascertain that the correct balance was being achieved. It took great care and a discerning palate to make really good pandy; it had to be yellow, soft, delicately flavoured, and as light as thistledown on the tongue. When you were sick or not feeling happy you judged how much your mother and the world loved you by the quality of her pandy. It was our antibiotic, our tranquilizer and our sleeping potion.

2 lb baking potatoes
butter
creamy milk or cream
salt

Boil the potatoes in boiling salted water until just cooked, peel immediately and mash with lots of butter. Season with salt and freshly ground pepper to taste and then whip in some cream. It should be light and fluffy. Eat while hot.

Dublin Parsnip Colcannon

Lutóga

Lutóga was the name given to potatoes baked in the embers of the fire on the Blaskets and other islands off Cork and Kerry. In her book Peig Sayers wrote:

Do bhí luthóg phrataí cois na tine, is iad brea rostaithe te. Thug mo mhathair cugham bluirín ime agus braon bainne…Ní raibh aon arán bán na té ag éinne on uair sin.

(There used to be ember-roasted potatoes at the foot of the fire and they were well roasted. My mother used to give me a little bit of butter and a drop of milk…Nobody had white bread or tea at the time.)

Deirdre Martin told me that when her father Donal (who came from Fanad in Co. Donegal) was in his teens, he used to put potatoes into the ash pit of the fire when he was going out to a dance. If his sister got home early she would smell the potatoes and eat them, then he'd be poking around in the ashes when he came home!

Strand Potatoes

A fisherman in the west of Ireland told me how they sometimes baked potatoes in the sand. They'd dig a shallow pit, 2 to 3 inches deep, lay the scrubbed potatoes in a single layer and cover them with sand. A fire would be lit on top, surrounded by a ring of stones. Water for the tea could be brought to a boil on top in a tin can or kettle and occasionally freshly caught fish was roasted over the fire or boiled in sea water.

In Donegal, fishermen sometimes took 'live' (smoldering) turf into their boats with them on calm days. This was used to bake potatoes and cook fish while they were out to sea.

Chips

Towards the end of the nineteenth century some of the poor Italian immigrants, who had brought fish and chips to England and Scotland, made their way to Ireland. Many arrived in the north and gradually traveled southwards to other parts of the country. The fish and chip business in Dublin is still securely in the hands of a thriving and prosperous Italian community. Homemade chips (called french fries in the United States) that start off with good potatoes and end up in hot beef dripping or good quality oil are still pretty sensational.

baking potatoes, e.g. Russet or Yukon Gold etc.(allow ¹/₂lb unpeeled potatoes per person)
beef drippings, lard, or good quality oil
table salt

Fill a deep fryer with drippings, lard or good quality oil and preheat it to 325°F.

Scrub the potatoes, peel or leave unpeeled according to your taste. Cut into equal sized chips so they will cook evenly. Dry meticulously in a tea towel or kitchen towel before cooking, otherwise they will splatter when they come in contact with the hot fat and will not brown so nicely.

Cook for a few minutes in the preheated fat or oil until they are soft and just beginning to brown, then drain. Increase the heat to 375°F and cook for 1 or 2 minutes more or until crisp and golden. Shake the basket, drain well, toss on paper towels, sprinkle with salt and serve the chips immediately.

Stovies

Serves 2 to 4

An ingenious traditional way of presenting the two basic ingredients, potatoes and onions, in a different guise. This recipe for stovies came from Co. Tyrone. Northern Ireland is an area particularly rich in potato variations.

4 tablespoons beef drippings
4 medium onions, peeled and sliced
2lb potatoes, peeled and cut into thick slices
salt and pepper
a little water

Melt the drippings in a good hot pan and fry the onions until nearly tender but not brown. Remove the onions, put in the potatoes and toss them in the fat. Return the onions, placing them on top of the potatoes. Season well and cover the pan; cook over a gentle heat for 4 to 5 minutes, shaking the pan now and again to prevent sticking. Add a very little water if the mixture gets too dry. Do not try to keep the slices whole; as much of the surface as possible should brown. Serve hot with a mug of buttermilk.

Fried Potatoes

Potatoes were regularly fried to use up leftovers. A favorite way was to mix them with golden fried onions. The secret of really crispy fried potatoes is to have patience and not to attempt to turn them over until they have a nice crust. This can take 5 to 10 minutes, but it's well worth it.

potatoes (allow ¹/₄ to ¹/₂lb per person)
lard, chicken fat or butter for frying
salt and freshly ground pepper
fried onions (optional)
chopped parsley

Scrub the potatoes and boil until just cooked. When they are cool, peel and cut into ¹/₂-inch slices.

Heat a little lard, chicken fat or butter in a heavy frying pan. Put in the potatoes in a single layer, season with salt and freshly ground pepper. Fry on a medium heat until golden, then turn over to brown on the other side. Serve in a hot dish, mixed with fried onions if liked, and sprinkled with freshly chopped parsley.

Griddle Potatoes

Co. Antrim is the source of this delicious, old-fashioned way of cooking potatoes.

cooked old potatoes (allow $^1/_4$ to $^1/_2$lb
    per person)
salt

Heat the griddle over the open fire, peel and slice the potatoes thickly. Sprinkle some salt over the griddle pan and put the potatoes on top. Cook first on one side, then the other until crisp and tasty. Eat with country butter. This also works very well in a non-stick pan.

Potato & Caraway Seed Cakes

Serves 6 (approximately)

The following description by Flurry Knox made my mouth water and inspired this recipe, now one of our favorites.

> While I live I shall not forget her potato cakes. They came in hot and hot from a pot-oven, they were speckled with caraway seeds, they swam in salt butter, and we ate them shamelessly and greasily, and washed them down with hot whiskey and water. I knew to a nicety how ill I should be next day, and I heeded not.
> *Some Experiences of an Irish R.M,* Somerville and Ross *(1899)*

1$^1/_2$lb baking potatoes (4 to 5 large potatoes,
    e..g. Russet or Yukon Gold)
3 tablespoons butter
$^1/_2$ cup finely chopped onion
1 to 2 teaspoons caraway seeds
1 tablespoon chopped parsley
salt and freshly ground pepper
$^1/_2$ cup flour
butter for frying

Cook the potatoes in their jackets in boiling salted water. Meanwhile melt the butter and sweat the onion in it over a gentle heat until soft but not colored. Peel and mash the potatoes while still hot. Add the onion and butter with the caraway seeds and chopped parsley. Season with salt and freshly ground pepper, add the flour and mix well. Knead a little until smooth, roll out and stamp into potato cakes with the top of a glass or a cutter. Alternatively, divide the dough into two rounds and cut into patties. Fry in melted butter on a hot pan until golden on both sides. Serve hot.

Fadge

Serves 4

These potato cakes are the way to an Ulsterman's heart, and often find their way into their suitcases on trips to friends and relatives far from home. One of my students from Belfast made them regularly in Cork to satisfy her craving for a taste of Ulster. Potato cakes, tatties and parleys are other names for fadge.

Florence Irwin tells us that in olden days the peeled potatoes were placed on the bakeboard and a flat bottomed mug or a pint can served to bruise them. This was then firmly grasped and pressed down on each potato in turn until no lumps remained.

1lb freshly cooked potatoes
$^3/_4$ to 1 cup plain white flour
$^1/_2$ teaspoon salt
2 tablespoons butter, melted

As soon as the potatoes are cooked, peel them, put them into a bowl and pound with a potato masher until free of lumps.

Sprinkle on the salt and gradually drizzle the melted butter over the mashed potatoes, then knead in enough flour to make a pliable dough. The potatoes I use take about $^3/_4$ cup of flour. Roll out the mixture into a round about $^1/_2$ inch thick, cut into patties.

Heat a griddle and bake the potato cakes until golden brown on both sides for about 3 to 4 minutes (a non-stick pan, though less romantic, also works well). Eat hot, spread with butter or butter and superfine granulated sugar. They are also very tasty fried in bacon fat and served for breakfast.

Note: *a piece of fadge or potato bread added to the Traditional Irish Breakfast (see page 118) forms the delicious Ulster Fry.*

Potato & Bacon Cakes

Serves 4

4 slices bacon, chopped
1 lb mashed potatoes
2 tablespoons plain white flour
salt and pepper
butter or fat drippings for frying

Mollie Keane, the indomitable Irish writer, includes this recipe in her book Mollie Keane's Nursery Cooking.

Fry the bacon without any additional fat until crisp. Remove and drain on paper towels. Stir the bacon into the mashed potatoes with the flour, salt and pepper. Form the mixture into four cakes. Heat the butter or drippings in a frying pan, add the cakes and fry for about 5 minutes on each side until golden and crisp.

Potato Oaten Cake

Makes 4 to 8

1 lb freshly cooked potatoes
2 to 4 tablespoons butter
2/3 to 3/4 cup fine oatmeal
salt

Not surprisingly, oatmeal, another staple ingredient, was sometimes added to potato cakes. The result was generally known as Pratie Oaten—Prataí being the Irish word for potato.

Mash the potatoes with the butter. Mix in the oatmeal and season with salt. Roll out into a round and cut into patties. Bake on a hot griddle for about 3 or 4 minutes on each side. Alternatively, cook in an iron pan in bacon fat. Eat hot with plenty of butter. Serve a few crispy slices of bacon with the potato oaten cakes.

Stampee or Stampy

May Fitzgerald from Ballycullane, Inch, Co. Kerry, sent me some recipes which her grandmother used to make with old potatoes in the spring. She had no scales or measures, but May vouches that the finished product tasted good.

She peeled some potatoes, and grated them on a coarse grater into a colander. She left them for a while until the clear liquid dropped out (incidentally she used that to stiffen grandfather's hard collars). Before supper she mixed potatoes with sufficient flour, seasoning (pepper and salt) and an egg to make a dough, which in turn she shaped into cakes, and fried in the large iron griddle over the fire. Then she served with a pat of homemade butter—delicious.

Boxty

Boxty vies with champ and colcannon as Ireland's best-known potato dish. It is particularly associated with the midland and northern counties, particularly Cavan, Tyrone, Fermanagh and Derry. It may have originated in the late eighteenth and early nineteenth centuries, when potato harvests began to fail, as a way of using poor quality potatoes which were useless for boiling. The watery, sometimes even rotting, potato flesh was put into a cloth and squeezed to remove as much liquid as possible. The remaining pulp was shaped into cakes and baked on heated flagstone or griddle.

Boxty on the griddle
Boxty on the pan
If you don't eat boxty
You'll never get your man.

When eaten instead of bread for the evening meal, milk and salt might be added to the mixture, which was then known as dippity.

Mollie Keane's Potato & Bacon Cakes

Whereas Leitrim and the Drumlin area seem to be the home of boxty, it crops up in many other places around the country under various names. In Co. Wexford and Co. Tipperary I was given recipes for 'grated cakes in the pan', both of which were essentially pan boxty. Granny Toye from Clones, Co. Monaghan, now 88 years of age, gave the recipe to me.

Scrub the potatoes well, but don't peel. Line a bowl with a cloth. Grate the potatoes into it, then squeeze out the liquid into the bowl and allow it to sit for about 20 minutes until the starch settles.

Drain off the water and leave the starch in the bottom of the bowl. Add the grated potato and a handful of flour and some salt.

Melt a nice bit of butter on a heavy iron pan and pour in the potato mixture. It should be ¾ to 1 inch thick. Cook on a medium heat. Let it brown nicely on one side before turning over and then on the other side, about 30 minutes depending on the heat. It's much better to cook it too slowly rather than too fast. It should be crisp and golden on the outside. Cut the boxty into four patties and serve.

Granny Toye says that pan boxty may be eaten hot or cold and may be reheated. A tablespoon of fresh herbs provide a delicious, if untraditional, flavoring to the dish.

Serves 4

Pan Boxty

6 medium potatoes
a handful of flour
salt
butter
fresh herbs (optional)

Boxty Pancakes

Serves 4

8oz freshly cooked potatoes
8oz peeled raw potatoes
2 cups white flour
1/2 teaspoon baking soda
1 to 1 1/2 cups buttermilk
pinch of salt (optional)
butter for frying

Peel the cooked potatoes while they are still hot. Drop them into a bowl and mash immediately. Grate the raw potatoes, add to the mash with the flour and sieved baking soda. Mix well and add enough buttermilk to make a stiff batter.

Heat a griddle or frying pan, grease with butter and drop in tablespoons on to the pan. Make large or small pancakes using anything from 1 to 3 to 4 tablespoons of mixture and cooking for about 5 minutes on each side. Eat them straight from the pan with butter, crispy slices of bacon or pure Irish honey.

Note: *Kat Clarke from Garbally, near Birr in Co. Offaly suggests serving the pancakes with superfine granulated sugar or corn syrup instead of the bacon or honey.*

Boiled Boxty

Serves 4 to 6

7lb raw potatoes
4 to 5lb mashed potatoes
4 to 6 cups flour
1 1/2 tablespoons salt

Phyl O'Kelly, the much admired cookery correspondent of the Cork Examiner, *was reared in Leitrim. She gave me details of the three types of boxty made in her area: pan boxty, boxty pancakes and boiled boxty.*

This is her version of the famous Leitrim boiled boxty, which she maintains is unique to Ireland, whereas versions of pan boxty can be found in many countries. Note the large quantities because of the large size of Irish families.

Wash, peel and grate the raw potatoes. Put them into a piece of muslin or a clean flour bag, squeeze out excess liquid into a bowl and leave to settle. Peel and mash the freshly boiled potatoes in a bowl. Add the grated raw potatoes, flour and starch that has separated out from the potato liquid. Season well with salt and shape into 5-inch rounds, 2 1/2 to 2 inches high with slightly flattened tops.

Bring a saucepan of water to a boil, add salt, gently drop in the boxty and cook until firm, about 45 minutes to 1 hour.

They will be greyish in color and not wildly appetizing to look at. When cold, slice into thick rounds and fry in butter or bacon fat until golden brown. Eat with country butter and a slice of bacon if you fancy.

This recipe, also for boiled boxty, came from Mrs Mary B. Kelly from Carrick-on-Shannon, Co. Leitrim:

7lb raw potatoes
3 1/2lb boiled potatoes
2 cups flour
1 1/2 tablespoons salt

Peel and grate the raw potatoes, squeezing out all the moisture you can. Peel and mash the boiled potatoes. Mix raw and mashed potatoes together, and add flour and salt. Mix all well together and make into dumplings the size of an orange and slightly flattened. Have a pot of boiling water ready and add the dumplings, bring back to a boil and simmer for one hour. Cool for a few hours or until the next day. Cut each dumpling into two half-moon shaped pieces, then cut each piece carefully into 2 or 3 slices. You should then have 6 half-moon shaped pieces. Fry these in butter until golden on both sides, eat as they are or with bacon for breakfast.

Baked Boxty or Boxty Loaf

Use the same recipe as above, but bake in two well buttered loaf pans in a moderate oven at 350°F for 1 hour.

Boxty Pancakes

Grated Cakes on the Griddle

1 teaspoon salt
³/4 cup plain white flour
1 lb raw potatoes
1 lb cooked mashed potatoes

Peel the raw potatoes and grate them into a linen tea towel. Squeeze and collect the liquid in a bowl and leave to stand. Mix the grated and mashed potatoes. When the starch has separated from the liquid, pour off the water and add the starch to the potatoes. Add the dry ingredients; mix well, adding enough flour to make a workable dough. Knead a little, then roll out and cut into 8 pieces. Bake on a hot griddle and serve the grated cakes warm with butter.

Grated Cakes in the Pan

1 teaspoon salt
1 teaspoon baking soda
4 cups flour
1 lb raw potatoes
1 lb cooked mashed potatoes
buttermilk

Peel the raw potatoes and grate them into a linen tea towel. Squeeze and collect the liquid in a bowl and leave to stand. Mix the grated potatoes and mashed potatoes. When the starch has separated from the liquid, pour off the water and add the starch to the potatoes. Add the dry ingredients and mix well, then add enough buttermilk to form a dropping consistency. Beat well and leave to stand a little before frying in spoonfuls in a greased frying pan. Fry on both sides and serve with butter and sugar.

Vegetables

In early Ireland and up to the late Middle Ages, vegetables appear to have been used mainly as salads or condiments. Charlock, *praiseach buí,* was eaten from the eleventh century onwards. Kale is mentioned in the eleventh century tale *Aislinge Meic Con Glinne* as the priest's fancy, but it was generally not highly regarded. Even in the famine years of the nineteenth century, it was only eaten under sufferance. A root vegetable called cerr-baccán, possibly referring to carrots, is also mentioned in *Aislinge Meic Con Glinne.*

In 1605, Harry Holland agreed to cultivate part of the gardens at Trinity College, Dublin (then known as the College of the Holy and Undivided Trinity) with turnips, parsnips, carrot, artichokes, onions and leeks. He provided vegetables for 'thirty person and eight messes as the cook hall think good'. In the eighteenth century, a wide variety of vegetables and fruit—asparagus, seakale, salsify, and vegetable marrows—began to be cultivated in the walled gardens of the large country house estates. This wider choice of vegetables seems not to have been adopted by poorer people, however: John Dunton, writing in 1699, described a typical peasant's garden as containing 'perhaps two or three hundred sheaves of oats and as much pease, the rest of the ground is full of those dearly loved potatoes, and a few cabbages'.

It seems likely that many other vegetables, such as turnips and carrots, did not become widespread in the Irish diet until the famine years.

Cabbage

A variety of brassicas, including cabbage, grow wild in Ireland and were used from early times mainly as a condiment or salad. Cultivated cabbage did not become widespread until the seventeenth century. In *Trinity College Dublin and the Idea of a University*, Charles Nelson points out that during the early seventeenth century, the scholars of Trinity dined ceaselessly on cabbages, which 'remained the constituent of the scholastic diet for a couple more centuries'. In 1683, the gardens of Trinity College were supplied with five hundred cabbage plants, along with other salads, herbs and vegetables, for the price of £1 16s 2d.

In *A Tour of Ireland 1776–79*, Arthur Young describes how cabbages were also used as cattle fodder:

> Cabbages Lord Farnham has cultivated three years; in 1774 he had 4 acres manured with lime and earth and of different sorts, flat Dutch, early Yorkshire, and green borecole, the seed was sown in the Spring, and planted out in June in rows three feet asunder, and horsehoed clean; found them for milch cows much better than turnips…the cabbages came to a good size, and the crop paid extremely well.

Cabbage is a relatively reliable crop and was therefore used extensively as an emergency food in the famine years of 1845 to 1848. In Castleisland, Co. Kerry, a particularly hard month during that period was known as 'July of the Cabbage'. Even up to the present day, cabbage is probably the most widely grown vegetable, from cottage gardens to huge vegetable farmers.

Until recently, the wisdom of the day advised cooking cabbage with bacon, ham or pig's head for 2 to 2½ hours. Later a pinch of baking soda was added 'to keep it green' and I even came across a recipe that suggested adding a lump of washing soda (see page 119)! These additions would have effectively destroyed most of the vitamins.

Boiled Cabbage

The traditional way of cooking cabbage. Remove the stalks and shred the cabbage fairly finely. Boil in salted water or, better still, water in which bacon has been cooked, until done. The cooking time varies depending on the variety of cabbage, so keep a watchful eye and drain the cabbage as soon as it is cooked. Add a nice lump of butter and season with lots of freshly ground pepper, adding a little more salt if necessary.

This recipe for quickly cooked cabbage has converted many an ardent cabbage hater!

Serves 6 to 8

Buttered Cabbage

1lb fresh Savoy cabbage
2 to 4 tablespoons butter
salt and freshly ground pepper
an extra knob of butter

Remove all the tough outer leaves from the cabbage. Cut the cabbage into four, remove the stalk and then cut each quarter into fine shreds, working across the grain. Put 2 or 3 tablespoons of water into a wide saucepan, together with the butter and a pinch of salt. Bring to a boil, add the cabbage and toss over a high heat, then cover the saucepan and cook for a few minutes. Toss again and add some salt, freshly ground pepper and the knob of butter. Serve immediately.

Buttered Cabbage and Glazed Carrots (see page 160)

Carrots

Traditionally carrots were cooked in the water in which bacon or corned beef had been boiled, which would give them a special flavor. On farms in the country, carrots and cabbage were pulled or cut just in time to be cooked for dinner. The clay was washed off in the barrel under the pump in the yard and five minutes later they were in the pot. No wonder they tasted so good. For many people cooking carrots straight from the garden is not now an option, so at least buy fresh unwashed carrots and cook them by this method to achieve maximum flavor.

Serves 4 to 6

Glazed Carrots

1 lb unwashed carrots
1 1/2 tablespoons butter
1/2 cup cold water
pinch of salt
a good pinch of sugar

Garnish
freshly chopped parsley or fresh mint

Cut off the tops and tips of the carrots, scrub them and peel thinly if necessary. Cut into slices 1/3 inch thick, either straight across or at an angle. Leave very young carrots whole. Put them in a saucepan with the butter, water, salt and sugar. Bring to a boil, cover and cook over a gentle heat until tender, by which time the liquid should all have been absorbed into the carrots. If it has not, remove the lid and increase the heat until all the water has evaporated. Taste and correct the seasoning. Shake the saucepan so the carrots become coated with the buttery glaze. Serve in a hot vegetable dish sprinkled with chopped parsley or mint.

'Green , White and Gold' and 'Sunshine' are some of the evocative names given to this popular vegetable combination, still widely made in Ireland.

Serves 4 to 6

Carrot & Parsnip Mash

8oz carrots
12oz parsnips
butter
salt, freshly ground pepper and sugar
chopped parsley

Wash and peel the carrots and parsnips. Slice the carrot into ¼-inch slices. Cook in a little boiled salted water with a pinch of sugar until soft.

Cook the parsnips separately in boiling salted water.

Strain both and mash or purée together. Add lots of butter, then the salt and freshly ground pepper. Sprinkle with chopped parsley.

Parsnips

In their valiant efforts to help the poor during the potato famines of 1845 to 1846, The Society of Friends encouraged the cultivation of parsnips, which may have been grown in Ireland since early Christian times. There are many references to *meacan* in early writings, which scholars believe may have meant parsnips. Traditionally parsnips were boiled and mashed with country butter. They are also delicious mixed with carrots, or cut into chunks and roast, either alone or around a joint of beef. Crispy parsnip cakes also make an irresistible and inexpensive treat.

The anonymous author of The Present State of Ireland, *written in 1673, writes that the Irish 'feed much upon parsnips, potatoes and watercresses'.*

The basis of this delicious recipe is simply mashed parsnips, which are made into plump little cakes and fried crispy on the pan.

Serves 6

Parsnip Cakes with Crispy Bacon

1lb parsnips
2 to 4 tablespoons butter
salt and freshly ground pepper
seasoned flour
1 beaten egg
white breadcrumbs
olive oil and butter for frying
bacon cut into ¼ inch cubes and fried until crisp in a little oil
watercress for garnish

Peel the parsnips thinly. Cut them into small chunks and cook in a little boiling salted water until soft. Mash with the butter, season with salt and freshly ground pepper to taste. Wet your hands and shape the mixture into six cakes. Dip each cake into the flour, then the egg, then coat with breadcrumbs. Heat a little olive oil with some butter in a wide frying pan. Fry the cakes on a gentle heat until golden on both sides. Serve hot with lardons of crispy bacon or as an accompaniment to a main course, garnished with sprigs of fresh watercress.

Swede Turnip

Probably because it was introduced to Ireland as cattle feed, the swede turnip, known to Americans as rutabaga, has humble connotations which it is still struggling to overcome. Lieutenant Joseph Archer's *Statistical Survey of County* Dublin in 1801 specifically recommends the use of turnips for animal fodder rather than human consumption:

> cabbages, potatoes or turnips would be better and more profitable for milch cows, than any, this is now used in Dublin.

However, it appears that turnip was unknown in many parts of Ireland up to the famine period. During the famine years, turnip seed was distributed, thereby establishing the popularity of the vegetable. One account from Barnesmore, Co. Donegal describes how in certain areas people ate so much of it that 'their skin turned yellow from the eating of swedes'.

As a result of eating turnips through necessity in the famine period, many imaginative adaptations of potato dishes developed, such as turnip boxty and turnip champ.

The unpretentious rutabaga is now becoming increasingly popular. It is a key vegetable in the movement towards hearty, rustic food. Besides being incredibly good value, rutabaga is much more versatile than many people suspect. If you are going to serve it mashed in the usual way, you should perk it up with caramelized onions. Remember, too, that farmers say rutabagas taste best after they have had a touch of frost.

Swede Turnips (rutabaga)

Heat the olive oil in a heavy saucepan. Toss in the onions and cook over a low heat until they are soft and caramelized to a golden brown (about 30 to 45 minutes).

Meanwhile peel the swede thickly in order to remove the thick outside skin. Cut into ¾-inch cubes and cover with water. Add in a good pinch of salt, bring to the boil and cook until soft. Strain off the excess water, mash the swede well and then beat in the butter. Stir in the soft and caramelized onions. Taste and season with lots of freshly ground pepper and more salt if necessary. Garnish with parsley and serve piping hot.

Serves about 6

Rutabagas
with Caramelized Onions

2lb rutabaga
salt and lots of freshly ground pepper
4 to 8 tablespoons butter

Caramelized Onions
1lb onions
2 to 3 tablespoons olive oil

Garnish
finely chopped parsley

Leeks are frequently referred to in early Irish manuscripts. The eleventh century poem *Aislinge Meic Con Glinne* speaks of 'a forest tall of real leeks of onions and carrots stood behind the house'. It is likely that the leek referred to was the perennial Babington leek (see page 18) which has a distinct garlic flavor and is still found growing wild at a number of locations on the west coast and the Aran Islands. It is thought to have been introduced to Ireland in pre-Christian times and now grows quite happily in my kitchen garden in Shanagarry. It tends to be rather tougher than modern varieties, so is perhaps best for flavoring broths and stews.

Leeks

Many people dislike leeks, possibly because they have only had them boiled. Try them this way—they are meltingly tender and mild in flavor.

Cut off the dark green leaves from the top of the leeks (wash and add to the stock pot or use for making green leek soup). Slit the leeks about half way down the center and wash well under cold running water. Slice into ¼ inch rounds. Melt the butter in a heavy saucepan; when it foams add the sliced leeks and toss gently to coat with butter. Season with salt and freshly ground pepper and add 1 tablespoon of water if necessary. Cover with a paper lid and a close-fitting saucepan lid. Reduce the heat and cook very gently for about 20 to 30 minutes, or until the leeks are soft and moist. Check and stir every now and then. Serve on a warm dish sprinkled with chopped parsley or chervil.

Note: *The pot of leeks may be cooked in the oven if that is more convenient, 325°F.*

Serves 4 to 6

Buttered Leeks

4 medium-sized leeks
3 tablespoons butter
salt and freshly ground pepper
1 tablespoon water, if necessary
chopped parsley or chervil

Globe Artichokes

In my research for this book a particular surprise was the discovery that globe artichokes have been grown in Ireland since the Anglo-Norman Conquest. They were, and still are, widely cultivated in the walled kitchen gardens of country houses, including Ballymaloe—where a particularly good variety has been grown since 1835 or even earlier. One of the loveliest Irish sights is a whole field of globe artichokes in bloom down near Allihies on the Beara Peninsula in West Cork.

Serves 6

Artichokes
with Melted Butter

6 artichokes
4 cups water
2 teaspoons salt
2 tablespoons white wine vinegar
12 tablespoons (1½ sticks) butter
freshly squeezed juice of ¼ lemon

Some restaurants prepare artichokes very elaborately. However, I merely trim the base of the artichoke just before cooking so it will sit steadily on the plate, then rub the cut end with lemon juice or vinegar to prevent it from discoloring.

Have a large saucepan of boiling water ready. Add 2 tablespoons of white wine vinegar and 2 teaspoons of salt to every 5 cups of water. Pop in the artichokes and bring the water back to a boil. Simmer steadily for about 25 minutes. After about 20 minutes test the artichokes to see if they are done by tugging off one of the larger leaves at the base. It should come away easily; if it doesn't continue to cook the artichokes for another 5 or 10 minutes. When cooked, remove the artichokes from the water and drain upside down on a hot serving plate.

While they are cooking, simply melt the butter and then add some lemon juice to taste. Serve the melted butter sauce in a little bowl beside the artichokes. Artichokes are eaten with the fingers, so you might like to provide a finger bowl. A spare plate to collect all the nibbled leaves would also be useful.

Asparagus

Asparagus is a rare, native plant in Ireland. The Viceroy, Lord Clarendon, commenting on the standard of cultivation in Dublin in 1685, notes that 'asparagus, here, is very good, large and green'. Jonathan Swift praised the vegetable as an excellent kidney stimulant, which was also good for gout and rheumatism.

Serves 4

Asparagus
with Hollandaise Sauce

16 to 20 spears fresh asparagus
Hollandaise Sauce (see opposite)
4 slices buttered toast

Garnish
sprigs of chervil

Trim the asparagus and cook in boiling salted water until a knife tip will pierce the root end easily. Meanwhile make the toast, butter it and remove the crusts. Place a piece of toast on a hot plate, place the asparagus on top and spoon a little Hollandaise sauce over it. Garnish with a sprig of chervil and serve immediately.

Globe Artichokes growing at Ballymaloe

Hollandaise Sauce

2 egg yolks, preferably free-range
8 tablespoons (1 stick) butter, cut into dice
2 teaspoons cold water
1 teaspoon lemon juice (approximately)

Put the egg yolks into a heavy stainless steel saucepan on a low heat, or in a bowl over hot water. Add water and beat thoroughly. Add the butter bit by bit, beating all the time. As soon as one piece melts, add the next. The mixture will gradually thicken, but if it shows signs of becoming too thick or of slightly 'scrambling', remove from the heat immediately and add a little cold water if necessary. Do not leave the pan or stop whisking until the sauce is made. Finally add the lemon juice to taste. If the sauce is slow to thicken it may be because you are excessively cautious and the heat is too low. Increase the heat slightly and continue to beat until the sauce thickens to coating consistency.

You will not be surprised to learn that our gourmet friend Amhlaoibh Uí Shúileabháin enjoyed 'cooked asparagus in melted butter on boiled new milk and salt', with his friend Father Hennebry in June 1828.

Celery

Celery is thought to have been one of the earliest vegetables grown alongside leeks, onions and kale in monastery gardens. It was probably used in pottages, with leeks, onion and wild garlic. In early Ireland every provincial king was apparently entitled to have 'three condiments supplied for his nursing; honey, fresh onions and an unlimited amount of celery'.

Serves 4 to 6

Celery with Cream

1 head of celery
salt and freshly ground pepper
roux (see page 40)
1/2 to 3/4 cup cream

Garnish
chopped parsley

Pull the stalks off the head of celery. If the outer stalks seem a bit tough, peel the strings off with a potato peeler or else use these tougher stalks in the stockpot. Cut the stalks into 1/2-inch chunks

Bring 1/2 cup water to a boil and season with salt and freshly ground pepper. Add the chopped celery, cover and cook for 15 to 20 minutes, or until a knife will go through the celery easily. Pour off most of the water into another pan. Add the cream to this water and thicken with roux. Strain the celery from its remaining cooking water and add the celery to the sauce. Allow the sauce to bubble for a few minutes. Put into a hot serving dish, sprinkle with chopped parsley and serve.

Onions

Onions have always been an essential ingredient in the Irish kitchen and they are a source of pride still in cottage gardens. Even people who would grow little else would buy a few sets and grow them every year.

Baked Onions

Baked or roast onions could be cooked long and slowly, either in the bastible or in the embers of the open fire. Don't be alarmed by the thought of eating a whole onion! This cooking method makes them mild, sweet and delicious. It is our very favorite way of eating onions and couldn't be simpler to prepare. You don't even have to peel them— just bung them into the oven.

Choose a number of small or medium-sized onions. Preheat the oven to 400°F. Place the unpeeled onions, on a baking tray, in the oven and bake until soft; this can take anything from 10 to 30 minutes, depending on size. Serve the onions in their jackets. To eat, cut off the root end, squeeze out the onion and enjoy with butter and sea salt.

Jonathan Swift had a different recipe for insuring against oniony breath:

> There is in every cook's opinion
> No savory dish without an onion
> But lest your kissing should be spoiled
> The onion must be thoroughly boiled.

Note: *stewed onions, eaten at night, were a folk remedy for constipation.*

This very simple dish of rutabagas, potatoes and onions is quite delicious—comfort food at its best. It was sent to me by Queenie Endersen from Ballyellis, Mallow, Co. Cork. Her grandmother used to make it for the boarders who lodged in her house.

Serves 4 hungry men

Beggarman's Stew

1 rutabaga, approx. 2lb when peeled
2 large onions, about 14oz
8 potatoes, 2lb 14oz
2¹/₂ cups chicken or lamb stock
salt and freshly ground pepper
lump of lamb fat (optional)
chopped parsley

Cut the rutabaga into thick fingers, peel the onions and slice into thick rings, peel the potatoes and leave whole. Mix the onions with the rutabagas and put into the base of a saucepan. Cover with potatoes, season well with salt and freshly ground pepper. Add about 2 cups chicken or lamb stock, or failing that water. Bring to a boil, cover and simmer until the vegetables are almost cooked (about 15 minutes).

Before the end of the cooking time a nice piece of lamb fat may be added. Watch carefully to ensure that the potatoes keep their shape and don't disintegrate. Add chopped parsley and serve the stew in deep plates with lots of country butter.

Peas

The Anglo-Normans introduced peas and beans to Ireland. These were a welcome addition to the Irish diet, which had relied heavily on milk products for protein since prehistoric times. Both peas and beans preserved well: we all here remember the packages of dried peas, the forerunner to mushy peas! Fields of peas are grown around our part of Ireland, so we feast on fresh peas for two or three weeks in July and August.

Serves 8 to 10

Garden Peas
with Fresh Mint

1lb garden peas or petits pois,
  freshly shelled
¹/₂ cup water
1 teaspoon salt
1 teaspoon sugar
sprig of mint
2 tablespoons butter
2 teaspoons chopped fresh mint

Bring the water to a boil. Add the salt, sugar, mint sprig and the peas. Bring the water back to a boil and simmer until the peas are cooked, for approximately 4 to 5 minutes.

Strain the peas, reserving the water for soup or gravy. Add the butter. Garnish with a little chopped fresh mint and add a little extra seasoning if necessary. Eat immediately.

Matter of Fact Peas

When I was a child there were just a few precious weeks in the year when we had fresh peas. For the remainder of the year it was marrowfats—called 'matter of fact peas' by Kevin Dunne's father, Terry, who lived in Rathgar in Dublin. Marrowfat peas are, of course, the basis for the now legendary mushy peas.

8oz dried split peas
¹/₂ teaspoon baking soda
salt and freshly ground pepper
sugar
butter

Put the marrowfats into a bowl, add the baking soda tablet and cover with 3¹/₂ cups of boiling water. Leave to soak overnight.

Next day, drain, and barely cover the peas with fresh boiling water. Bring to a boil and simmer for 15 to 20 minutes until tender.

When the peas are cooked, strain. Add salt, freshly ground pepper, sugar and a big blob of butter to taste. Serve hot.

Cut and Come Kale

Serves 4

This type of kale (Brassica oleracea) *is thought to be more than 2000 years old and is of tremendous interest to botanists. It was unknown to me until I came across it in the eighteenth century walled garden at Glin Castle in Co. Limerick. May Liston, one of the cooks at Glin, had originally brought slips of this vegetable from her home in Lower Athea and she gave me some to plant. The gardener, Tom Wall, called it 'Cut and Come'. Since I have begun to grow it myself in the kitchen garden several people have recognized it from their childhood and given it different names—Winter Kale, Winter Greens, Cut and Come, Cottier's Kale or Hungry Gap, because it was the only green available between the end of the winter and the arrival of the first spring vegetables. It is quite different from curly kale and is much more melting and tender when cooked.*

2lbs cut and come kale
5 cups water
1 teaspoon salt
butter
salt and freshly ground pepper

Wash and trim the sprigs of kale. Bring the water to a boil, add the salt and kale. Cook the vegetable with the lid off, for about 25 minutes or until tender. Drain off all the water. Chop well, add a big lump of butter and plenty of freshly ground pepper and salt.

Note: *cut and come kale, like spinach, reduces a lot during cooking, like spinach, so you need to start off with a large pot-full.*

Curly Kale

Serves 4 to 6

1lb curly kale, destalked (1lb 10oz with stalks)
salt, freshly ground pepper and a little grated nutmeg
4 tablespoons butter
²/₃ cup cream

Bring a large saucepan of salted water to a boil, (14 cups to 3 teaspooons salt). Add the curly kale, minus its stalks, and boil uncovered on a high heat until tender. This can vary from 5 to 10 minutes depending on how tough the kale is.

Drain off the water and purée the kale in a food processor. Return to the saucepan. Season with salt, freshly ground pepper and a little nutmeg if you fancy.

Add a generous lump of butter and some cream, bubble and taste.

Serve hot.

Seakale

Seakale, one of the most exquisite of all vegetables, seakale is known as strand cabbage *(praiseach trá)* in parts of Co. Donegal and Antrim. It grows wild on sandy, pebbly strands around the coast. Traditionally, devotees kept an eye out for the first leaves towards the end of February and into March. Knowing that seakale was best when the young stalks were excluded from the light, they would draw sand and pebbles over the plant as it grew. Weeks later, provided the same spot could be located, the pale yellow, tender stems were uncovered and harvested.

Seakale was a sought-after vegetable in country house gardens in the eighteenth and nineteenth centuries. It is rarely if ever seen for sale, but is relatively easy to grow, so is well worth cultivating. You can buy replicas of the old seakale blanching pots with lids, but a brick chimney liner covered by a slate works perfectly well. Even a simple black plastic bucket will suffice. Exclude the light from about November, then you will be rewarded with delicate shoots in the early part of April. Seakale is a perennial plant and is altogether beautiful, with white flowers in summer and lots of bobbly seed heads in autumn. It thrives with a mulch of cinders.

Seakale growing at Glin Castlein Co. Limerick

Serves 4 to 6

Seakale
with Melted Butter

1 lb seakale
4 to 6 tablespoons butter
salt and freshly ground pepper

Wash the seakale gently and trim into manageable lengths—about 4 inches. Bring about 2½ cups water to a fast boil and add a generous ½ teaspoon of salt. Add the seakale, cover and boil until tender—about 15 minutes. Just as soon as a knife will pierce the seakale easily, drain it and then serve on hot plates with a little melted butter and perhaps a few small triangles of toast.

Normally served as a course on its own, an abundance of seakale makes a wonderful accompaniment to fish, particularly poached salmon with Irish butter sauce (see page 50).

Cauliflower

Cauliflower was one of the later brassicas to be introduced to Ireland. It seems to have reached England during the sixteenth century from Spain and is likely to have reached Ireland soon afterward. It is known that one Nicholas Shepherd sold cauliflower seeds in Dublin in 1685 to the gardener at Trinity College, Dublin.

When I was a child, we grew cauliflowers in the garden. It was still considered a great treat. I remember helping Pad, our gardener, to bend the leaves up over the heads to protect the delicate white curds from the sharp midland frost.

I have failed to find the name of the old variety which we ate as children. Cauliflower varieties seem to have suffered more, flavorwise than most other vegetables. The leaves are more flavorsome than the curd so make sure not to discard them. Even a mediocre cauliflower can be made to taste delicious in a bubbling cheese sauce.

Serves 6 to 8

Cauliflower in Cheese Sauce

1 medium-sized cauliflower with lots of fresh green leaves
table salt

Cheese Sauce
2¹/2 cups milk with a dash of cream
a slice of onion
3 to 4 slices of carrot
6 peppercorns
thyme or sprig of parsley
roux (see page 40)
salt and freshly ground pepper
1 cup grated cheese, e.g. Cheddar or a mixture of Gruyère, Parmesan and Cheddar
¹/4 teaspoon dry mustard
salt and freshly ground pepper
1 oz grated Cheddar cheese

Garnish
chopped parsley

Remove the outer leaves and wash both the cauliflower and the leaves well. Put not more than 1 inch (2.5cm) water in a saucepan just large enough to take the cauliflower; add a little salt. Chop the leaves into small pieces and cut the cauliflower into quarters or eighths. Place the cauliflower on top of the green leaves in the saucepan, cover and simmer until cooked (about 10 to 15 minutes). Test if the cauliflower is cooked by piercing the stalk with a knife: there should be just a little resistance. Remove the cauliflower and leaves to an ovenproof serving dish.

Meanwhile make the cheese sauce. Put the cold milk into a saucepan with the onion, carrot, peppercorns and thyme or parsley. Bring to a boil, simmer for 3 to 4 minutes and remove from the heat and leave to infuse for 10 minutes. Strain out the vegetables, then bring the milk back to a boil and thicken with roux to a light coating consistency. Add the grated cheese and a little mustard. Season with salt and freshly ground pepper, taste and correct the seasoning if necessary. Spoon the sauce over the cauliflower and sprinkle with more grated cheese. The dish may be prepared ahead to this point.

Put into a hot oven, 450°F, or under the grill to brown. If the cauliflower cheese is allowed to get completely cold, it will take 20 to 25 minutes to reheat in a moderate oven, 350°F.

Serve sprinkled with chopped parsley.

Beets were often grown side by side with potatoes, carrots and onions in cottage garden plots. They appear to have lost popularity, partly, I imagine, because of the frightfully vinegary pickled variety on sale in jars,

Beets

To prepare the beets, chop off the leaf stalks, leaving 2 inches of leaf stalk on the top and the whole root on the beet. Hold the beet under a running tap and wash off the mud with the palms of your hands, so that you don't damage the skin. Cover with cold water into which a little salt and sugar have been added. Cover the pot, bring to a boil and simmer on top, or in an oven at 400°F, for 1 to 2 hours depending on size. They are cooked when the skin rubs off easily and if they dent when pressed with a finger.

Serves 5-6

Pickled Beets and Onion Salad

Dissolve the sugar in water, bringing it to a boil. Add the sliced onion and simmer for 3 to 4 minutes. Add the vinegar, pour over the peeled sliced beet and leave to cool.

Note: *The onion may be omitted if desired.*

For 1lb cooked beets:
1¹/4 cups sugar
2¹/2 cups water
1 onion, peeled and thinly sliced
1¹/4 cups white wine vinegar

Moore Street Market, Dublin

Serves 4

Old-fashioned Salad

with Shanagarry Cream Dressing

2 free-range eggs
1 Boston lettuce
watercress sprigs
4 tiny scallions
2 to 4 tomatoes, quartered
16 slices of cucumber
4 slices of home-pickled beets
(see page 171)
4 sliced radishes
chopped parsley

Shanagarry Cream Dressing
2 eggs, free-range if possible
1 tablespoon dark soft brown sugar
pinch of salt
1 level teaspoon dry mustard
1 tablespoon brown malt vinegar
$1/4$ to $1/2$ cup cream

This simple old-fashioned salad is the sort of thing you would have had for tea on a visit to your Granny on a Sunday evening—perhaps with a slice of meat left over from the Sunday roast. It is one of my absolute favorites.

It can be quite delicious made with a crisp lettuce, good home-grown tomatoes and cucumbers, free-range eggs and home-preserved beets. If, on the other hand, you make it with pale battery eggs, watery tomatoes, tired lettuce and cucumber and (worst of all) vinegary beets from a jar, you'll wonder why you bothered.

We serve this traditional salad as a starter in Ballymaloe, with an old-fashioned salad dressing which would have been popular before the days of mayonnaise. This recipe came from Lydia Strangman, the last occupant of our house.

Hard-boil the eggs for the salad and the dressing. Bring a small saucepan of water to a boil, gently slide in the eggs and boil for 10 minutes (12 if they are very fresh). Strain off the hot water and cover with cold water. Peel when cold.

Wash and dry the lettuce, scallions and watercress.

Next make the dressing. Cut two eggs in half and sieve the yolks into a bowl. Add the sugar, a pinch of salt and the mustard. Blend in the vinegar and cream. Chop the egg whites and add some to the sauce. Keep the rest to scatter over the salad. Cover the dressing until needed.

To assemble the salads, first arrange a few lettuce leaves on each of four plates. Scatter a few tomato quarters and two hard-boiled egg quarters, a few slices of cucumber and a radish on each plate, and (preferably just before serving) add a slice of beet to each. Garnish with scallions and watercress. Scatter the remaining egg white (from the dressing) and some chopped parsley over the salad.

Put a tiny bowl of cream dressing in the center of each plate and serve immediately, while the salad is crisp and before the beet starts to run. Alternatively, serve the dressing from one large bowl.

Food from the Wild

Our early ancestors, the hunter-gatherers, lived on the bounty of wild foods which were provided by the land and sea. They understood the pattern of the seasons, and moved from place to place in pursuit of different foods at different times of the year. In spring they camped around the estuaries and ate fish and shellfish, and the eggs of seabirds. Towards summer they moved inland, following the salmon up river, and in autumn there was a proliferation of nuts and berries to enjoy.

Nowadays, in times of relative plenty, many of these wild foods are neglected and often left to rot in the hedgerows. Fortunately it is now becoming more fashionable for restaurants to feature such things as wild mushrooms, wild garlic, samphire, damsons and other free foods from nature on their menus. For years Ballymaloe House has encouraged local children to forage in the countryside and to bring their finds to the kitchen door for use in the restaurant.

Wild Garlic

Wild garlic has been used in Ireland as a condiment or as part of a relish since earliest times. In the heyday of many large Irish estates it was apparently quite common to plant it on the edges of woodland and pasture. In late spring, when the cattle and sheep were put out to grass after the long winter indoors, the garlic was thought to have a beneficial effect on them. There are two types: wild garlic *(Allium ursinum)*, which grows in shady places along the banks of streams and in undisturbed mossy woodland, and snowbells *(Allium triquestrum)*, which resemble white bluebells and usually grow along the sides of country lanes.

Serves 10 (approximately)

Lamb

Braised with Wild Garlic

Myrtle Allen gave me this delicious recipe which she serves at Ballymaloe when the wild garlic is just about to bloom in May.

Leg of young lamb
oil, butter or lamb fat
salt and freshly ground black pepper
3 to 6 wild garlic heads, picked preferably just before they flower
4 bunches scallions, peeled
1 lb small potatoes, peeled

Set the oven to 350°F.

Brown the lamb in a little oil, butter or lamb fat. Season with salt and freshly ground black pepper. Chop up the wild garlic plants and press into the skin of the meat with the herbs (if used). Sauté the scallions and potatoes in the same fat and then put them around the meat and herbs in a heavy cast iron casserole. Cover with a tight fitting lid.

Cook in the oven for 1½ to 2 hours or until cooked through. Strain off the juices and pour off the fat. Serve the juices separately as a gravy. A little good stock may be added if not enough juices are left in the pot. More chopped fresh herbs may be added to the gravy.

Note: *later in the season, garlic cloves can be used with fresh herbs, such as thyme or marjoram, making a good substitute for garlic's own green leaves.*

Sorrel

Throughout the sixteenth and seventeenth centuries, a number of visitors to Ireland commented on the Irish practice of eating shamrock. These references to shamrock have been variously interpreted: one suggestion is that shamrock was, in fact, sorrel. One of the first to record the consumption of shamrock/sorrel was Edmund Campion in *A History of Ireland, 1571*, who observed that 'shamrotes, watercresses, rootes and other herbes they feed upon'.

In his Irish herbal of 1735, the *Botanalogia Universalis Hibernica*, the Reverend John K'Eogh makes the following entry for sorrel:

It is beneficial for the heart, mouth and liver because it induces perspiration, it is also good against jaundice. It cleanses and heals rotten ulcers.

I first learned about the existence of this recipe from Jane Grigson. Charles J. Haughey tracked it down for me in the book Bean an Oileáin *by Máire Ní Guithín (1986) and had it translated from Irish. The author's aunt, who was born and reared on Inis Mhic Uibhleáin, was apparently the first and only woman to use this recipe. The pie was baked in a three-legged pot set over an open fire, with hot coals placed on top of the lid. According to* Bean an Oileáin *young children on the Great Blasket Island used to eat sorrel leaves, even though they found them very bitter.*

We preheated the oven to 450°F. We used a 9-inch x 2-inch deep pot with a cover, buttered it well and proceeded according to the recipe.

> Put flour into bowl, add baking soda and salt. Rub in the butter and wet with buttermilk to a soft mixture. Knead lightly on a lightly floured table. Cut in two halves. [Meanwhile, heat oven (3 legged pot) on an open fire.] Flatten dough with hand. Place sorrel leaves on one half of the flattened dough. Sprinkle with brown sugar. [We put some underneath and on top of the sorrel.] Flatten the second half of dough and cover the sorrel mixture. Press the edges together. Place in a hot buttered and floured (pot) with lid and bake until nicely browned.

The pie took 1 hour to bake and cooked to a pale golden color in the covered pot. It had a bitter-sweet flavor and was quite delicious.

Sorrel Pie
from Inis Mhic Uibhleáin

large mug of flour (we used 4 cups flour)
3/4 teaspoon baking soda
a knob of butter (we used 1 tablespoon)
buttermilk (we used 1 1/4 to 1 1/2 cups)
half a mug brown sugar (we used 3 heaped tablespoons)
sorrel leaves (amount not given—we used 4 to 6oz)
we also added a little salt to the dough

Wild Garlic growing at Glin Castle, Co. Limerick.

Nettles

Nettles have always been one of the most important and abundant wild foods in Ireland.

On Cape Clear, Oilean Céire, an island off the West Cork coast, there was an annual feast on 1 May called Féile na Neantóg. On that day all the children would have great sport chasing each other with bundles of stinging nettles. If they wet the nettles beforehand it put 'extra heat' in them. They stung every inch of each others' bodies. This was done with great glee and without a shred of remorse.

Older people also believed that nettle stings helped to cure 'the pains'. I have heard this in many parts of the country; on Cape Clear, Donncadh O'Driscéoil remembered how people would throw off their clothes and roll in a bed of nettles, not happy until their entire body was covered with the blisters. They were convinced that this would cure rheumatism. It would certainly divert your attention from the pain of the rheumatism for a while!

The tradition of eating nettles still lives on in many rural areas, particularly among the older generation. Many people still eat several 'feeds' of nettles during May to clear the blood and 'keep the rheumatics away' for the rest of the year.

Islanders also fed nettles to the pigs and hens. Donncadh O'Driscéoil described in his book *Aistí O Chléire* how he would search around the edge of the house and sheds for young nettles. The nettles were scalded and mixed with cornmeal to entice the pig to eat them, and it was highly prized as a cheap and healthy food. He also believed that the nettle supplement encouraged the hens to go broody and hatch bigger and healthier clutches of chickens—a very desirable thing in what was virtually a self-sufficient community.

To Cook Young Nettles

This recipe comes from Catherine Dowd-Rohan, from Annascaul, Co. Kerry:

Fill a 2 quart bowl with young nettles, just only the top of them, not more than 6 leaves, wash well and drain. Have ready an enamel saucepan and into it put about 1oz of fresh butter and a little seasoning of salt and pepper. Sometimes a tiny bit of spice of clove. pack in nettles. Put lid on saucepan for a few minutes over fire and then stir and chop vigorously with large wooden spoon. Put on lid again and in less than 10 minutes this dish is ready and can be rubbed through a sieve and can be served with poached egg if liked.

Mushrooms

The mere mention of wild mushrooms evokes nostalgic memories for most Irish people, who recall racing out at dawn with aluminum cans to search for wild mushrooms in the dewy fields. Many remember cooking them over embers on the hearth, and on the cool plate of the range, with nothing more than a few grains of salt for seasoning. Sometimes the mushrooms were stewed in milk and occasionally, when there was a glut in warm humid autumn weather, we'd collect bucketsful and make mushroom ketchup.

Nowadays the common field mushroom is scarcer than ever, because of modern intensive farming, but the Irish woods are peppered with wild mushrooms, chanterelles, morels, deceivers, hedgehog mushrooms and many more. There is a deep suspicion of unusual wild mushrooms in Ireland, which may come from folklore memories of cases of mushroom poisoning during famine times. However, people are now becoming much more adventurous and wild mushrooms are beginning to appear on the menus of more innovative restaurants.

If you choose to pick wild mushrooms yourself, always be sure to have expert help with identification.

Chanterelles on Buttered Toast

Serves 4 to 6

1lb chanterelles
1 to 2 tablespoons butter
salt and freshly ground black pepper
1 tablespoon chopped parsley
hot buttered toast

Trim off the earthy part of the stems. Then wash the caps quickly but carefully, and drain them well. Slice or keep whole, depending on the size. Melt some butter in a frying pan, add the mushrooms and fry over a high heat. The mushrooms will begin to exude their juice, but continue to cook on a very high heat until the juices are reabsorbed. Season with salt and pepper, sprinkle with parsley and serve immediately on hot buttered toast.

Sloe Gin

Sloes are very tart berries that resemble tiny purple plums in appearance. They grow on prickly bushes on top of stone walls and are in season in September and October. They make a wonderful drink, ready for consuming at Christmas.

1½lb sloes
1²/₃ cups white sugar
5 cups gin or poteen

Wash and dry the sloes and prick in several places (we use a clean darning needle). Put them into a sterilized 2 quart glass canning jar and cover with sugar and gin. Cover and seal tightly. Shake during this time—initially every couple of days and then every so often for 3 to 4 months, by which time it will be ready to strain and bottle. It will improve on keeping, so try to resist drinking it for another few months!

Note: *delicious damson gin can be made in exactly the same way.*

Damson Jam

Damson jam was a great favorite of mine as a child. My friends and I collected damsons every year in a field near the old castle in Cullohill, Co. Laois. First we ate so many we almost burst! The rest we brought home to be made into jam or fruit pies.

6lb damsons
15 cups sugar
3 cups water

Pick over the fruit carefully. Wash and drain well and discard any damaged damsons. Put the damsons and water into a greased stainless steel preserving pan and stew them gently until the skins break. Heat the sugar in a low oven, add it to the fruit and stir over a gentle heat until the sugar is dissolved. Increase the heat and boil steadily, stirring frequently. Skim off the stones and scum as they rise to the top. Test for a set after 15 minutes' boiling. Pour a teaspoonful on to a cold plate and push the jam gently with your finger. It should wrinkle when the jam has set. Pour into hot sterilized jars, cover, and seal. Store in a cool dry place.

Crab Apples

Crab apples are still easy to find in the autumn. Native to Ireland, they are extremely bitter, but make a delicious jelly. The entry for crab apple in John K'Eogh's *Botanalogia Universalis Hibernica* of 1735 reads:

> Crab tree grows frequently in hedges and flowers in April and May, with the fruit ripening in September. [Its juice] is used for burns, scalds and inflammations.

Wash the apples and cut into quarters. Do not remove peel and core. If you use windfalls, make sure to cut out the bruised parts. Put the apples into a large saucepan with the water and the thinly pared rind of the lemons. Cook until reduced to a pulp (about 30 minutes).

Turn the pulp into a jelly bag. Allow it to drip until all the juice has been extracted (overnight is best). Measure the juice into a preserving pan and weigh out 2½ cups sugar to each 2½ cups of juice. Warm the sugar.

Squeeze the lemons, strain the juice and add to the preserving pan. Bring to a boil, add the sugar (and the flavorings if used). Stir over a gentle heat until the sugar is dissolved. Increase the heat and boil rapidly without stirring for about 8 to 10 minutes. Skim and test to see if setting point has been reached by placing a teaspoonful on a cold plate and pushing it gently with your finger (if the jelly wrinkles, it is ready). Pour into sterilized jars, cover and seal immediately.

Note: *flavor with sweet geranium, mint or cloves as desired.*

Makes 6 to 7 pots

Crab Apple Jelly

6lb crab apples or windfall cooking apples
10 cups water
2 lemons
sugar
sweet geranium, mint or cloves to flavor (optional)

The profusion of wonderful white elderflower blossom turns in autumn into black elderberries which the birds feast on and most people ignore. Why not try this delicious jelly? If you can't find crab apples, use cooking apples instead. This recipe was given to me by Catherine O'Connor and is served at Strokestown House in Co. Roscommon.

Wash the apples well and remove any blemished parts. Cut into pieces and put into a pan with the elderberries. Add water, cover the pan and simmer to a pulp. Pour into a jelly bag or cloth and leave to drip. Measure the juice and weigh out 2½ cups sugar to each 2½ cups juice. Put the sugar and juice into a pan and stir over a moderate heat until the sugar is dissolved. Tie the orange rind and cinnamon together and add to the pan. Boil rapidly for about 15 minutes, then test for setting. Put a teaspoonful on a cold plate; the jelly should wrinkle when pressed with a finger. If it doesn't, carry on cooking a bit longer. Remove the cinnamon and orange rind and pour the jelly into warm sterilized jars, cover, and seal. This jelly should be of a soft rather than a too firm consistency.

Elderberry & Crab Apple Jelly

3lb crab apples or cooking apples
10 cups elderberries
5 cups water
peeled rind of 1 orange
½ stick cinnamon
sugar

Wild crab apple trees blossom and fruit all through the Irish countryside, year in, year out. I came across many recipes for crab apple jelly and even wine, but this recipe, the only one for a crab apple cake, came from Mrs Carrow from Togher, near Drogheda in Co. Louth. She was given it by her mother.

Mix the flour, sugar and baking soda together in a bowl and rub in the butter. Peel, core and cut the crab apples in halves and put into the mixture. Beat the eggs well with a fork and add to the sour milk, then to the flour. Knead the mixture into a round cake and bake in a pot oven over a slow fire for one hour.

Note: *no doubt this would be delicious served with soft brown sugar and cream.*

Crab Apple Cake

4¾ cups flour
1¼ cups sugar
1 teaspoon baking soda
16 tablespoons (2 sticks) butter
1 dozen crab apples
2 duck eggs
sour milk

Medlar

The medlar, a type of wild apple tree, was probably introduced into Ireland in the sixteenth century. In the spring the trees are covered with pale pink flowers which produce the bizarre-looking fruit from which this jelly is made; in autumn they provide a feast of rich color. The fruit is similar to a crab apple and needs to be half-rotten (bletted) before it can be eaten.

Medlars are another fruit mentioned in John K'Eogh's 1735 work, *Botanalogia Universalis Hibernica*:

> Medlars have a cold dry astringent nature. When hard and green, they are useful in stopping diarrhoea. If the crushed stones of the Medlar are drunk in a solution, they break up bladder stones.

Don't let this riveting description put you off, because medlar jelly is quite delicious! Serve it with game or pork, or with cream cheese.

Medlar Jelly

ripe medlars—slightly soft (bletted)
sugar
piece of cinnamon stick
2 cloves
2 strips of lemon peel

Cut the fruit into quarters, put into a stainless steel saucepan. Cover with water, bring to a boil and cook until soft. Pour into a jelly bag and leave to drip overnight. Don't squeeze the jelly through the bag or the juice will be cloudy. Next day measure the juice and allow 2½ cups sugar to every 2½ cups juice. Warm the sugar and add to the hot juice. Add the spices and lemon peel and boil until setting point is reached. Pour into hot sterilized jars ,cover, and seal immediately. Serve with game.

Clonbrock Medlar Jelly

This jelly was made from the medlars which grew in the walled garden at Clonbrock in Co. Galway, and the recipe is from the Kitchen Book of Clonbrock:

> Take sufficient ripe medlars, they need not be yellow but must be quite ripe. Place in a preserving pan with the peel of a lemon and enough water to cover. Simmer very gently until the fruit is pulped. Pour the contents of the pan into a large sieve and allow the liquid to strain off gradually. Do not press the pulp through or the jelly will be cloudy. Measure the liquid and allow ¾lb of sugar to every pint. Pour the liquid into a clean pan and boil rapidly for thirty minutes, skimming off the scum if necessary. Heat the sugar in the oven and add to the contents of the pan, stir until the sugar is dissolved and continue boiling for ten minutes. Drop a little on a plate to see if it sets. If not, boil for a few minutes longer or until the syrup jellies when cold. Pour the jelly into small jars and stand in a sunny window for several hours. The next day put a round of white tissue paper dipped in the white of an egg on top of the jelly and cover with transparent paper in the usual way.

Rowanberries

Rowan trees are native to Ireland. Rowans were not cultivated for their fruit, however, but for their powers to ward off evil spirits, often planting a rowan beside a house. Nevertheless, our ancestors clearly did not ignore the fruit of this magical tree. In a twelfth century Fenian poem it is said 'I will eat good apples in the glen and fragrant berries of rowan tree'.

Dr John Rutty, writing in his 1772 *An Essay towards a Natural History of the County of Dublin*, states that frost-bitten rowanberries possess a 'sweet, acid, not an ungrateful taste'.

Rowanberry & Apple Jelly

crab apples or windfall cooking apples
rowanberries
white sugar

Chop the apples (windfalls are fine) into chunks and barely cover with cold water. Bring to a boil and cook until they are soft and pulpy. Strain the juice through a jelly bag.

Crush the rowanberries. Add a very little water and cook them in a heavy bottomed saucepan until they are soft. Strain through a nylon sieve.

Combine the juices and measure, using equal quantities of both. Bring to a boil. Use 2½ cups sugar for every 2 cups of juice. Warm the sugar and add to the boiling juice. Stir until all the sugar is dissolved, then boil rapidly until the liquid reaches setting point. (To test this, drop a little liquid on to a plate. The jelly should wrinkle when pressed with a finger.) Pot into sterilized jars, seal, and store in a cool place.

Fraughans or Blueberries

Fraughans, blueberries, herts or bilberries are the names used in different parts of Ireland for the intensely flavored wild blueberries that grow on the acid hilltops. Fraughans are inextricably linked with the festival of Lugnasadh, the first Sunday in August, which came to be known as Garland Sunday or Fraughan Sunday. It was the tradition in many places for the whole community to take off to a chosen place in the mountains, or beside a lake or stream or holy well, for a carefree day of picnicking, singing, dancing, sports and picking wild fraughans, which would either have been eaten crushed, with sugar and cream, as here, or baked into cakes. It was also a time for serious courting, as is clear from the maxim 'Many a lad met his wife on Blaeberry Sunday'. Blueberries were also used to make a drink called *fraochán*.

Crushed Fraughans

This is quite the most delicious way to eat these little wild berries!

fraughans or blueberries
superfine granulated sugar
softly whipped cream

Crush the berries with a pounder or potato masher and sweeten to taste with sugar. Serve with softly whipped cream. Alternatively, fold in about half their volume of whipped cream to make a tasty fraughan fool.

Blackberries

There is evidence from the Iron Age site settlement of Rathinaun in Lough Gara, that our ancestors were enjoying blackberries as long ago as 150 B.C. In the eighth century Brehon Laws, the blackberry bush is given legal protection, presumably because of the importance of its fruit.

Reliably, Amhlaoibh Uí Shúileabháin of Callan in Co. Kilkenny notes in his diary for August 30, 1827 'I ate ripe blackberries today', and three days later he comments 'I went for a stroll along the fences between the Fair Green and the Owbeg, picking blackberries for my four children, Dennis, Anastasiette, Humphrey and James.'

It is a popular and wide-held folk belief that is dangerous to pick wild fruits, including blackberries, after the feast of Samhain (Hallowe'en), because the *púca* had spat on the fruits.

Makes 9 or 10 1lb (450g) jars

Blackberry & Apple Jam

*5lb blackberries
2lb cooking apples (Bramley or Grenadier in season)
10 cups sugar
about 1³/4 cups water (in total)*

Blackberry picking takes on a rosy glow of nostalgia in retrospect. The reality was often less pleasurable—scratched fingers, stained deep purple with blackberry juice— but it was always worth it for the wonderful jams and tarts that resulted.

Blackberries are a bit low in pectin, so the apples help the jam to set as well as adding valuable extra flavor.

Wash, peel and core the apples. Stew them until soft with 1¼ cups water in a stainless steel saucepan; beat to a pulp.

Pick over the blackberries and cook until soft, adding about ²/3 cup water if the berries are a little dry. It is a good idea to push them through a coarse sieve to remove the seeds.

Warm the sugar. Put the blackberries into a wide stainless steel saucepan or preserving pan, together with the apple pulp and the heated sugar. Stir over a gentle heat until the sugar is dissolved.

Boil steadily for about 15 minutes. Skim the jam and test for a set by dropping a little on to a cold plate and pushing it with your finger. The surface should wrinkle when it is ready. Pour into warm sterilized jars, cover and seal.

Elderberry & Crab Apple Jelly and Blackberry & Apple Jam

Wild Food from the Seashore

'Poor people need never be hungry when you have the strand.' Bridget Guerin, who lives in Ballyheighue, Co. Kerry, recalls how they picked *bairneachs* (limpets), winkles, and seaweeds, such as dilisk, *sliúhāne* and carrigeen off the seashore and sold them. Enterprising and hardworking people all around the coast of Ireland collected what they could to feed themselves and to supplement what was often a meager income. They well knew the value of seafood and seaweeds in the diet, and the practice of chewing seaweeds is still very strong on the western and northern seaboard. Indeed there is currently a mini seaweed revival, now that the healthy properties of the seaweed that flourishes in Ireland's clean waters are being recognized abroad.

Sloke or Sliúhāne
Porphyra laciniata

Sliúhāne is a short, thin ribbon seaweed that only grows on sloping rock flag—hence the name sliú meaning slant. The flags are washed daily by the tide which makes them very slippery so the picking of sliúhāne is highly dangerous. Sliúhāne has a very short growing season from January to early March and old people say that it is best gathered after a spell of frost. This traditional recipe for sliúhāne *is supplied by John Francis Guerin of Ballyheigue, Co. Kerry. He tells me that* sliúhāne *is reputed to be an aphrodisiac! It is certainly a particularly delicious seaweed.*

Cut the *sliúhán*e into small pieces with a scissors. Place in a saucepan with water and boil slowly for one hour. Then pound or knead the *sliúhāne*, using a specially prepared stick with a pared, tapered end, until the whole lot becomes semi-liquid. Boil slowly for a further hour and thicken to taste by adding more water. Finally add a knob of butter and some pepper. Eat on its own or with fish, ham or roast lamb.

Samphire

Also known as Peter's cress or rock samphire (Crithmum maritimum)*, this fleshy-leaved plant with small yellow flowers grows wild on salt marshes in many places around the coast of Ireland and is still there free for the picking. A few years ago a group of us scrambled excitedly down the steep rocky slope to Goat Island near Ardmore in Co. Cork, where rock samphire grew in abundance. Patricia Cockburn showed us how to cook the samphire, which we ate with a succulent salmon in cream.*

A different species called marsh samphire (Salicornia europaea) *can be found around Carlingford Lough. It is cooked in the same way. To eat it, hold it by the stem end and pull through your teeth to separate the flesh from the stem inside. Marsh samphire is now much sought after and creative young chefs are putting it onto their menus.*

samphire
water
butter

Cover the samphire with cold water, bring to a boil and simmer for about 15 to 20 minutes until tender. Drain off the water, season with freshly ground pepper and toss in lots of butter, no salt will be needed because samphire has a natural salty tang.

Pickled Samphire

Anne Kennedy from Rostrevor in Co. Down sent me this recipe.

Gather the samphire and soak for 3 hours in brine. Place in a pan, cover with a mixture of a little salt and 3 parts of white wine vinegar to 1 part of water. Cover and simmer for 30 minutes. Allow to cool and pack into jars. Carefully cover with liquid mixed with a little fresh vinegar. The samphire should remain a good green color.

Carrigeen Moss

Carrigeen moss is a seaweed which can be gathered off the south and west coasts of Ireland. It is rich in iodine and trace elements, and is also full of natural gelatine. *Carraigín* means 'little rock' in Gaelic.

Myrtle Allen writes in *The Ballymaloe Cookbook:*

> Ballyandreen is a tiny fishing village by a rocky inlet four miles south of Ballymaloe. For generations the inhabitants there have gathered and sold Carrigeen Moss. It is picked from the farthest out rocks at low water during spring tides in June. This means that it is almost always covered by sea water. It is then laid out on the short grass on the cliff top to dry and bleach in the sun. It has the reputation of being a health giving food. It is a source of agar jelly. It certainly contains iron and minerals. Traditionally, it was fed to calves and made into cough syrups and milk puddings. I have used it all my life. I have thickened milk for babies with it at weaning time. For more sophisticated meals I serve it topped with whipped cream and coffee sauce strongly laced with whiskey.

Chocolate carrigeen has nostalgic memories for me. I first encountered it at Sunday night supper in this house, long ago, when it was still clad in its Victorian décor and life was very different.

A product that is hard to measure, however, is hard to market. This is so with carrigeen moss. The success of this dish lies in using only just enough carrigeen needed to get a set—so that you don't taste it in the pudding, as a less than enthusiastic friend pointed out!

Carrigeen sometimes comes mixed with grass and other seaweeds; these should be carefully removed before use.

Carrigeen Moss Pudding

Serves 4 to 6

¼oz cleaned, well dried carrigeen moss (1 semi-closed fistful)
3¾ cups milk
½ teaspoon pure vanilla extract or a vanilla pod
1 egg, preferably free-range
1 tablespoon superfine granulated sugar

Soak the carrigeen in tepid water for 10 minutes. Strain off the water and put the carrigeen into a saucepan with the milk and vanilla pod, if used. Bring to a boil and simmer very gently with the lid on for 20 minutes. At that point, and not before, separate the egg and put the yolk into a bowl. Add the sugar and vanilla extract (if you are using it) and beat together for a few seconds, then pour the milk and carrigeen moss through a strainer on to the egg yolk mixture, beating all the time. The carrigeen will now be swollen and exuding jelly. Rub all this jelly through the strainer and beat it into the liquid. Test for a set in a saucer. Put it in the fridge—it should set in a couple of minutes. Rub a little more through the strainer if necessary. Beat the egg white stiffly and fold it in gently; it will rise to make a fluffy top. Leave to cool.

Serve chilled with soft brown sugar and cream, or with a fruit compote e.g. poached rhubarb.

Dulse

Rhodymenia palmata

This winey-brown seaweed—also called dillisk, dilisk, dillesk and *dílís*—is found all around the Irish coast, particularly on the western seaboard. It is mentioned in the eighth century Brehon Laws, which describe a penalty for consuming another person's dulse without their permission. It is picked on the rocks at low tide and spread out on a tin roof or on the grass or shingle to dry in the sun. Once sold at fairs and markets all over the country, it is now found in shops close to the coast. Many people told me of sending little parcels of it to relatives who had emigrated and retained a craving for it. Dulse can be eaten raw or added to fish soups or stews. It was also mixed with potatoes for dulse champ (see page 144).

Dulse and yellowman (a homemade crunchy toffee) were and still are sold at stalls at the famous Ould Lammas Fair in Ballycastle, Co. Antrim, held on the last Tuesday of August every year.

> At the auld Lammas Fair, were you ever there?
> Were you ever at the fair of Ballycastle, oh?
> Did you treat your Mary Anne to dulce and 'yallaman'?
> At the auld Lammas Fair of Ballycastle, oh?

Pepper dulse *(Laurencia pinnatifida)* was also eaten on the Blaskets and Bere Island.

Shell Dilisk

Shell dilisk has a distinctive little mussel shell attached to the base. John Francis Guerin showed me how to identify the shell dilisk on the rocky Kerry coast. After the dilisk is picked, it should be spread out on the grass or on a flat tin roof to dry for a few days. Then store and chew a little whenever the fancy takes you.

Dilisk Sandwiches

In Co. Antrim an old man told me about dilisk sandwiches. Simply put a good layer of dilisk between two slices of buttered bread—for a nutritious and delicious snack.

Florence Irwin includes a Portaferry recipe which is one hundred years old at least for stewed dulse in her 1937 publication *Irish Country Recipes*.

Carrigeen Moss Pudding

Desserts

Most traditional Irish desserts are based on the fruits readily available in the garden or orchard, or on those found in the wild. Fruit pies, tarts and crumbles, or simple stewed fruit, would have been prepared over the open fire, in the bastible, or, more recently, in the oven. The recipes vary slightly from one household to another, and would have been passed down orally in the farmhouses across the country. My own mother taught me many of the recipes I still use; she would vary the fillings according to the season, from rhubarb to green gooseberries, blackberries and apple.

Wild raspberries and strawberries have grown in Ireland since early times. In our garden there rarely seemed to be enough fruit for us children to have a real feast – all I remember was our gardener, Pad, chasing us any time he spied us in the strawberry patch. Poor Pad – there were nine of us! Fortunately for us he had a bad leg and we were all pretty agile. Not surprisingly, there never seemed to be a lot of fruit for the kitchen, and when the berries actually made it to the table it was often in the form of a delicious fruit fluff.

Steamed suet puddings are another great Irish tradition. They are the best kind of comfort food. By contrast, I have also included here some more elegant dishes from the great country house tradition, which we still serve at Ballymaloe. What they have in common is their use of the fruits and dairy products for which Ireland is justly famous.

Apple Dumpling

Serves 6 to 8

A Dublin taxi driver once told me about an apple dumpling that his mother used to make. The apples were peeled and put into the saucepan with some sugar, then a cake or scone mixture was put on top. The pot was covered, put directly on to the heat and cooked on top of the stove until the apples were soft and fluffy and the topping had cooked in the steam. It was a wonderful way of producing a delicious apple dessert in homes that had no oven.

3lb apples
1¼ cups sugar
⅔ cup water
2 or 3 cloves, optional

Topping
8 tablespoons (1 stick) butter
⅔ cup superfine granulated sugar
2 eggs, free-range if possible
1½ cups flour
⅔ teaspoon baking powder

Peel and core the apples and cut into chunks. Put the apple pieces into a deep saucepan (we use a 9 x 4 inch stainless steel saucepan). Add the sugar and water and cloves, if you wish.

Cream the butter until really soft. Add the superfine sugar and beat until white and creamy, using a wooden spoon. Beat the eggs and gradually add to the creamed butter and sugar. Beat well. If preferred the eggs may be broken and beaten into the mixture one at a time. A little sieved flour may be added between each addition of egg. Fold in the remainder of the flour, adding a little water or milk if necessary, to make to a dropping consistency. Add the baking powder mixed with the last addition of flour.

Spread the cake mixture as evenly as possible over the top of the apples. Put the lid on the saucepan and cook over a medium heat for 15 minutes then reduce the heat to the minimum for a further 15 to 20 minutes, by which time the apples should be soft and juicy and the topping cooked in the steam. Serve with soft brown sugar and cream or custard.

Apple Fritters

Serves 6 to 8

Food memories are so evocative! Apple fritters were another delight, every bit as delicious today as they were when we all stood round as Mummy cooked them, excitedly guessing what each one looked like. The little wisps of batter at the edges cooked into legs, tails, ears and horns as we let our imagination run riot.

1lb cooking or eating apples

Batter
1 cup flour
pinch of salt
1 egg, free-range if possible
⅔ cup milk

good quality oil for frying
superfine granulated sugar

To make the batter, sieve the flour and salt into a bowl. Make a well in the center and drop in the egg. Use a whisk to bring in the flour gradually from the edges, slowly adding in the milk at the same time. Leave the batter in a cool place for about an hour. Heat the oil in a deep fryer to 350°F.

Peel and core the apples with an apple corer. Cut into rings not more than ½ inch thick. Hold each ring on a skewer to dip into the batter then lift out with a skewer and allow any surplus batter to drain off. Drop the rings straight into the hot fat. Don't put too many fritters into the fat at the same time. Fry until golden brown. Drain well on paper towels and sprinkle with sugar. Serve immediately with softly whipped cream.

Note: *the fritters can be shallow-fried in a pan if more convenient.*

Stewed Apples
with Cream or Custard

Serves 4 to 6

2lb cooking apples
⅔ cup sugar
2 tablespoons water

Peel and core the apples, cut into quarters and put into a castiron or stainless steel saucepan. Add the sugar and water, cover and cook on a gentle heat until the apples break down into a fluff. Stir, pour into a serving bowl and allow to cool. Serve with softly whipped cream or custard.

Patrons of my family's pub, the Sportsman Inn in Cullohill, Co. Laois, will be familiar with this apple tart. The pastry is made by the creaming method, so people who suffer from 'hot hands' don't have to worry about rubbing in the butter.

Preheat the oven to 350°F.

First make the pastry. Cream the butter and sugar together by hand or in a electric mixer. Add the eggs and beat for several minutes. Reduce speed and mix in the flour. This pastry needs to be chilled for at least 1 hour otherwise it is difficult to handle.

To make the pie, first roll out the pastry to about ⅛ inch thick and use about two-thirds of it to line a loaf pan, 7 x 12 x 1 inches in depth. Peel, quarter and slice the apples into the tart. Sprinkle with sugar and add the cloves. Cover with a top crust made of the remaining pastry, seal the edges and decorate with pastry leaves. Brush with egg wash and bake in the oven until the apples are tender, about 45 minutes to 1 hour. When cooked cut into squares, sprinkle lightly with superfine granulated sugar and serve with softly whipped cream and dark brown sugar.

Serves 8 to 12

Cullohill Apple Pie

Pastry
16 tablespoons (2 sticks) butter
⅓ cup superfine granulated sugar
2 eggs, free-range if possible
3 cups white flour, preferably unbleached

Filling
1½lb Bramley Seedling cooking apples
¾ cup sugar
2 or 3 cloves

egg wash
superfine granulated sugar for sprinkling

To serve
softly whipped cream
dark brown sugar

The most delicious apple tart with a 'built in' custard topping.

Preheat the oven to 350°F.

First make the shortcrust pastry and set aside. Cream the butter and sugar together by hand or in a food mixer. Add the eggs and beat for several minutes. Reduce the speed and mix in the flour. This pastry needs to be chilled for at least 1 hour, otherwise it is difficult to handle.

Peel and core the apples and chop into chunks. Put into a 3¾ cup pie dish. Add sugar and perhaps a clove a two.

Roll the pastry into a sheet ⅛ inch thick and cut several strips to fit on to the lip of a 3¾ cup pie dish. Brush the tip of the dish with cold water and press the strips of pastry firmly on. Brush the pastry strips with cold water and then press the pastry lid firmly down onto the edges. Trim off the excess pastry. Flute the edges and scallop with the back of a knife. Brush the pie with beaten egg. Cut some pastry leaves from the excess pastry and use to decorate the pie. Cut a hole in the center. Brush with egg again.

Bake in a preheated oven at 350°F for 30 minutes until the apple is almost cooked (test with a skewer). Beat the egg and sugar together, then mix in the cream and vanilla extract. Open up the hole in the center of the pie if necessary and pour in the custard from a jug. Put the pie back into the oven for a further 25 to 30 minutes or until the custard has set. Sprinkle the pastry with a little sugar and serve.

Serves 4

Apple Custard Pie

2lb apples
⅔ cup sugar
2 or 3 cloves (optional)

Shortcrust Pastry
8 tablespoons (1 stick) butter
2 tablespoons superfine granulated sugar
1 egg, free-range if possible
1⅓ cups flour

beaten egg to glaze

Custard
1 large egg, free-range if possible
1 tablespoon sugar
⅔ cup cream
½ teaspoon vanilla extract

Serves 6 to 8

Apple Crumble

1¹/₂lb apples, peeled, cored and chopped
¹/₄ cup to ¹/₃ cup sugar
1 to 2 tablespoons water

Crumble
4 tablespoons butter
³/₄ cup flour
¹/₃ cup superfine granulated sugar
¹/₂ cup rolled oats

Another simple pudding that finds favor all over the country.

Stew the apples gently with the sugar and water in a covered casserole or stainless steel saucepan for 5 to 10 minutes until about half cooked.

Taste and add more sugar if necessary. Turn into a 5 cup pie dish. Allow to cool slightly while you make the crumble.

Rub the butter into the flour just until the mixture resembles coarse breadcrumbs, then mix in the sugar and oats. Sprinkle this mixture over the apple in the pie dish. Bake in a preheated moderate oven at 350°F, for 30 to 45 minutes or until the topping is cooked and golden. Serve with whipped cream and soft brown sugar.

Serves 6

Apple Snow

1lb cooking apples
1 to 2 tablespoons water
¹/₃ cup approx. sugar
2 egg whites

Peel and core the apples, cut into chunks and put into a saucepan. Add the sugar and water, cover and cook on a gentle heat, stirring every now and then until the apples dissolve into a fluff. Rub through a nylon sieve or liquidize. If the apples seem very sour, add a little more sugar.

Beat the egg whites until stiff then fold in gently. Pour into a glass bowl, put in the refrigerator and serve chilled with cream and soft brown sugar.

Serves 4 to 6

Apple Soufflé

2lb approx. large cooking apples
²/₃ cup sugar
1 egg

This recipe comes from Anne Kennedy in Rostrevor, Co. Down.

Preheat the oven to 425°F.

Peel, core and slice the apples and cook in a covered saucepan on a low heat with the sugar and about 2 tablespoons of water until tender. When the apples dissolve into a fluff, beat into a purée with a wooden spoon. Separate the egg and beat the yolk into the apple purée. Whisk the egg white until light and fluffy and fold into the apple. Pour into a buttered soufflé dish and bake in the preheated oven for 15 to 18 minutes. Serve immediately with softly whipped cream and dark brown sugar.

Serves 4

Roast Apples

4 large cooking apples
5 tablespoons sugar
butter
a little water

Nowadays roast or baked apples are often stuffed with 'exciting' mixtures which may include dried fruit, lemon rind, nuts and spices. While this is nice occasionally, my favorite is still the simple roast apple of my childhood, so beloved of my grandfather.

Core the apples and score the skin of each around the 'equator'. Put the apples onto an ovenproof dish large enough to take them in a single layer without touching. Fill the center of each apple with sugar and put a little dab of butter on top of each one.

Pour a little water around and roast in a preheated moderate oven 350°F for about 1 hour, depending on size. They should be fluffy and burst slightly, but still fat and puffy, not collapsed. Serve immediately with softly whipped cream and soft brown sugar.

Apple cakes like this one are the traditional dessert in Ireland. The recipe varies from house to house and the individual technique has been passed from mother to daughter in farmhouses all over the country for generations. It would originally have been baked in a bastible or pot beside an open fire and later in the oven or stove on tin or enamel plates. These are much better than ovenproof glass because the heat travels through and cooks the pastry base more readily—worth remembering, as a pie with a soggy base is not attractive! In Ireland all apple cakes are made with cooking apples.

Serves 6 (approximately)

Irish Apple Cake

Sieve the flour and baking powder into a bowl. Rub in the butter with your fingertips until it resembles the texture of breadcrumbs. Add ¹/₂ cup sugar, then make a well in the center and mix together with the beaten egg and enough milk to form a soft dough. Divide in two. Put one half on to a greased ovenproof plate (9 inches in diameter) and pat it out to cover. Peel, core and chop up the apples. Place them on the dough with the cloves, if used, and add the remaining sugar, depending on the sweetness of the apples. Roll out the remaining pastry and fit it on top. (This is easier said than done as this 'pastry' is very soft like scone dough. You may need to do a bit of patchwork if it breaks.) Press the sides together and cut a slit through the top crust. Brush with beaten egg wash and bake in a moderate oven at 350°F for about 40 minutes, or until cooked through and nicely browned. Dredge with superfine sugar and serve warm with dark brown sugar and softly whipped cream.

2 cups flour
¹/₃ teaspoon baking powder
8 tablespoons (1 stick) butter
²/₃ cup superfine granulated sugar
1 egg, free-range if possible, beaten
¹/₂ to ²/₃ cup milk, approx.
1 to 2 cooking apples
2 or 3 cloves (optional)
beaten egg to glaze

Blackberry & Apple Pie

1lb approx. puff pastry (see opposite)
3 to 4 cooking apples
1 cup blackberries
³/4 to 1 cup sugar (depending
on the sweetness of the apples)
3 or 4 cloves
beaten egg to glaze
superfine sugar

Blackberries and apples were referred to in glowing terms in the Irish medieval Fionn Mac Cumhaill legends. 'Beautiful golden yellow apples' and 'beautiful blackberries' are frequently mentioned in the twelfth century Fianna text Agallamh na Seanórach *(The Colloquy of the Ancients). It's nice to think of all those brave warriors feasting on blackberries and getting scratched on the brambles just as we do nowadays when we go blackberry picking!*

Roll out half the pastry and line a 10 inch Pyrex plate. Trim the excess pastry, but leave about ³/4 inch overlapping the edge. Peel and quarter the apples, cut out the cores and cut the quarters in half (the pieces of apple should be quite chunky). Put the apples on to the pastry and pile them up in the center. Put the blackberries on top, leaving a border of 1 inch around the edge. Sprinkle with sugar, then add the cloves to taste.

Roll out the remainder of the pastry, a little thicker than the base. Wet the 1 inch strip around the bottom crust and press the pastry lid down on to it. Trim the pastry, again leaving a ¼ inch edge. Crimp up the edges with a knife and then scallop them. Make a hole in the center to allow steam to escape. Brush with beaten egg. Roll out the pastry trimmings and cut into leaves to decorate the top of the tart. Brush with egg wash.

Bake in a hot oven at 475°F for 15 to 20 minutes, then turn the heat to moderate for a further 40 to 45 minutes, depending on how hard the apples are. Test the apples to see if they are cooked by inserting a skewer through the hole.

Sprinkle with sugar and serve hot with soft brown sugar and softly whipped cream.

Damson Tart

Substitute 1½lb damsons (do not remove stones) for the apple and blackberries. You may need more sugar, depending how ripe they are.

Worcesterberry Tart

We first discovered worcesterberries in an old lady's garden when she replied to our advertisement in the local paper for *fraughans* (see page 183). She assured us that she had an abundance of them growing at the end of her garden, but they turned out to be quite a different fruit. These are, in fact, an old-fashioned species of black gooseberry. We used them for this tart and found them absolutely delicious.

Rhubarb Tart

Make in exactly the same way, but use about 1lb of finely chopped red rhubarb and 1 cup sugar.

Other Suitable Fillings:
Rhubarb and Strawberry
Apple and Mincemeat
Apple and Raspberry
Apple and Mixed Spice
Apple, Golden Raisins and Cinnamon
Green Gooseberry and Elderflower
Worcesterberry
Plum
Damson

Makes about 2lb 10oz

Puff Pastry

Homemade puff pastry takes a little time to make, but it is more than worth the effort for the wonderful flavor which bears no relation to the commercial equivalent. It is essential to use butter.

1lb chilled flour (use strong or bread flour if possible)
pinch of salt
1¼ to 1½ cups cold water
squeeze of lemon juice
4 sticks butter, firm but pliable

Sieve the flour and salt into a bowl and mix to a firm dough (called detempre) with water and a squeeze of lemon juice. Cover with wax paper or plastic wrap and rest for 30 minutes in the refrigerator.

Roll the chilled dough into a square about ½ inch thick. If the butter is very hard, beat it (still in the wrapper) with a rolling pin until pliable but not sticky. Unwrap the butter and shape into a slab roughly about ⅛ inch thick. Place this in the center of the dough and fold the dough over the edges of the butter to make a neat parcel. Make sure your chilled marble slab or pastry board is well floured, then flatten the dough with a rolling pin, and roll it out into a rectangle about 18 inches long and 6½ inches wide (this is approximate, so don't worry if it's not exactly that measurement). Fold neatly into three, with the sides as accurately aligned as possible. Seal the edges with a rolling pin.

Give the dough a one-quarter turn (90°): it should now be on your pastry bench as though it was a book with the open ends facing north/south. Roll out again, fold in three and seal the edges with the rolling pin. cover with plastic wrap or wax paper and rest in the fridge for 30 minutes. The pastry has now had two rolls or 'turns'. Repeat the rolling process another two times, giving the dough six rolls altogether, with a 30-minute rest in the fridge between every two turns.

Chill for at least 30 minutes before using.

Note: *each time you start to roll the pastry, place it on the worktop with the open ends north/south as if it were a book. In hot weather it may be necessary to chill the pastry slightly longer between rollings.*

Roscommon Rhubarb Pie

Serves 8

Country Rhubarb Cake

2¹/2 cups flour
a pinch of salt
³/4 teaspoon baking soda
¹/4 cup superfine sugar
6 tablespoons butter
1 egg, free-range if possible
²/3 cup milk, buttermilk
or sour milk
1 to 2lb rhubarb, finely chopped
1 to 1¹/4 cups granulated sugar
beaten egg to glaze
superfine sugar for sprinkling

This delicious juicy rhubarb cake, based on an enriched bread dough, was made all over the country. Originally it would have been baked in the bastible or baking oven beside an open fire. My mother, who taught me this recipe, varied the filling with the seasons. First there was rhubarb, followed in May by green gooseberries. Eventually we had the first of the cooking apples in Grandad's garden, then if we were lucky Victoria plums from a neighbor's walled garden, and finally blackberries and apple in the autumn.

Preheat the oven to 350°F.

Sieve the flour, salt, baking soda and superfine granulated sugar into a bowl and rub in the butter. Whisk the egg and mix with the milk or buttermilk. Make a well in the center of the dry ingredients. Pour in most of the liquid and mix to soft dough; add the remainder of the liquid if necessary.

Sprinkle a little flour on the work surface. Turn out the dough and pat gently into a round. Divide into two pieces: one should be slightly larger than the other; keep the larger one for the top crust.

Dip your fingers in flour. Spread the smaller piece of pastry on to a 10-inch enamel or Pyrex pie plate. Scatter the finely chopped rhubarb all over the base, sprinkle the rhubarb with sugar. Brush the edges of the pastry with beaten egg. Roll out the other piece of dough until it is exactly the size to cover the plate, lift it on and press the edges gently to seal them. Make a hole in the center for the steam to escape. Brush again with beaten egg and sprinkle with a very small amount of superfine granulated sugar.

Bake in the oven for 45 minutes to 1 hour or until the rhubarb is soft and the crust is golden. Leave it to sit for 15 to 20 minutes so that the juice can soak into the crust. Sprinkle with superfine sugar. Serve still warm, with a bowl of softly whipped cream and some moist, brown sugar.

This is a perfect example of the way in which recipes originally cooked on an open fire can be adapted to produce the most delicious results today. Anna Dodd of Castlebaldwin in Co. Sligo, who gave it to me, remembers how her grandmother would strew the bastible with chopped rhubarb, sweeten it with a sprinkling of sugar and cover it with an enriched bread dough. When the cake was baked, it was turned out so that it landed upside down, with the sweet juice soaking into the soft, golden crust. It was served warm, with soft brown sugar and lots of softly whipped cream. It is certainly one of the most delectable traditional recipes I have come across while researching this book, and has already become a firm favorite.

You will need a 9 x 2 inch round pan. We use a heavy stainless steel baking pan which works very well.

Preheat the oven to 450°F.

Trim the rhubarb, wipe with a damp cloth and cut into pieces about 1 inch in length. Put into the base of a pan and sprinkle with the sugar.

Sieve all the dry ingredients for the scone dough into a bowl. Cut the butter into cubes and rub into the flour until the mixture resembles coarse breadcrumbs. Beat the egg with the milk. Make a well in the center of the dry ingredients, pour in the liquid all at once and mix to a soft dough. Turn out on to a floured board and roll into a 9 inch round, about 1 inch thick. Place this round on top of the rhubarb and tuck in the edges neatly. Brush with a little beaten egg and sprinkle generously with sugar.

Bake in the fully preheated oven for 15 minutes then reduce the temperature to 350°F for about a further 30 minutes, or until the top is crusty and golden and the rhubarb soft and juicy.

Remove the pan from the oven and allow to sit for a few minutes. Put a warm plate over the top of the pan and turn it upside down so that the pie comes out on to the plate. Be careful of the hot juices.

Serve warm with soft brown sugar and cream.

Note: this recipe may also be made with cooking apples, in which case Anna Dodd suggests adding a little cinnamon or mixed spice to the sugar.

Serves 8-10

Roscommon Rhubarb Pie

2lb red rhubarb
1¹/3 to 1¹/2 cups granulated sugar

Scone Dough
2¹/4 cups flour
1¹/2 tablespoons superfine
    granulated sugar
2 teaspoons baking powder
pinch of salt
4 tablespoons butter
1 egg
about ³/4 cup full cream milk

beaten egg
granulated sugar

Rhubarb Fool

Put the rhubarb into a stainless steel saucepan with the sugar and water. Stir, cover, bring to a boil and simmer until soft, about 20 minutes. Stir with a wooden spoon until the rhubarb dissolves into a mush. Allow the mixture to get quite cold, then fold in the softly whipped cream. Serve chilled, with shortbread (see page 258).

1lb red rhubarb, cut into chunks
1¹/4 cups sugar
2 tablespoons water
1¹/4 cups cream, whipped

Blackcurrant Fool

Serves 8

12oz blackcurrants, strings removed
whipped cream

Stock Syrup
^{1}/$_3$ cup sugar
^{1}/$_3$ cup water

Leftover stewed blackcurrants will make a delicious fruit fool. Years ago stiffly whipped cream was folded straight into the crushed blackcurrants, but nowadays they should be puréed and sieved first.

Cover the blackcurrants with stock syrup. Bring to the boil and cook until the fruit bursts—this will take about 4 to 5 minutes. Liquidize in a blender and sieve the stewed fruit and measure how much purée there is. When the purée has cooled, swirl in up to an equal quantity of softly whipped cream, according to taste. Serve with thin shortbread (see page 258).

Gooseberry & Elderflower Fool

Serves about 6

1lb green gooseberries
stock syrup (see above)
2 elderflower heads, tied in muslin
whipped cream

Tart green gooseberries picked in May make the best gooseberry fool.

Poach the gooseberries with the elderflowers as above, until the fruit bursts—about 5 to 6 minutes. Remove the elderflower heads. Liquidize in a blender or purée the fruit and measure the amount. When the purée has cooled, add up to an equal volume of softly whipped cream, according to taste.

A little stiffly beaten egg white may be added to lighten the fool. The fool should not be very stiff, more the texture of softly whipped cream. If it is too stiff, stir in a little milk rather than more cream. Pour into a glass serving dish and serve with cookies.

Gooseberry & Elderflower Compôte

Serves 6 to 8

2lb green gooseberries
2 or 3 elderflower heads
2^1/$_2$ cups sugar
2^1/$_2$ cups cold water

'Gooseberries, currants and cherries for children, gingerbread for grown girls, strong beer and maddening whiskey for wranglers and busybodies,' wrote Amhlaoibh Uí Shúilleabháin of the fare at a Pattern Day (a kind of fair) held near Callan in Co. Kilkenny in 1829.

Elder bushes, which grow freely in the hedges all around Ireland, produce a mass of blooms in May and early June. They smell strangely musty, but have the most magical muscat flavour when cooked with green gooseberries.

First trim both ends of the gooseberries. Tie the elderflower heads in a little square of muslin and put in a stainless steel or enameled saucepan. Add the sugar and cover with cold water. Bring slowly to a boil and continue to boil for 2 minutes. Add the gooseberries and simmer just until the fruit bursts, for approximatley 5 or 6 minutes. Allow to get cold. Serve in a pretty bowl and decorate with fresh elderflowers.

Everyone seems to become wistful when you mention summer pudding. Bursting with soft fruit, served with lots of softly whipped cream, it's one of the very best puddings of summer. At Ballymaloe, summer pudding was, and still is, made with cake. We traditionally use blackcurrants, but you could use a mixture of summer fruits flavored with sweet geranium leaves. Cook the blackcurrants and redcurrants until they burst and then add the soft fruit. Remember to pour the syrup and fruit into the sponge-lined bowl while still boiling hot, otherwise the syrup won't soak through the sponge properly.

First make the sponge cake.

Cut each sponge round in half, horizontally. Line a 8 cup bowl with the cake, crusty side inwards. It doesn't matter if it looks like patchwork as it will blend later.

Dissolve the sugar in the water and boil for 2 minutes. Add the blackcurrants and boil until they burst—about 3 or 4 minutes. Immediately, ladle some of the hot liquid and fruit into the sponge-lined bowl. When it is about half full, if you have scraps of cake put them in the center. Then fill to the top with fruit. Cover with a layer of sponge.

Put the bowl into a dish with sides. Put a plate on top of the bowl and press down with a heavy weight. Allow to get cold. If some of the juices escape, they will gather together in the dish and can be served spooned over the pudding as a delicious sauce.

Store the pudding in the refrigerator for a minimum of 24 hours before serving. It will keep for 4 or 5 days.

To serve, unmold the pudding onto a deep serving dish. Serve with any leftover fruit and syrup around it, and lots of softly whipped cream.

Serves 8

Blackcurrant Summer Pudding

2lb blackcurrants
3¹/4 cups granulated sugar
3¹/4 cups water
1 sponge cake (see recipe for Great-Grandmother's Sponge Cake, page 257)

This very simple dessert uses two of Ireland's most delicious fruits.

Crush the berries roughly, sprinkle with superfine sugar and fold in the softly whipped cream.

Serves 6

Strawberry or Raspberry Fluff

1lb strawberries or raspberries
superfine granulated sugar
whipped cream

After apple or rhubarb tarts, stewed fruit served with custard was, and perhaps still is, the most common family dessert. It varies with the seasons and the fruit available. Apple and rhubarb are top of the list, but in the old days anyone fortunate enough to have a kitchen garden, as we had at home, would also have stewed gooseberries and blackcurrants during their short summer season.

Stewed Seasonal Fruit

Almond Rock

This recipe comes from the beautifully written receipt book of Mrs Dot Drew, Mocollop Castle, Ballyduff, Co. Waterford, dated 1801:

> A lb of butter just fresh from the churn, beat to a cream, mix with it a lb of almonds well pounded add ½lb of sugar finely pounded when well mixed heap it up high on a dish, stick with almonds and citron and oranges mix a little sugar and lemon juice in a pint of cream, whip it up put it between the rows of sweetmeats and round the dish. Half this quantity will make a side dish.

Fluffy Lemon Pudding

Serves 4 to 6

This is an old-fashioned family dessert which separates into two quite distinct layers when it cooks; it has a fluffy top and a creamy lemon base. If the lemons are very pale, use the zest of 1½ or 2 to give a sharper lemon flavor.

2 tablespoons butter
¾ cup superfine granulated sugar
1 or 2 lemons
2 eggs, free-range if possible
½ cup flour
1¼ cups milk

Decoration
confectioners' sugar

Cream the butter well. Add the sugar and beat well. Grate the rind of the lemon and squeeze and strain its juice. Separate the eggs and add the yolks one by one, then stir in the flour and gradually add the finely grated rind and juice of the lemon (or lemons). Lastly add the milk. Whisk the egg whites stiffly in a bowl and fold gently into the lemon mixture. Pour into a 2½ cup pie dish and bake in a moderate oven at 350°F, for about 40 minutes. Dredge with confectioners' sugar and serve immediately with softly whipped cream.

Burnt Cream

Serves about 6

This delicious recipe also comes from the receipt book of Mrs Dot Drew of Mocollop Castle near Ballyduff in Co. Waterford. It was lent to me by Diana Sandles.

> To one quart of Cream, beat up the yolks of Eight Eggs a little Flour and some Sugar, put it over a fire with a little lemon or orange Peel and some Cinnamon, keep it stirring 'till it boils, then take it up and let it cool take out the cinnamon and peel and let it be put in the dish you intend to serve it up on grate a good deal of Sugar on it and brown it with a Salamander.

We tried this version and found it quite delicious.

2½ cups heavy cream
rind of ½ or 1 lemon or orange, cut in strips
1½ inch piece of cinnamon bark
4 egg yolks
4 tablespoons sugar
2 teaspoons flour
superfine granulated sugar to glaze

Put the cream, lemon or orange rind and cinnamon into a saucepan and bring slowly almost to boiling point. Turn off the heat and allow to infuse for 15 minutes.

Meanwhile beat the egg yolks with the sugar and stir in the flour. Beat in the cream and return this mixture to the saucepan. Bring back to a boil, stirring all the time (beat occasionally if necessary). Pour immediately into a serving dish. Cool, cover and chill well.

Several hours later or next day, sprinkle the top with a layer of superfine granulated sugar and caramelize under a hot grill (or cheat and use a blow torch!).

Serve as soon as the sheet of caramel solidifies.

Suet and steamed puddings were great winter favorites throughout the country. My mother made three or four different kinds which we adored as children. She had got the recipes from her mother, who had cooked the same puddings for her.

Steamed Puddings

For almost a week during the cold January days the whole house smells of marmalade as we lay down our store for the coming year. My father-in-law looks forward every year to the final day when the last of the oranges have been turned into marmalade, because by tradition on that day there is marmalade pudding for lunch. This recipe was given to me by Myrtle Allen.

Mix the flour, suet, breadcrumbs, sugar and baking powder together. Add the beaten eggs, marmalade and a little milk to moisten if necessary (the mixture should have the consistency of plum pudding). Spoon into lightly greased 7-inch earthenware pudding bowls and cover with a double sheet of wax paper with a pleat in the center. Tie the paper firmly with string under the lip of the bowl. Place each bowl in a saucepan of boiling water. Cover and cook for 2 to 3 hours, topping up the water in the pan from time to time to make sure that it does not boil dry.

To make the sauce, put the water and marmalade into a saucepan. Warm them together for 15 minutes and then bring slowly to the boil. Continue to boil for 5 minutes. Add a few drops of lemon juice and sugar to taste.

When the puddings are cooked, turn them out onto warm serving dishes and pour the sauce around them.

Serves 10 to 12

Marmalade Pudding

3¹/4 cups flour
1 lb chopped beef suet
4 cups breadcrumbs
2¹/2 cups sugar
5 teaspoons baking powder
4 eggs, free-range if possible
10 tablespoons homemade marmalade
milk

Sauce
8 oz marmalade
2 tablespoons water
a few drops of lemon juice
sugar (optional)

Cream the butter, add the sugar and beat until white and creamy. Beat the eggs with the vanilla extract and beat, a little at a time, into the creamed mixture. Stir in the flour and baking powder and add a little milk or water if necessary to make a dropping consistency.

Grease a 5 inch earthenware pudding bowl. Spread raspberry jam over the bottom and sides. Carefully spoon the cake mixture into the bowl. Cover with pleated wax paper, tied on firmly, and steam the pudding for about 1¹/2 hours.

Meanwhile make the raspberry jam sauce. Heat the jam with the water, add the lemon rind and juice and a little extra sugar if necessary.

Turn the pudding on to a hot dish and serve with the sauce.

Serves 4

Jam Pudding

8 tablespoons butter, at room temperature
²/3 cup superfine granulated sugar
2 eggs, free-range if possible
few drops of pure vanilla extract
1¹/2 cups flour
²/3 teaspoon baking powder
about 1 tablespoon milk or water
4 or 5 tablespoons homemade raspberry jam
(see page 265)

Raspberry Jam Sauce
6 to 8 tablespoons homemade raspberry jam
rind and juice of half a lemon
²/3 cup water
sugar (optional)

Serves about 6

Currant & Apple Roly-Poly

8oz apples
1/3 cup currants
1/3 cup sugar
nutmeg or mixed spice
2oz suet
1 1/2 cups flour
pinch of salt
1/2 teaspoon baking powder
cold water

These seriously filling puddings were a great favorite in years gone by, before all the anxiety about cholesterol and the momentum of low-fat diets. They are beginning to find favor again among those who realize that a little of what you fancy every now and then doesn't do any harm!

Peel, core and chop the apples, then wash the currants. Mix the fruits together with the sugar and spice. Chop the suet finely and put it into a bowl with the flour, salt and baking powder. Mix well, then add cold water to make a stiff paste. Roll out to 1/4 inch thickness, spread the fruit mixture on the paste, wet the edges and roll up neatly.

Scald a cloth in boiling water, wring it out then sprinkle flour onto it. Wrap the pudding in the cloth and tie securely. Boil a large saucepan of water and lower the pudding in. Boil it gently for 1 1/2 hours. Carefully unwrap the roly-poly. Serve on a very hot plate, with cream and soft brown sugar.

Serves 8

Grandmother's Fierling

4 eggs, free-range if possible
5 tablespoons flour
5 tablespoons milk
5 tablespoons superfine granulated sugar
3 to 4 tablespoons butter

This recipe was given to Lucy Madden of Hilton Park, Co. Monaghan by her grand-mother, who suggested that it was a good dessert for a last-minute lunch in the kitchen. We found it absolutely delicious—certainly good enough to share with friends in the dining-room.

Separate the eggs. Put the yolks into a bowl, add the flour and milk and mix until you have achieved the consistency of thick cream. Whisk the egg whites stiffly with the sugar and fold into the mixture.

Gently heat two frying pans (I used 10 inch non-stick pans with good results). Add half the butter to each. Divide the batter mixture between the pans and cook until the bottom is golden brown. Slide one of the 'fierlings' on to a warmed serving dish, crispy side down and fluffy side uppermost. Gently place the other fierling on top, brown side upwards. Pour the pan juices over the top and serve immediately, just as it is or decorated with some summer berries.

Serves 6 to 8

Bread & Butter Pudding

8 slices good quality white bread, crusts removed
1/4 to 1/2 cup raisins soaked in hot water and then drained
butter
1/4 cup sugar
1 teaspoon ground cinnamon
5 eggs, free-range if possible
5 cups milk
2/3 cup cream
1 teaspoon freshly grated nutmeg
1 teaspoon ground ginger

She made May collect the crusts and pieces of broken bread to help to make Tuesday's bread pudding.

James Joyce, *Dubliners*

This rich version of bread and butter pudding is hardly what May's landlady would have had in mind for her boarders!

Butter the bread. Break it up into smallish pieces and put into an oven-proof dish. Add the raisins. Mix one quarter of the sugar with the cinnamon and sprinkle over the bread. Whisk the eggs with the remainder of the sugar and add milk, cream, nutmeg and ginger. Pour over the bread, put the dish in a *bain marie* of hot water and bake at 350°F for 1 to 1 1/4 hours.

Serve warm with lots of softly whipped cream.

There was always trifle as well as plum pudding for Christmas Day in our house. My mother's trifle was famous. She made two huge glass bowls of it, using trifle sponges and lashings of sherry. She used to hide it because my brothers would get up in the night to eat trifle. As each year passed she was forced to become more and more ingenious with her hiding place and eventually 'hunt the trifle' became a traditional Christmas game.

Sandwich the rounds of sponge cake together with homemade raspberry jam. If you use trifle sponges, sandwich them in pairs. Next make the egg custard. Beat the eggs with the sugar and vanilla extract. Heat the milk to the 'shivery' stage and add it to the egg beating all the time. Put into a heavy saucepan and stir over a gentle heat until the custard coats the back of the wooden spoon lightly. Don't let it boil or it will curdle.

Cut the sponge into ¾ inch slices and use these to line the bottom of a 7½ cup glass bowl, sprinkling generously with sherry as you go along. Pour in some homemade egg custard and then add another layer of sponge. Sprinkle with the remainder of the sherry. Spread the rest of the custard over the top. Cover and leave for 5 or 6 hours, or preferably overnight, to mature.

Before serving, spread whipped cream over the top, pipe rosettes if you like, and decorate the trifle with glacé cherries or crystallized violets and diamonds of angelica.

Serves 8 to 10

Traditional Irish Sherry Trifle

2 layers homemade sponge cake (see page 252) or 1lb bought sponges
8oz homemade Raspberry Jam
⅔ to ¾ cup best quality sweet or medium sherry—don't spare the sherry and don't waste your time with cooking sherry

Custard

5 eggs, free-range if possible
1½ tablespoons superfine granulated sugar
¾ teaspoon pure vanilla extract
3 cups rich milk

Garnish

2½ cups whipped cream
8 glacé cherries or crystallized violets
8 diamonds of angelica

Irish Coffee Meringue

Serves 6 to 8

2 egg whites
³/4 cup confectioners' sugar
*2 teaspoons instant coffee powder
(not granules)*

Filling

1¹/4 cups whipped cream
2 tablespoons approx. Irish whiskey

Decoration

chocolate coffee beans (optional)

This is a recent Irish recipe served to guests on the sweet trolley at Ballymaloe House. It is so extraordinarily popular that it is definitely a tradition there.

Draw 2 x 7 inch circles on to a sheet of parchment paper.

Put the egg whites into a spotlessly clean and dry bowl. Add all the confectioners' sugar except 2 tablespoons. Whisk until the mixture stands in firm dry peaks. It may take 10 to 15 minutes. Sieve the coffee with the remaining sugar and fold in carefully.

Spread the meringue carefully with a palette knife onto the circles of the wax paper. Bake in a very low oven at 300°F for about 1 hour or until crisp. The discs should peel easily from the paper. Allow to get quite cold.

Stir the whiskey into the whipped cream. Sandwich the meringue discs together with whiskey flavored cream. Pipe five rosettes of cream on top. Decorate with chocolate coffee beans if available.

Balloons

Makes about 10

1¹/4 cups flour
3 teaspoons superfine granulated sugar
pinch of salt
1 teaspoon baking powder
milk
extra superfine granulated sugar

This cheap and simple doughnut recipe has been passed down for generations in my husband's family. Children adore these balloons because they cook into exciting shapes. Grown-ups hang about hoping they'll be allowed some too!

Sift the dry ingredients into a bowl. Mix to a thick batter (dropping consistency) with milk. Meanwhile, heat fat in a deep fryer to 385°F. Take a tablespoon of the mixture and push it gently off with your finger so that it drops in a round ball into the fat. Repeat with the rest of the mixture. Fry until golden, then remove and drain. Roll the balloons in sugar and serve at once.

Old-fashioned Rice Pudding

1/4 cup short grain rice
2 tablespoons sugar
knob of butter
2¹/2 cups milk

A creamy rice pudding with a tender golden skin is one of the greatest treats on a cold winter's day. Resist the temptation to put in dried fruit or other flavorings—just eat it at the peak of perfection, with lots of soft brown sugar and cream.

Put the rice, sugar and a little knob of butter into a 2¹/2 cup pie dish. Bring the milk to the boil and pour over. Bake in a moderate oven at 350°F for 1 to 1¹/2 hours.

It is quite tricky to catch the pudding at exactly the right stage. The skin on top should be golden, the rice underneath should be cooked through and have soaked up the milk, but still be soft and creamy underneath. Time it, so that it is ready just in time for dessert. If it has to wait in the oven for ages it will be dry and dull and you'll wonder why you bothered. Serve with cream and soft brown sugar.

Boiled Rice for a Black Fast Day

I couldn't resist this recipe from Annie Kiely's manuscript of 1908:

Wash ½ pound rice in three waters, remove any black grains that are in it, then put into a quart of boiling water, boil for one hour, add one tablespoon of sugar, put into the shape, wet with cold water, allow it to set, turn out and serve with raspberry jam around it.

Eamonn Mac Thomáis described how his family would sometimes have a rice dinner during Lent that consisted of rice pudding made on water.

Elizabeth O'Connell's Plum Pudding

It was always the tradition in our house to eat the first plum pudding on the evening it was made. As children we could hardly contain ourselves with excitement—somehow that plum pudding seemed all the more delicious because it was our first taste of Christmas. The plum pudding was usually made about mid-November and everyone in the family had to stir so they could make a wish! Mummy put silver plum pudding charms in the pudding destined to be eaten on Christmas Day.

This recipe makes 2 large or 3 medium puddings. The large size will serve 10 to 12 people, the medium size will serve 6 to 8.

2½ cups raisins
2½ cups golden raisins
2½ cups currants
2½ cups brown sugar
2½ cups white breadcrumbs
2½ cups finely-chopped suet
¾ cup candied peel (preferably homemade)
2 cooking apples, diced or grated
rind of 1 lemon
3 pounded cloves (¾ teaspoon)
a pinch of salt
6 eggs
½ cup Jamaica rum
1 cup chopped almonds

Mix all the ingredients together very thoroughly and leave overnight. Don't forget, everyone in the family must stir and make a wish!

Next day, stir again for good measure. Fill into earthenware pudding bowls; cover with a double thickness of wax paper which has been pleated in the center, and tie it tightly under the rim with cotton twine, making a twine handle also for ease of lifting.

Steam the puddings in covered saucepans of boiling water for 6 hours. The water should come half way up the side of the bowl. Check every hour or so, and top up with boiling water if necessary. After 6 hours, remove the puddings. Allow to get cold and re-cover with fresh wax paper. Store in a cool dry place until required.

On Christmas Day, or whenever you wish to serve the plum pudding, steam for a further 2 hours. Turn the plum pudding out of the bowl on to a very hot serving plate. Pour over some whiskey or brandy and ignite. Serve immediately on *very hot plates* with brandy butter (see below).

You might like to decorate the plum pudding with a sprig of holly; however take care, because the last time I did that I provided much merriment by setting the holly and my bangs on fire, as well as the pudding!

Brandy Butter

6 tablespoons butter
¾ cup confectioners' sugar
2 to 6 tablespoons brandy

Cream the butter until very light. Add the sugar and beat again. Then beat in the brandy, drop by drop. If you have a food processor, use it: you will get a wonderfully light and fluffy result.

Makes 8 jars (approximately)

Lady Levinge's Mincemeat

*3lb cooking apples, peeled,
cored and chopped
grated rind and juice of 1 orange
and 1 lemon
2¹/₂ cups cider
2¹/₂ cups soft brown sugar
1 teaspoon ground cinnamon
1 teaspoon grated nutmeg
1 teaspoon ground cloves
3 cups raisins
3 cups currants or 1¹/₂ cups currants
and 1¹/₂ cups golden raisins
1¹/₂ cups glacé cherries, halved (natural
color ones if possible)
¹/₃ cup dark Jamaica rum*

Originally mincemeat got its name because it included meat and later suet. Lady Maria Levinge of Clohamon House in Co. Wexford gave me this delicious recipe— which uses neither!

In a large saucepan bring the apples, juice and rinds of orange and lemon and cider to the boil. Reduce the heat and simmer, stirring occasionally, for 10 minutes.

Stir in the sugar, cinnamon, nutmeg, cloves, raisins and currants. When the sugar has dissolved, simmer for a further 15 minutes.

Remove the pan from the heat and stir in the glacé cherries. Allow the mixture to cool and then stir in the rum. Spoon into sterilized jars, cover, seal, and store in a cool, dark place.

Makes 7lb

Ballymaloe Mincemeat

*2 cooking apples
2 lemons
1lb finely chopped beef suet
³/₄ cup mixed peel (preferably
homemade, see page 264)
3 tablespoons orange marmalade
1¹/₂ cups currants
3 cups raisins
1¹/₂ cups golden raisins
5 cups moist, soft, dark brown sugar
¹/₃ cup Irish whiskey*

Core and bake the whole apples in a moderate oven at 350°F for about 45 minutes. When they are soft, remove the skin and mash the flesh into a pulp. Grate the rind from the lemons on the finest part of a stainless steel grater and squeeze out the juice. Add the other ingredients one by one, and as they are added, mix everything thoroughly together. Put into jars, cover with jam covers and leave to mature for 3 weeks before using. This mincemeat will keep for months or a year in a cool, airy place.

Make the shortcrust pastry in the usual way (see page 191), and refrigerate for one hour. Roll out the pastry until quite thin and stamp out into rounds 3 inches in diameter. Line shallow muffin pans with the pastry rounds and put a good teaspoonful of mincemeat into each pan. Damp the edges with water and put another round on top. Brush with egg and decorate each pie with holly leaves and berries made from the pastry trimmings.

Bake the mince pies in a preheated moderate oven at 350°F, for about 30 minutes. Allow them to cool slightly, then dredge with sugar.

Serve with a dollop of whiskey flavored cream.

Fold the sugar and whiskey into the whipped cream.

Makes 20 to 24 mince pies

Ballymaloe Mince Pies

with Irish Whiskey Cream

Pastry

2 cups (225g) plain flour
8 to 12 tablespoons (1 to 1¹/₂ sticks) butter
a pinch of salt
1 tablespoon confectioner's sugar
a little beaten egg or egg yolk and water to bind
1 lb Ballymaloe mincemeat (see opposite)
superfine granulated or confectioners' sugar

Irish Whiskey Cream

1 cup whipped cream
1 teaspoon confectioners' sugar
1¹/₂ to 3 tablespoons Irish whiskey

Pancakes

As most cooking was traditionally done over the open fire, Ireland has a wide variety of recipes for pancakes and other griddle cakes. These are easily made from readily available ingredients—such as flour, cornmeal or potatoes mixed with milk or buttermilk and perhaps an egg.

Shrove Tuesday has always been seen as a last chance for merriment before the rigors of lenten fasting began. During Lent, Catholics were urged to abstain not only from meat, but also from eggs, milk, butter and cheese—hence the tradition of using up these ingredients in pancakes on Shrove Tuesday. An early (decidedly lavish) recipe in Sheila Newcomen's manuscript book of 1717 from Co. Longford includes eggs, flour, milk, brandy, nutmeg, ginger, butter, sugar and salt.

It was a common folk belief that an unmarried girl's skill in tossing pancakes was an indication of her future prospects—if she dropped it, she had no hope of marriage during the coming year. As weddings were forbidden during Lent, there was a tremendous rush to the altar on Shrove Tuesday. A great deal of pressure was put on marriageable bachelors and spinsters as the day approached—with plenty of pranks and practical jokes!

Pancakes are still made in virtually every household in Ireland on Shrove Tuesday and are enjoyed by young and old alike. My children queue up beside the Aga for theirs and eat them hot off the pan with a brush of melted butter, a squeeze of lemon juice and a sprinkling of sugar.

Buttermilk Pancakes

Makes about 20

4 cups flour
1 teaspoon baking soda
large pinch salt
$^1/_3$ cup sugar
1 egg, free-range if possible
$2^1/_2$ cups buttermilk

'Run round to the dairy and fetch me a jug of buttermilk and sure we'll make pancakes.' My great aunt in Tipperary would put on the griddle to heat and within minutes she'd be mixing the batter. We would drop big spoonfuls of batter on to the hot griddle and watch the bubbles rise and burst. Then we'd carefully flip them over and wait impatiently for them to be cooked on the other side. We would eat them straight off the griddle with butter and homemade jam.

Mix the dry ingredients together in a bowl. Make a well in the center, add the egg and enough buttermilk to make batter of a dropping consistency (it usually takes the full amount). Drop spoonfuls of the mixture onto a lightly greased hot griddle and cook for 3 to 4 minutes on one side before turning over. The pancakes are ready to turn when the bubbles burst. Flip over gently and cook until golden on the other side. Serve warm with butter and jam or honey for tea.

Note: *we cook the pancakes rather less romantically on a non-stick pan at a medium heat and use a generous tablespoon of batter for each pancake.*

Snow Pancakes

This unique recipe was sent to me by Elizabeth MacKevitt from Waterford. It originated with Miss Nancy McCoy who, with her sister Ursula, catered for large events and weddings in the Kilkenny region for many years. Nancy used to recommend putting a clean tray out in the garden to collect the snow so that it was not dirtied. This recipe would not necessarily be an annual event in Kilkenny, even though it is supposed to be the coldest city in the south—her words, not mine!

Beat the milk and flour together. Add ³/4lb of fresh light snow. Mix in gently and leave for some hours to melt, so that the snow aerates the flour and milk. This makes a very light but very pale pancake. It can be made richer by adding some egg yolks, but the egg whites are not needed for the pancakes. They can be used for meringues.

3³/4 cups milk
5 cups flour
egg yolks (optional)

Makes about 20

Beestings Pancakes

Beestings is the name of the very rich milk which the cow produces immediately after a calf is born. In some parts of the country it was never used for human consumption but in others it was highly prized and shared with the neighbors. It was made into pancakes and beestings curds. The third milking was considered to be best for these recipes.
Last year, much to the amazement of my long-suffering husband, I bought a little black Kerry cow, partly to protect an endangered species and also because of my happy memories of the house cow we had when I was a child. To my great delight and the amusement of all my neighbours and friends she duly produced a heifer calf, so I had the opportunity to try these beesting pancakes.

Sieve the flour, baking soda and salt into a bowl. Whisk in enough beestings to make a thin or slightly thicker batter, depending on whether you want thin or thick pancakes. Drop tablespoonfuls on to a hot greased griddle and cook for about 5 minutes on each side. Serve hot with butter for tea.

6 cups flour
1 teaspoon baking soda
pinch of salt
1 tablespoon sugar
beestings
butter for frying

Breads

The baking tradition is one of the richest and most varied aspects of Ireland's culinary heritage. From earliest times, breadmaking was an integral part of daily life in almost every home, and it is now undergoing a huge revival across Ireland.

For centuries, thin oatcakes were made on a bakestone or griddle over an open fire. Later, breads were leavened with sourdough and barm made from beer, sowans (the fermented juice of oat husks) and fermented potato juice. It was only in the first half of the nineteenth century that baking soda was introduced, enabling cooks to bake the wide range of soda breads for which Ireland is now so famous.

Even in the poorest country cabin, fresh soda bread would have been mixed on a wooden baking board and baked on the griddle, or in the pot oven or bastible, over the embers of the turf fire.

The traditional skills of breadmaking were passed on from mother to daughter, and were a great source of pride. It was a compliment of the highest order to be described as having 'a light hand with baking'. Try your own hand at griddle cakes, treacle or potato bread, as well as the delicious soda breads!

Food of the Monasteries

Many monasteries were almost self-sufficient. The monks grew wheat which was stoneground on a mill wheel and then baked into bread to feed both the community and the poor. People flocked in their hundreds to the monasteries to be shrived and then to have bread and tea in the guesthouse. There was no charge, but it was understood that one should leave a donation according to one's means. The Cistercian Abbey at Mount St. Joseph in Roscrea keeps up this tradition to the present day.

There are many references in early literature to hermits and monks fasting on a meager diet of dry bread. Many of these holy men fasted on barley bread and water on weekdays and feasted on wheaten bread, salmon and ale on Sundays and feast days.

Flour

The flour, often ground from home-grown wheat, was traditionally stored in a wooden meal chest close to the fire. Such chests were robustly built with a sloping lid and perhaps two or three divisions inside to store white flour, wheaten meal and oatmeal, and on occasion some cornmeal (maize meal). Many had a narrow shelf in the back near the top to store baking soda, cornstarch and the precious, expensive sugar. The chest was kept locked in many households to guard against not only two-legged invaders, but also four-legged pests. Some good examples of these meal chests still survive.

This revealing account from Eric Cross's *The Tailor and Ansty* describes the goings on in a West Cork tailor's house in the early 20th century:

> Upstairs are the bedroom, with the great box bed, and the small room beyond where Ansty keeps the meal and corn so that even at night when she is asleep, she can still guard it from the pilfering of the rats and the mice.

When times were hard, as they were more often than not, the woman of the house scrimped to try to ensure that the supply of meal lasted from one harvest to the next. The ability to produce freshly baked bread in the months of July and August was a source of great pride to a housewife.

Well-to-do households and farmers with several farm laborers to feed would have bought white flour by the sack. Originally farmers who grew their own wheat would have taken it to a local stone mill to be ground into flour. White flour was sold in white cotton flour bags. These were a great bonus and had a myriad of uses.

Thrifty housewives made them into tablecloths, sheets, pillow cases, nightdresses, tea towels…The Christmas plum pudding, for example, was boiled in one. Some more artistic housewives hand-painted them, or they embroidered the bags and transformed them into tablecloths or fancy cushion covers for use in the parlor.

A Buttermilk Plant

Traditionally most farmers would have had their own cows and used buttermilk, left over from churning the butter, in the breadmaking. Every year, my husband Tim and I proudly teach hundreds of students from all over the world how to make our Irish soda breads, which soon become addictive. Many students worry about the difficulty of funding a regular supply of buttermilk back at home, so we now pass on this miraculous recipe, taken from Kind Cooking *by Maura Laverty. This buttermilk starter will increase and after a few weeks you will be in a position to pass some on to your friends.*

2 tablespoons sugar
1 oz yeast
5 cups tepid milk and water

Cream the yeast with the sugar, gradually add the tepid milk and water. Put the mixture in some vessel that may easily be washed and scalded, cover it, and leave it in a warm place for a couple of days or until the milk smells and tastes like buttermilk, put a piece of muslin in the bottom of a strainer and strain the milk through this. The funny-looking thing like lumpy cornstarch which remains will be the plant. Rinse every drop of milk off it, by pouring a cup of tepid water over it. Let the water run through the strainer into the buttermilk—it will all make excellent liquid for mixing cake bread. To start a new lot , scrape the plant off the muslin and put it back into the scalded and well rinsed vessel. Add another 5 cups of tepid milk and water, cover and leave it as before.

That first ounce of yeast will go on growing and multiplying, giving you buttermilk until the end of time. But the plant needs care.

It must be strained at least every five days. If you don't want the milk for baking, you can always drink it. I knew a woman so crippled with rheumatics that she couldn't kneel down to say the rosary. After six months of drinking this buttermilk, she was able to do the Lough Derg Pilgrimage on her knees.

Make sure the milk and water is never more than lukewarm. Strong heat kills yeast.

Cleanliness is very important. Careful rinsing after straining, and the scalding of the container must be done if the plant is to live.

Soda Bread

Like many other children I began my cooking career at my mother's side while she made the daily soda bread. As soon as she reached for the mixing bowl, I'd don my apron and pester her for a little piece of dough to make a *cístín beag*. This was a tiny loaf shaped into a round just like my Mammy made. I'd solemnly cut a cross on top with a knife and my little *cístín* was baked beside her big loaf in the range. The result was often a bit tough and rather too crusty from over-enthusiastic handling, nonetheless I was delighted with it. Fortunately all the grown-ups who were invited to taste 'my bread' were always careful to be encouraging and lavish in their praise as they sampled and chewed!

White Soda Bread

Makes 1 large loaf

4 cups flour
1 teaspoon salt
1 teaspoon baking soda
1¹/2 to 1³/4 cups buttermilk

Originally baked in a pot oven or bastible beside the open fire, white soda bread is often referred to as cake bread. The word bastible seems to be a bastardization of the name Barnstaple, the town in Devon where these iron baking pots were made.

First preheat your oven to 450°F.

Sieve the dry ingredients. Make a well in the center. Pour most of the milk in at once. Using one hand, stir in a full circle to mix in the flour from the sides of the bowl, adding more buttermilk if necessary. The dough should be softish, not too wet and sticky. When it all comes together, turn it out on to a floured board and knead lightly for a second, just enough to tidy it up. Pat the dough into a round about 2 inches deep and cut a cross on it to let the fairies out! Let the cuts go over the sides of the bread to make sure of this. Bake in preheated oven for 15 minutes, then turn down the oven to 400°F for a further 20 to 30 minutes or until cooked. If in doubt, tap the bread bottom; it should sound hollow.

Cool on a wire rack or on the windowsill in the time-honored way.

Fresh crusty bread makes my mouth water, but some people prefer a soft crust. Years ago a clean flour bag would have been wrapped around the hot bread to soften the crust. A tea towel will produce the same result.

Goaty Bread

Brid Mahon, in her book *Land of Milk and Honey*, mentioned a bread made with goat's milk called goaty bread, but I have not been able to trace a recipe for it. It is likely that it was soda bread made with soured goat's milk rather that cow's milk.

Brown Soda Bread

Makes 2 loaves

4 cups brown wholewheat flour
(preferably stone ground)
4 cups flour
3 rounded teaspoons salt
2 rounded teaspoons baking soda, sieved
3 to 3¹/4 cups sour milk
or buttermilk

The warm and comforting smell of brown soda bread wafting from the kitchen has cheered and nourished countless generations of Irish people after a hard day's work in the fields and bogs. It is the quintessential Irish bread.

Occasionally we add a small fist of fine stoneground oatmeal, 1 egg or 2 table-spoons butter to make a richer soda bread dough. Irish wholemeal flours are coarse and nutty with a rich wheaten flavor. The various textures will produce different types of bread.

First preheat the oven to 450°F.

Mix the dry ingredients together. Make a well in the center and add most of the sour milk or buttermilk all in one go. Working from the center, mix with your hand and add more milk if necessary. The dough should be soft but not sticky. Turn out on to a floured board and knead lightly, just enough to shape into a round. Flatten slightly to about 2 inches deep. Put on to a baking sheet. Mark with a deep cross and bake in the hot oven for 15 to 20 minutes, then reduce the heat to 400°F for about 20 to 25 minutes, or until the bread is cooked and sounds hollow when tapped.

Brown Soda Scones

Make the dough as above. Flatten the dough into a round about 1 inch deep. Cut into scones. Cook for about 20 minutes in a hot oven.

White Soda Bread

Surely the first Irish pizza! Margaret Breen, now aged 73, from Lahard Upper, Beaufort in Co. Kerry, describes how 'my grandmother baked a cake made with white flour, sour milk and bread soda. She put 8 bacon slices criss-crossed on top of it in the pot oven. No one would want butter or jam with that bread. It was cut up when hot and devoured.'

Soda Bread with Bacon

Nowadays a new kind of soda bread is made with a more moist dough and baked in a pan. This delicious version has won several bread competitions for its proud creator.

Breda Power's Bread

Preheat the oven to 400°F.

Grease a large loaf pan with oil. Mix all the dry ingredients together and make a well in the center. Beat the oil, honey, buttermilk and egg together and pour into the dry ingredients. Mix to a nice soft dough and knead lightly. Place the dough in the pan, cover with foil, and bake in the pre-heated oven for 1 hour, or until the bread sounds hollow when tapped. Cool on a wire rack.

3¹/₂ cups wholewheat flour
1¹/₃ cups plain white flour
1 teaspoon baking soda
1 teaspoon cream of tartar
1 rounded teaspoon salt
1 teaspoon pure Irish honey
1 tablespoon cooking oil
2 cups buttermilk
1 egg, free-range if possible

Bocáire

Catherine O'Drisceóil from Cape Clear told us about this bread which was made from wheat grown on the island and milled on the mainland. Soda bread was called cake bread or just 'a cake', not only on the islands, but also in many parts of the country. The term still lingers to this day.

Catherine explained that 'bocáire was made when you'd find yourself running short of bread and you didn't have the time to make a big loaf of cake bread'.

Bocáire was normal bread dough mixture 'patted out very thin'—so thin that there was very little dough in the center between the two crusts. It was much thinner than normal griddle bread. It was cooked on a heavy iron pan and was eaten immediately after it was cooked.

1³/₄ cups wholewheat flour
1³/₄ cups plain white flour
1 level teaspoon salt
1 level teaspoon baking soda
1¹/₂ cups sour milk or buttermilk

Heat a heavy iron pan over the fire.

Mix the dry ingredients together. Make a well in the center and add most of the sour milk or buttermilk. Working from the center, mix with your hand and add more milk if necessary. The dough should be soft but not sticky. Turn out on to a floured board and knead lightly, just enough to shape into a round. Roll out very thinly. Grease the pan with a butter wrapper. Bake for 20 minutes on one side, turn over and cook on the other side. Cool on a wire rack. Eat freshly baked with country butter.

Nancy Ellis's Griddle Bread

Serves 4 to 8

Afternoon tea served in Madame Fitzgerald's kitchen at Glin Castle in Co. Limerick was a memorable experience for me recently. There was thinly sliced homemade bread, jam, a comb of honey from the beehive in the orchard, tiny scones with homemade raspberry jam and cream, a chocolate cake and a moist plum cake. However, the pièce de résistance was Nancy Ellis's warm griddle bread, which she made on a heavy iron pan on the side of the Aga.

Nancy Ellis cooked at Glin for over 40 years and her food was legendary.

1 lb flour (2 fists)
1 scant level teaspoon baking soda
no salt
fresh milk to bind (1¹/₄ to 1¹/₂ cups)

Nancy seived the flour on to a tray rather than into a bowl. She then added a level teaspoon of baking soda, which she first rubbed between the palms of her hands to eliminate any lumps.

She mixed dry ingredients well and then added enough fresh milk to make a softish but not sticky dough. This was flattened out to about 1¹/₂ inches thick and baked on a preheated pan on the cool plate of the Aga. It took about 30 minutes in total (approx. 15 minutes on each side). Originally it would have been baked on a griddle.

Note: *a non-stick pan works very well for griddle bread.*

Gátarí

Small griddle cakes (*gátarí* in Irish) smeared with molasses were sold at country markets and fairs and on the streets of Dublin. Smear some black molasses over the griddle cakes and serve warm if possible.

Mrs McGillycuddy's Yellowmeal Bread (top)
and Kerry Treacle Bread (see page 220)

Mrs McGillycuddy's Yellowmeal Bread

This bread tastes just as delicious today as it did over a hundred years ago and it deserves to be much better known. I've made it over and over again since Mrs McGillycuddy, from Caragh Lake in Co. Kerry, first showed me how to make it. I've also heard it referred to as 'Yalla Male' bread.

Other recipes from West Cork use equal quantities of yellowmeal and flour, which produces a slightly yellower bread with a grittier texture.

1¹/₂ cups yellowmeal, known as cornmeal
2¹/₂ cups plain white flour
1 level teaspoon salt
1 level teaspoon baking soda
1¹/₂ to 1³/₄ cups sour milk or buttermilk

First preheat your oven to 450°F.

Sieve the dry ingredients. Make a well in the center. Pour most of the milk in at once. Using one hand, mix in the flour from the sides of the bowl, adding more milk if necessary. The dough should be softish, not too wet and sticky. When it all comes together, turn it out on to a floured board and knead lightly to tidy it up. Flip over the edges with a floured hand. Pat the dough into a round about 1¹/₂ inches deep and cut a cross on it to let the fairies out! Bake in the hot oven for 15 minutes, then turn down the oven to 400°F for 30 minutes or until cooked. If you are in doubt about this, tap the bottom of the bread: if it is cooked it will sound hollow.

Yellow Buck

Another version of yellowmeal bread comes from the Tralee area in North Kerry.

1 cup cornmeal
4 cups plain white flour
1 small teaspoon salt
2 heaped teaspoons sugar
1 teaspoon baking soda
1 teaspoon cream of tartar
4 tablespoons butter
2 cups approx. sour milk or buttermilk

Mix all the dry ingredients together. Make a well in the center and rub in the butter. Pour in the milk and mix to a nice soft dough. Turn on to a floured board and knead gently. Put on a floured baking sheet. Score with a knife and bake for 30 minutes in a hot oven at 425°F. Turn off the heat, leaving the cake in the oven for a further 10 minutes.

Slim Bread

This old recipe was given to me by George McCartney of McCartney's family butchers in Moira, Co. Down:

It's one bread I remember well from my school days. My mother would have had the griddle on when we arrived home to cook slim bread which we ate warm with lots of butter and home made strawberry jam. She lives next door to the shop, even yet when there is slim being made I slip round for some.

4 cups plain white flour
1 teaspoon baking soda
1 level teaspoon salt
$^1/_3$ cup superfine granulated sugar
4 tablespoons butter
1 egg, free-range if possible
1 cup buttermilk

Sieve the flour, soda and salt into a bowl. Add the sugar.

Rub in the butter and mix to a firm dough with the beaten egg and the buttermilk. Shape the mixture into two rounds and cut each one into four patties. Bake on a heated griddle for 6 to 10 minutes on each side, depending on the thickness. Eat hot or cold, split in half and spread with butter and homemade strawberry jam.

Fruit Slims

Add 1 cup golden raisins to the dry ingredients before starting to mix in the liquid. Bake as above.

Makes about 10

Slim Cakes

Many recipes have turned up under this name. One version seems to have been made from freshly rendered lard, the week after the pig was killed (see page 114). I'm not sure where the name comes from; perhaps it refers to the fact that the bread is rolled thinly. There's certainly nothing slimming about this recipe!

3 cups flour
good pinch of salt
1 cup freshly rendered lard

Sieve the flour and salt into a bowl. Rub in the lard and continue to work until the mixture comes together. Roll out thinly. Bake on a hot griddle or non-stick pan until brown on both sides. Serve the cakes straight off the griddle, hot and buttered.

Kerry Treacle Bread

This recipe was described to me by Mrs McGillycuddy from Glencar in Co. Kerry, who still makes it occasionally. A richer treacle bread, closer to gingerbread, was and still is widely made in Ulster.

1 to 2 tablespoons molasses (treacle)
1 egg (optional), free-range if possible
1$^1/_4$ cups approx. sour milk
or buttermilk to mix
4 cups white flour,
preferably unbleached
1 level teaspoon salt
1 level teaspoon baking soda

First fully preheat your oven to 450°F.

Heat the molasses until it begins to run. Beat the egg, if you are using it, add to the molasses and mix well. Then add the buttermilk.

Sieve the dry ingredients. Make a well in the center. Pour in most of the liquid all at once. Using one hand, mix in the flour from the sides of the bowl, adding more liquid if necessary. The dough should be softish, not too wet and sticky. When it comes together, turn it out on to a floured board. Tidy it up and flip over the edges with a floured hand. Pat the dough into a round about 1 inch deep and cut a cross on it. The cuts should go over the sides of the bread. Bake in the hot oven for 15 minutes, then turn down the oven to 400°F for 30 minutes or until cooked. If you are in doubt, tap the bottom of the bread; it will sound hollow if cooked. Cool on a wire rack.

Oaten Bread

In Clones, Co. Monaghan, I talked to Granny Toye, whose memory, at 88, is crystal clear. 'People going to America would always take a few cakes of oaten bread with them on the ship,' she told me. 'It sustained them and kept them from getting sick. Sure there's nothing in the making of it—use fine oatmeal and it must be well cooked.' This is the method which she described to me.

Put oatmeal into a bowl, soak with water, add salt. Roll in a ball, then put on a bakeboard. Roll into a round approx. 10 inches across. Leave it to sit for an hour or so to dry out, by which time it will be possible to lift it. Put onto the harden griddle propped up by the fire and keep it turned as it browns. It will take about half an hour to cook, but the time depends on the heat of the fire. It should be dry and crisp. It keeps very well.

Oatmeal Soda Bread

For this early soda bread the oatmeal was steeped in buttermilk overnight. It makes a light, pale bread with quite a different flavor—also absolutely delicious. This recipe was given to me by Honor Moore from Dublin.

$2^1/2$ cups fine stoneground oatmeal
2 cups sour milk or buttermilk
$2^1/2$ cups white flour
$^1/2$ teaspoon salt
1 teaspoon baking soda

Steep the oatmeal in the buttermilk overnight.

Next day, preheat the oven to 350°F. Mix the flour, salt and baking soda together, then stir into the oatmeal. If necessary add a little more milk, but don't make the dough too wet. Put into a large well greased loaf pan (we use one which is $5^1/2$ x $9^1/2$ x $2^1/2$ inches and bake in a moderate oven for 1 to $1^1/4$ hours.

Note: *John Dunton, writing in 1698, recalls a meal he enjoyed in the west of Ireland:*

The oaten cake was sett next to me, at the lower end of our table was placed a greate roll of fresh butter of three pound at least, and a wodden vessell full of milk and water.

Joan Twomey (standing) shows Darina how to bake bread in a bastible

Rye Bread

Makes 2 or 3 loaves

Rye is mentioned in the seventh/eighth century. Brehon Laws and there is substantial archaeological evidence for its cultivation in the fifth to eleventh centuries. In her book Land of Milk and Honey, *Brid Mahon says that rye bread continued to be part of the traditional Irish diet right up to the nineteenth century. A popular rhyme advises:*

> Rye bread will do you good
> Barley bread will do you no harm
> Wheaten bread will sweeten your blood
> Oaten bread will strengthen your arm.

Charles Etienne Coquebert de Montbret, on a visit to Cork in 1790, noted that 'In the South of Ireland bread is made with oats, in Wicklow with rye and in Meath with a mixture of rye and wheat.'

Rye straw was used for thatching, a use for which it is second only to wheat straw. It was grown specifically for this purpose in Donegal, and still is on the Aran Islands.

1/4oz fresh yeast
warm water at blood temperature
2 2/3 cups bread flour
1 cup dark rye flour
3/4oz caraway seeds
1 teaspoon salt
1 egg, free-range if possible, beaten
poppyseeds

Crumble the yeast and mix with 1¼ cups lukewarm water. Mix the flours, caraway seeds and salt in a bowl. Add the yeast liquid, with extra warm water if necessary, to make a soft but not sticky dough. Knead until smooth (for about 10 minutes). Cover and leave to rise in a warm place until doubled in bulk. Punch down and knead again for 4 or 5 minutes. Shape into two or three loaves. Cover and allow to rise again.

Brush the loaves with beaten egg. Sprinkle with poppyseeds and slash the tops in a cross with a razor blade or sharp knife. Bake in a preheated oven at 450°F for about 25 minutes or until the bread sounds hollow when tapped underneath.

Potato Bread

White flour was scarce in the earlier part of this century, so was considered a luxury. There were many recipes for potato bread, potato pastry etc. to help to 'stretch' the flour. Paddy the 'Cope' Gallagher from Co. Donegal recalled that in the 1870s, when he was a child, 'flour bread was rare, we had oat bread and boxty instead. Boxty was looked on as a rare treat, probably because there was white flour in it.'

1/2 cup flour
1/2 teaspoon salt
1/2 teaspoon baking powder
1 cup mashed potatoes
2 tablespoons bacon fat

Mix the flour, salt and baking powder together. Add the potatoes, melt the fat and pour in. Knead lightly and roll out, cut into four patties. Bake on a greased pan or griddle, or in the oven.

We cook this bread in a preheated oven at 350°F for about 30 minutes, or until golden on both sides.

In Cork city this bread was traditionally eaten on Christmas Eve. Paddy Ormond, whose family were bakers in Shandon Street for three generations, told me how people would eat seed loaf after Midnight Mass, presumably following 'a feed of salted Ling' (see page 53), and also on Christmas Day. 'A glass of port and seed cake after Christmas dinner and you were perfect.' Caraway seeds are a splendid aid to digestion.

Recently I enquired about this bread in a local bakery, but the reply was 'Yerra not at all girl, sure that's been discontinued. The modern housewife would have no meas on that, sure she'd think it was mouse droppings that was in it!'

Mix the yeast with ½ cup lukewarm water. When the yeast is dissolved, add a further 1 cup tepid water.

Sieve the flour into a bowl and add the salt, sugar and caraway seeds. Make a well in the center and pour in most of the lukewarm liquid. Mix to a loose dough, adding the remainder of the liquid or more flour if necessary. Turn the dough on to a floured board, cover and leave to relax for 5 to 10 minutes. Knead until smooth and springy (about 10 minutes). If using a food mixer with a dough hook, 5 minutes is usually long enough.

Put the dough to rise in the bowl covered with a damp cloth or tightly sealed with plastic wrap. Yeast dough rises best in a warm moist atmosphere, e.g. near your stove, on top of a radiator, or in an oven turned to minimum heat with the door open (use a thick pottery bowl if rising in a fan oven). Rising time depends on the temperature, but it is much better to err on the side of having it too cool rather than too hot. Remember that cold won't kill yeast, but heat over 110°F will.

When the dough has more than doubled in size, knead again for about 3 to 4 minutes until all the air has been forced out—this is known as 'knocking back'. Leave the dough to relax again for 10 minutes. Shape the bread into two loaves and place on a baking tray. Allow to rise again in a warm place, this time for only 20 to 30 minutes. The dough is ready for baking when a small dent remains in it when pressed lightly with the finger.

Brush the loaves with water and sprinkle with flour. Bake in a preheated hot oven, 450°F for 30 to 35 minutes.

Note: *you can also bake the loaves in pans. If so, brush the pans well with oil before*

For two 1 lb loaves
Seed Loaf

³/₄oz fresh yeast
2 cups warm water, or more as needed
5 ¼ cups strong white flour
2 level teaspoons salt
1 tablespoon sugar
1 to 2oz caraway seeds

Yeast Bread

In the *Irish Country Women's Association Cookbook*, published in 1978, Patrick Staunton asks

And does anyone make yeast bread now? A familiar sight one time was the big bucket by the fire and in it the mysterious dough that seemed to have a life all of its own. But not everybody could make it. Some people had the touch—and if you had, you were looked on as a kind of rural Cordon Bleu.

Cooking in a bastible

I was delighted to have an opportunity recently to watch an elderly Corkwoman cook in the traditional Irish way—in a bastible over an open fire. Joan Twomey, from Ballingrane near Shanagarry, was '80 years', as she says herself, in November 1994. She cooked absolutely everything on the fire: bread, apple cakes, geese, turkeys, chickens, stews, roast potatoes…often for large numbers of hungry men who helped with the haymaking or harvesting. Her house has always been known for 'a warm welcome'. Long ago, as Joan says, they played cards every night for tuppence and thruppence, and no one ever left her house without a cup of tea and a slice of sweet cake or apple tart.

When I first contacted Joan she was surprised to discover that I was interested in the old ways of cooking. However, when I explained my wish to pass on recipes and cooking methods to the next generation, she spoke excitedly about all the things she'd cooked through the years, and we set a date to cook bread and apple tarts.

When I arrived on the appointed day the fire was blazing in the big open fireplace in the old-fashioned, whitewashed kitchen. Joan already had the bastible, a heavy iron pot with three legs and a flat base, heating over the open fire. Nowadays Joan is troubled by arthritis in her hands so she instructed me on how to make her currant bread.

We put a round of brown paper and a round of buttered parchment paper into the base of the bastible, which was hanging from a crane about 14 inches above the fire. Then the loaf of currant bread was laid on top. While we were making the bread the lid of the bastible had been heating on the open fire, so we lifted this on to the top of the bastible and then shovelled 'spleece'—hot embers from the wood fire—over the lid. Joan showed me how to test the heat with my hand and how to lift off the lid carefully so that no hot embers dropped into the oven while I checked the bread. The bastible was held securely in position over the fire by a pronged stick called a *gaulóg* propped against the chimney's back wall.

In no time the currant bread was baked and we rested it on its side to cool. My first effort was a bit scorched on the base, but Joan assured me I'd get better at it with practice and she was right. While the kettle was coming to the boil for tea, we made an apple cake which Joan rightly said would take 10 to 15 minutes in the bastible. On my first attempt I cut the apple into chunks so it took longer to bake, but Joan explained to me that she would normally slice the apples and not pile them so high. The apple cake cooks amazingly quickly on a tin plate. Joan brushes the surface with milk and adds a few dabs of butter. Both the bread and apple cake had soft and tender crusts, quite different from their oven-baked relatives.

The satisfaction of mastering this much more skilful way of cooking on the open fire was terrific. I am absolutely hooked, and have put an open fire into my house in Ballycotton specially to cook on!

Note: Mrs Bridget Guerin, of Ballyheigue, in North Kerry, described to me how she made yeast bread in the bastible back in the 1940s. This was an interesting discovery, as I had always associated the bastible with soda breads rather than yeast breads.

Seedy Bread

Many Americans are convinced that Irish soda bread traditionally contains caraway seeds. I was baffled by this assumption until I discovered that seedy bread was certainly made in Donegal and Leitrim. The tradition of putting caraway seeds in bread must have been taken to the United States by Irish emigrants.

4 cups plain white flour
1 level teaspoon salt
1 level teaspoon baking soda
1 tablespoon sugar
4 tablespoons butter
2 teaspoons caraway seeds
1¼ to 1½ cups buttermilk

First fully preheat your oven to 450°F.

Sieve all the dry ingredients and add the caraway seeds. Rub in the butter, if using. Make a well in the center and pour in most of the milk at once. Using one hand, mix in the flour from the sides of the bowl, adding more milk if necessary. The dough should be softish, but not too wet and sticky. When it all comes together, turn it out on to a floured board and knead lightly for a second, just enough to tidy it up. Pat the dough into a round about 1½ inches deep and cut a cross on it to let the fairies out! (Let the cuts go over the sides of the bread to make sure of this.) Bake in the hot oven for 15 minutes, then turn down the heat to 400°F for 30 minutes or until just cooked. If you are in doubt, tap the bottom of the bread: if it is cooked it will sound hollow.

Table laid for afternoon tea at Glin Castle, Co. Limerick.

These scones with their sweet sugary tops are still one of my favourite things in the whole world! When I was a child, our enormous family of nine regularly polished off a tray of them after school.

First preheat your oven to 475°F.

Sieve all the dry ingredients together in a nice roomy bowl. Make a well in the center and rub in the butter. Beat the eggs with the milk, add the liquid all in one go and mix to a soft dough. Turn out on to a floured board. Knead lightly, just enough to shape into a round. Roll out to about 1 inch thick and stamp into scones. (Mummy always cut them into squares or diamond shapes.) Brush the tops with egg wash and dip in granulated sugar. Bake in the hot oven for 10 to 12 minutes, until golden brown on top. Cool on a wire rack.

Serve the scones split in half with butter and homemade jam or, better still, with homemade raspberry jam and a dollop of whipped cream.

Add 4oz plump sultanas to the above mixture when the butter has been rubbed in. Continue as above.

Makes 18 to 20 scones using a 3-inch cutter

Mummy's Sweet White Scones

8 cups flour
pinch of salt
^{1}/$_3$ cup superfine granulated sugar
4 teaspoons baking powder
12 tablespoons (1^1/$_2$ sticks) butter
3 eggs, free range if possible
approximately 1^3/$_4$ cups milk to mix

To glaze
1 egg, beaten with a pinch of salt
granulated sugar

Fruit Scones

A friend from West Cork told me that scones were aptly named Lightning Buns in his house when he was a child, because his mother 'had them in and out of the oven as fast as lightning', not to mention the speed at which they disappeared as soon as they were out of the oven.

Lightning Buns

Currant Squares

The carts were big and box-like, filled with double rows of shallow trays on which rested row after row of steaming loaves, tuppence or tuppence-farthing each…Underneath a deep deep drawer, going the whole length of the cart, filled with lovely white an' brown squares, soda squares, currant squares, and brown loaves, covered with their shining golden crust.

Sean O' Casey, *The Street Sings*.

6 cups plain white flour
1 teaspoon baking soda
$^1/_2$ teaspoon salt
$^1/_4$ cup superfine granulated sugar
4 tablespoons butter
$^3/_4$ cup currants
$^3/_4$ cup golden raisins
$^1/_3$ cup chopped mixed peel
1 egg, optional; free-range if possible
2 to 2$^1/_4$ cups buttermilk

Preheat the oven to 450°F.

Sieve all the dry ingredients into a nice roomy bowl. Rub in the butter, then add the dried fruit and chopped peel and toss well in the flour. Whisk the egg if using and add the buttermilk. Make a well in the center and pour in the liquid all at once. Quickly mix to a soft dough. Turn out on to a floured board and tidy it around the edges with a floured hand. Flip the mixture over and flatten into a round, 2 inch thick. Cut into four patties. Bake in the preheated oven for 15 minutes, then reduce the temperature to 350°F for a further 20 to 30 minutes or until golden brown. The bread should sound hollow when tapped on the base. Serve freshly baked with butter.

Spotted Dog

At times of the year when the men were working particularly hard in the fields, the farmer's wife would go out of her way to reward them with a richer bread than usual for tea. According to her means she might throw in a fistful of currants or raisins, some sugar and an egg, if there was one to spare. The resulting bread, the traditional Irish 'sweet cake', had different names in different parts of the country—spotted dog, currie cake, railway cake and so on. Currant bread was not just for haymaking and threshing, but was also a treat for Sundays and special occasions.

4 cups plain white flour
1 to 2 tablespoons sugar
1 level teaspoon salt
1 teaspoon baking soda, sieved
$^3/_4$ cup raisins, currants, or golden raisins
1$^1/_4$ to 1$^1/_3$ cups sour milk or buttermilk
1 egg, free-range if possible (optional— you will not need all the milk if you use the egg)

First fully preheat your oven to 450°F.

Sieve the dry ingredients, add the fruit and mix well. Make a well in the center and pour most of the milk in at once with the egg. Using one hand, mix in the flour from the sides of the bowl, adding more milk if necessary. The dough should be softish, not too wet and sticky. When it all comes together, turn it out on to a floured board and knead it lightly for a few seconds, just enough to tidy it up. Pat the dough into a round about 1$^1/_2$ inches deep and cut a deep cross on it. Bake for 15 minutes, then turn down the oven to 400°F and continue to cook for approximately 30 minutes. If you are in doubt, tap the bottom: if it is cooked, it will sound hollow.

Serve spotted dog freshly baked, cut into thick slices and generously smeared with butter. Simply delicious!

Spotted Dog

Fraughan Bread

Fraughans, fraochans, herts and bilberries are all names for the little wild blueberries that grow in Ireland on moorland and mountain. They have become scarcer in recent years, but are still collected in late July and early August. They have an intense flavor which is quite delicious and are much prized, particularly by older people. Crushed with a little sugar and eaten with cream they are a feast (see page 183).

During the Second World War, when dried fruit was scarce, fraughans were often used for making spotted dog (see opposite).

Substitute 1 to 2 cups wild blueberries fraughans for the dried fruit. Add the fraughans to the dry ingredients and proceed as above.

The Stations

'The Stations' is a lovely Irish tradition which dates back to Penal times, when religious persecution forbade Catholic priests to say Mass. They went into hiding, and Mass was often said rather furtively on Mass rocks in the woods or in people's houses.

The custom has lived on in country areas. People take turns every few years to have Mass said in their home for neighbors, friends and relatives —usually in the kitchen, with the kitchen table, covered with a starched linen cloth, serving as the altar. It is considered a great honor to be the chosen household. The woman of the house and one or two friends would traditionally be up at dawn, lighting fires, baking breads, making butter balls from freshly churned butter and undertaking all the final preparations for the breakfast after the Mass. This feast would include hot cereal with thick cream followed by bacon, sausages, black and white puddings, tomatoes, fried farm eggs and sometimes wild mushrooms. These were served with a mountain of buttered toast, soda bread and copious cups of strong sweet tea. 'Shop bread' or 'priest's bread' (a buttered loaf from the local bakery) was bought for this special occasion.

When the priests left, the Stations were officially over, but in many parts of the country it was only then that the real party began. Often there would be a sing-song with music on a melodeon or even a few whistles. Stories were told and eventually people made their way home with a few sugar lumps as a treat for the children.

Priest's Bread

For 2 1 lb (450g) loaves

¾oz fresh yeast
2 cups water, more as needed
2 tablespoons butter
2 teaspoons salt
1 tablespoon sugar
5 cups bread flour

White yeast bread became known as 'priest's bread' in many parts of the country, as it was associated with these special occasions.

Mix the yeast with ½ cup lukewarm water until dissolved. Put the butter, salt and sugar into a bowl with ½ cup of very hot water. Stir until the sugar and salt are dissolved and the butter has melted. Add ½ cup of cold water. By now, the liquid should be lukewarm or blood heat, so combine it with the yeast.

Sieve the flour into a bowl. Make a well in the center and pour in most of the lukewarm liquid. Mix to a loose dough, adding the remainder of the liquid, or more flour or liquid if necessary. Turn the dough on to a floured board, cover and leave to relax for about 5 minutes. Then knead for about 10 minutes or until smooth and springy (if you use a food mixer with a dough hook, 5 minutes is usually long enough). Put the dough somewhere warm and moist to rise, in a pottery bowl sealed with plastic wrap.

When the dough has doubled in size, knead it again for about 4 or 5 minutes until all the air had been forced out. Leave it to relax again for 10 minutes, shape into loaves and put into two well greased bread tins.

Cover with a tea towel and allow to rise again in a warm place for about 20 minutes. The loaves are ready for baking when they have doubled in size and a small dent remains in the dough if pressed lightly with a finger. Brush with warm water and dredge lightly with white flour.

Bake in a preheated hot oven at 450°F for 30 to 35 minutes. The bread should be crusty and sound hollow when tapped. Cool on a wire rack.

Barry's Bakery in Midleton still make this traditional bread as a special order for people having 'the Stations' in their houses.

Mix the yeast with ²/₃ cup lukewarm water until dissolved. Put the butter, salt and sugar into a bowl with ²/₃ cup of very hot water. Stir until the sugar and salt are dissolved and butter melted. Add ²/₃ cup of cold water. By now, the liquid should be lukewarm or blood heat. Combine it with the yeast.

Sieve the flour into a bowl. Make a well in the center and pour in most of the lukewarm liquid. Mix to a loose dough, adding the remainder of the liquid, or more flour if necessary. Turn the dough on to a floured board, cover and leave to relax for 5 to 10 minutes. Then knead for about 10 minutes or until smooth and springy (if you use a food mixer with a dough hook, 5 minutes is usually long enough). Put the dough to rise in a pottery bowl covered tightly with a damp cloth or pure plastic wrap (yeast dough rises best in a warm moist atmosphere, e.g. close to your stove or on top of a radiator). When the dough has doubled in size, knead it again for about 2 or 3 minutes until all the air has been forced out—this is called 'knocking back'. Leave the dough to relax again for 10 minutes.

Shape the bread into a loaf and put it into a well greased 2lb loaf pan. Cover with a tea towel and allow to rise again in a warm place. This rising period will be much shorter, only about 20 to 30 minutes. The loaf is ready for baking when a small dent remains in the loaf when the dough is pressed lightly with the finger.

Brush the surface of the loaf lightly with egg wash. Bake in a preheated hot oven at 450°F for 30 to 35 minutes.

For a 2lb loaf

Buttered Loaf

³/₄ oz fresh yeast
2 cups water or more as needed
4 tablespoons butter
1 rounded teaspoon salt
1 tablespoon sugar
5³/₄ cups bread flour
light egg wash, made from beaten egg
*   and water*

Oatmeal &
other Grains

From the time that Ireland became a society of farmers rather than hunter-gatherers, oatmeal has been a staple food. Early Irish literature contains many references to various kinds of porridge made, depending on the wealth of the household, with water, milk or buttermilk. Oaten bread, or oatcakes, were also common fare. The oats were probably ground at home with a rotary quern, and the bread or cakes baked on a hot stone by the hearth.

Cereals ground in this way were exceedingly abrasive, as pieces of stone and grit inevitably found their way into the flour. Porridge, or stirabout, made from oats, wheat or barley was a more palatable and easier way of consuming grain. Nourishing additions rich in protein, such as milk, butter and eggs, could usefully be incorporated into the porridge.

A more recent introduction to Ireland was maize—imported from America to relieve starvation during the famine. Known as Indian corn, or yellowmeal, it still plays a part in some traditional Irish recipes, though as a 'famine food' it fell into disrepute in the years of comparative plenty that followed. Recently these foods have been taken up again and their delicious and nutritious qualities recognized. Carefully made porridge, served with milk or cream and soft brown sugar, or crisp Donegal oatcakes with lashings of Irish butter and homemade jam, are hard to beat!

Pinhead Oatmeal Porridge

Porridge

Porridge is one of the oldest Irish foods. Eaten for breakfast and supper, it could be made not just from oatmeal, but also from wheat or barley. It could be cooked in water, milk or buttermilk and flavored with salt, butter or honey and, in later years, sugar and eaten with milk or cream. The seventh/eighth century Brehon Laws regulate the types of porridge taken by the children of different classes who were being fostered:

> The children of inferior grades are to be fed on porridge or stirabout made of oatmeal on buttermilk or water taken with old butter and are to be given a bare sufficiency; the sons of chieftains are to be fed to satiety on porridge made of barley meal upon new milk, taken with fresh butter, while the sons of kings and princes are to be fed on porridge made of wheaten meal, upon new milk, taken with honey.

In the eleventh century tale *Aislinge Meic Con Glinne,* the hero dreamed of 'fair white porridge made of sheeps' milk' and of 'porridge the treasure that is smoothest and sweetest of all'.

Gruel

Gruel, which was strained oatmeal, was mentioned in the ninth century Monastery of Tallaght as part of the fasting fare of the Culdee monks.

Their abbot, Maelruain, laid down a rule that 'if a festival happened to fall on certain days the monks were given leave to make gruel of meal and water'. Wow!

This was always made using a teacup as a measure.

Serves 4

Pinhead Oatmeal Porridge

1 cup pinhead oatmeal
4 cups water
1 level teaspoon salt

Soak the oatmeal in one cup of cold water. Meanwhile bring three cups of water to a boil and pour on to the oatmeal. Put in a pan over a low heat and stir until the water comes to a boil.

Cover and simmer for 15 to 20 minutes, stirring occasionally. Stir in the salt. Cover again and leave aside overnight. The oatmeal will absorb all the water. Reheat and serve with single cream or milk and soft brown sugar.

Stirabout

I have always been baffled by the fact that the Irish never took to gruel made from the yellowmeal (cornmeal) sent in to relieve hunger during the famine. In essence this is the same as *polenta,* so beloved of Italian peasants for generations.

According to Luke Dodd, curator of the Famine Museum at Strokestown Park, in Co. Roscommon, there were two factors responsible for this. Firstly, the Irish had been accustomed to cooking oatmeal which cooked relatively quickly, so they frequently undercooked the yellowmeal and therefore it was indigestible and often sickened people. Secondly, Irish peasants of that period had become accustomed to eating 10 to 14lb of potatoes at a sitting, and so they were accustomed to bulk and were far from satisfied by the yellowmeal stirabout. In fact it is said that Irish men's stomachs were unusually large because of this factor.

An indication of the scale of yellowmeal imports during those times is given by the purchase of £100,000-worth of meal from America, ordered by Sir Robert Peel in 1845.

Rye porridge was also eaten extensively during the famine period.

Wheat Pudding

This recipe has been handed down from famine times. I found it in an undated booklet entitled Galway Homegrown Foodstuffs:

Gather ears of wheat when turning ripe or better still quite ripe about late August. Rub them between the hands to remove the outside layer. Boil in water or milk for about 1 hour, stirring occasionally like porridge.

Use 2oz grain to 2½ cups liquid. Add sugar or salt according to taste and serve with milk or cream.

Próinsimín

Right up to the 1970s Diarmuid Ó'Drisceoil would be given *próinsimín* as a special treat when he went back to Cape Clear, an island off West Cork, to visit his relations. Home-grown wholewheat grains were roasted on a dry pan, almost like popcorn, except it didn't pop. (The pan was rubbed with a butter wrapper first.) As a special treat for the city kids, Diarmuid's gran-aunt would first melt some sugar in a little water, then she would toss the hot wheat straight off the pan in the syrup. This, according to Diarmuid, gave the mixture a sort of sweet 'crystally' coating which they loved. *Próinsimín* was hard and crunchy, a challenge for the teeth even though the wheat grains were cooked into the center. It was always eagerly looked forward to and much enjoyed.

Ríobún

Another fascinating recipe from Cape Clear (Oileán Chléire)—an island located off Schull in West Cork.

Donncha Ó'Drisceoil spoke evocatively of ríobún *in his book* Aistí ó Chleíre, *published by An Clóchomhar, Dublin, 1987. Diarmuid Ó'Drisceoil described* ríobún *as 'a sort of cold porridge with a delicious nutty flavour'.*

To make *ríobún*, wholewheat grains were ground on a rotary quern on the table in the kitchen. This roughly ground wheat was called *minbhró*. This was eaten with milk and sometimes sprinkled with a little sugar as a special treat for the children.

Grainseachán

Grainseachán, a porridge made of home-grown wholewheat grains boiled in milk, was still made up to the 1930s on Cape Clear Island.

Oatcakes

Makes about 30

These delicious biscuits keep for several weeks in a tin.

4 cups rolled oat flakes
16 tablespoons (2 sticks) butter
³/4 cup superfine granulated sugar
1 cup plain white flour
pinch of salt
1 level teaspoon baking powder

Melt the butter in a saucepan. Mix all the dry ingredients together. Take the saucepan off the heat and stir the dry ingredients into the melted butter. Roll out the mixture until it is about ¼ inch thick, and either cut into 2½-inch rounds or place in one piece in a swiss roll tin.

Bake in a preheated oven at 350°F for about 20 minutes. Cool on a wire rack.

Mealie Greachie or Durgan

Armando Certuccelli, the Italian post-master in Ballycastle Post Office, on the North Antrim coast, told me about this dish which was one of the dinners expected by farm laborers at harvest time. It is still eaten in that area to this day. The problem is, nowadays, where to buy decent fatty bacon, so that there is some fat rather than nitrates left in the pan after you fry it.

coarsely ground oatmeal
bacon fat

Add some dry oatmeal to the bacon fat in a frying pan after you have cooked bacon slices in it. Fry, stirring, until the oatmeal is nicely toasted. Serve with the bacon and potatoes. Fried onion is sometimes added to this meal also.

Donegal Oatcakes

Serves 4

2 cups fine oatmeal
2 tablespoons butter or lard
pinch of salt
³/4 to 1 cup boiling water

Put the oatmeal into a bowl. Put the butter and salt into a measuring jug, pour boiling water on to it and stir until melted and dissolved. Pour this into the oatmeal and mix to a pliable dough. You may need a little more liquid to obtain the right consistency.

In Donegal the mixture was then left for several hours, or overnight, until it was dry enough to press out into a thin sheet. Press out with your fingers into a pan about 10 x 8 inches. You may not manage to get it quite that thin on your first attempt, because the dough is rather difficult to handle.

Leave it to dry for another hour or two before you bake it. Bake in a very low oven at 250°F. (I use the coolest oven—half of a four-door Aga) for 3 to 4 hours. The more slowly it cooks, the better the flavor will be. Oatcakes keep for ages in an airtight container and can be reheated. Eat with butter or butter and jam.

Note: *we use fine stoneground oatmeal from Macroom.*

Cakes & Cookies

The tradition of baking cakes for ceremonies and festivals—weddings, baptisms and funerals, harvest, Christmas, Easter, Mothering Sunday—is an important one in Ireland. Originally, no doubt, it arose from the practice of adding a few precious, luxury ingredients, such as a handful of dried fruit, to the daily bread, to celebrate a special occasion. The traditional Irish barm brack, a fruited yeast bread or cake, is probably the direct descendant of these early celebration breads.

Having 'a light hand with a sponge' used to be the highest compliment a woman could be paid. Indeed, her status in her village or community would virtually depend on how high her sponge cake rose! Some of the most delectable recipes I have collected in the course of writing this book have been for tea-time dainties that remind me of an almost forgotten era when women would have time to sit down together, chat, sip tea and eat a slice of some feather-light homemade confection.

Children always love helping with cake-making. I think it particularly appeals to them because of the almost magical way in which the raw, runny ingredients puff up in the oven into delicious buns or cakes. I adored helping my mother when she baked and I have included here some of the recipes that I would make with her, following the time-honoured Irish tradition of passing the recipes down the generations.

To make Barm

This recipe, taken from Eliza Helena Odell's manuscript receipt book, is dated August 26th, 1851:

Take one ounce of hops with a plateful of malt and boil in two gallons of water for an hour and then strain them, when milk is warm add 2lbs of flour with a pint of old barm, jug it up well and set it in a warm place and it will be fit for use next day. 1 pint and about a wine glass will be sufficient for 4 quarts of flour.

Accounts from the nineteenth century show that barm bracks were associated with New Year's Eve festivities. Pieces of baked loaf were dashed against the back of the house door to ward off poverty in the coming year.

Halloween Barmbrack

The word 'barm' comes from an old English word beorma, *which means yeasted fermented liquor. This was used to raise the cake and is now replaced by yeast. 'Brack' comes from the Irish word* brac, *meaning speckled—which is exactly what this cake is, with dried fruit and candied peel.*

Halloween has always been associated with fortune-telling and divination, so various objects are wrapped up and hidden in the cake mixture. They may include a wedding ring, a coin, a pea (for poverty), a thimble (signifying spinsterhood) or a piece of matchstick (which means that your husband will beat you!)

3¹/2 cups bread flour
¹/2 teaspoon ground cinnamon
¹/2 teaspoon mixed spice
pinch of salt
¹/4 teaspoon nutmeg
2 tablespoons butter
³/4oz fresh yeast
¹/2 cup superfine granulated sugar
1 cup tepid milk
1 egg, free-range if possible, beaten
1¹/2 cups golden raisins
³/4 cup currants
¹/3 cup chopped candied peel

To glaze
1 tablespoon sugar
2 tablespoons water or milk

For Halloween
Ring, coin, stick, pea, thimble, all wrapped in parchment paper

All utensils should be warm before starting to make barmbrack.

Sieve the flour, spices and salt into a bowl. Rub in the butter. Mix the yeast with 1 teaspoon of sugar and 1 teaspoon of tepid milk and leave for 4 or 5 minutes, until it becomes creamy and slightly bubbly. Add the rest of the sugar to the flour mixture and mix well. Pour the tepid milk and the beaten egg on to the yeast mixture; add to the flour. Knead well, either by hand or in the warmed bowl of an electric mixer for 5 minutes at high speed. The batter should be stiff but elastic. Fold in the dried fruit and chopped peel, cover with a cloth and leave in a warm place until the dough is well doubled in size.

Punch down the dough and knead well for 2 or 3 minutes, then divide it into two equal portions. Grease two 7-inch loaf pans and put one portion in each pan. Add the ring, coin, stick, pea and thimble at this stage. Cover the pans with a cloth and leave to rise for about 30 minutes to 1 hour. Bake in a preheated moderate oven at 350°F for about 1 hour or until golden and fully cooked.

Dissolve 1 tablespoon of sugar in 2 tablespoons of boiling water or milk and brush this over the loaves to glaze them. Put them back into the oven for about 2 or 3 minutes. Turn out to cool on a wire tray. When cool, serve cut into thick slices, with butter.

Note: *barmbrack keeps well, but if it gets a little stale, try it toasted.*

Mixed spice can be made by grinding together 1 tablespoon coriander seeds, 1 crushed cinnamon stick, 1 teaspoon allspice berries and 1 teaspoon whole cloves. Stir in 1 tablespoon freshly grated nutmeg and 2 teaspoons ground ginger.

This is a more modern version, now commonly called a tea brack, because the dried fruit is soaked in tea to plump it up. Even though it is a very rich bread, it is traditionally served buttered.

Soak the raisins and currants in cold tea overnight. Next day, preheat the oven to 350°F. Add all the remaining ingredients to the fruit and tea and stir well. Put the mixture in a 1lb loaf pan which has been lined with greased parchment paper. Cook in the oven for about 1½ hours. Cool on a wire rack. Keeps very well in an airtight tin. Serve buttered.

Makes 1 loaf

Irish Barm Brack

3/4 cup golden raisins
3/4 cup raisins
3/4 cup currants
1/3 cup crystallized cherries (undyed)
1/3 cup homemade candied peel
1 cup soft brown sugar
2 cups self-rising flour
1 cup cold tea
1 egg, free-range if possible, beaten
1 teaspoon mixed spice

Irish Barm Brack (left) and
Hallowe'en Barm Brack

Lana Pringle's Barmbrack

2³/4 cups raisins and golden raisins
1³/4 cups tea
1/3 cup glacé cherries, halved
1/3 cup chopped candied peel,
(see page 264)
2/3 cup soft brown sugar
2/3 cup granulated sugar
1 egg
3³/4 cups plain white flour
1/4 teaspoon of baking powder

Lana Pringle comes from Clydaville near Mallow in Co. Cork, where her breads, cakes and biscuits are legendary among her friends. Lana's confections are truly hand-made. She dislikes the din made by food processors, so all her cakes are creamed, beaten and whisked laboriously by hand and baked in the temperamental Aga. Her recipe for barmbrack came from her husband Gerald's family, who lived in Dublin. It keeps wonderfully well in a tin and is traditionally served sliced and buttered.

You will need either three pans 4 x 6¼ x 3 inches deep or two pans 5 x 8 x 2½ inches deep.

Put the raisins and sultanas into a bowl and cover with tea. (Lana occasionally uses a mixture of Indian and Lapsang Souchong, but any good strong tea will do.) Leave overnight to allow the fruit to plump up. Next day add the cherries, chopped candied peel, sugars and egg; mix well. Sieve the flour and baking powder and stir in thoroughly. The mixture should be softish; add a little more tea if necessary (¼ cup).

Grease the pans with melted butter. Lana uses old pans, of a heavier gauge than is available nowadays, so light modern pans may need to be lined with parchment paper for extra protection.

Divide the mixture between the pans and bake in a moderate oven at 350°F for about 40 minutes.

Lana bakes her barmbracks in the Aga. After 40 minutes she turns the pans around and gives them a further 10 minutes. If you are using two pans the barmbracks will take about 1 hour. Leave in the pans for about 10 minutes and then remove and cool on a wire rack.

Note: *in the early twentieth century, Lady Gregory would distribute barmbrack to the actors and actresses of the Abbey Theatre in Dublin.*

Barm Tea Cakes

4 cups flour
6 tablespoons butter
1 egg
1¼ cups warm milk
—only blood heat
1/2oz yeast

This recipe, dated Christmas 1918, comes from Mrs Anglin's hand-written cookbook:

Rub butter to flour, add salt. Dissolve yeast in a little sugar, add milk and beaten egg, beat all the barm together and add flour.

Put the basin in a warm place, cover with a tea towel and leave 2 hours to rise—when surface has cracked, roll out lightly and cut into rounds the size of a saucer. Place before the fire for ¼ hour to rise again—then bake without turning, 20 minutes. When needed split and toast and butter—will keep.

Rich Plum Cake

Practically all the manuscript cook books I came across had one, or indeed several, recipes for plum cake. The name sounded so evocative I couldn't wait to try them. The earlier ones, from about 1800, just had currants in the recipe, and some called for fat drippings instead of butter. Later entries were often richer and included a mixture of dried fruit. None mentioned plums or even prunes. Rich cakes like these would have been made in the summer when eggs and butter were plentiful. This one comes from a manuscript cookbook which belonged to Annie Kiely of York Street, Cork, dated about 1910. It makes a huge cake.

1 lb (4 sticks) butter
2 1/2 cups soft, dark brown sugar
12 eggs
4 cups flour
2 cups ground almonds
3 cups golden raisins
3 cups Valencia raisins, stoned
3 cups currants
2/3 cup mixed peel
rind and juice of 1 lemon
1 glass whiskey or brandy

Line a 12-inch (30.5cm) round cake pan carefully with both brown and wax paper.

Cream the butter in a nice big bowl, add the sugar and beat until soft and light. Add the eggs one at a time, beating well between each one. Mix half the flour and the ground almonds with the fruit and peel. Stir the other half of the flour into the cake mixture, then carefully stir in the fruit with the lemon juice and rind, and mix all very thoroughly. [You'll be quite exhausted by this stage if you've performed the whole operation by hand!] Pour the cake mixture into the lined pan, smooth the top and bake in a preheated moderate oven at 350°F for 2 hours, then reduce the temperature for about a further half hour or until a skewer comes out clean. Allow the cake to cool in the pan. Poke holes in it with a skewer and pour the whiskey or brandy over it. Wrap next day in greaseproof or brown paper. Keeps very well.

Plum Cake

A recipe from Eliza Helena Odell's manuscript receipt book, dated 26 August 1851:

1 lb (4 sticks) fresh butter, beaten to a cream
2 1/2 cups granulared sugar, finely powdered
rinds of 2 lemons, grated
6 cups flour, well dried
6 cups currants
3/4 lb citron, cut into pieces
8 or 9 eggs, yolks and whites beaten together.

Mix all well and when ready for the pan add a large glass of whiskey—it will take two hours and a half in a brick oven to bake it well.

L. Croker

Bride Cake

The bride cake of former years was much less rich than the fruitcake of the present day. When white flour was still a luxury, bride cake was often just a simple wheaten cake or one made from honey and fruit. No matter how simple, it denoted prosperity and good fortune and was an important part of the wedding festivities.

When the bride entered her home after the wedding ceremony her mother broke the cake over her head for good luck. The pieces were then divided amongst the guests. In Irishtown and Ringsend in Dublin they broke cake over the bride's head up to recent times, for luck and fertility.

Christmas Cake

For many people the Christmas Cake was, and to a great extent still is, the most important cake of the year. For weeks thrifty women all over the country scrimped and saved to gather up enough dried fruit—golden raisins, currants, candied peel, crystallized cherries, perhaps even a few plump muscatel raisins—to make the cake of cakes. Eventually when all the ingredients had been collected, a day towards the end of October or early November was chosen. Excitement was in the air. Making the cake was always a family affair and in our family there was no shortage of eager helpers. As children we stoned the muscatel raisins, washed and halved the jewel-like cherries, diced the chunks of candied peel and citron and even helped with the laborious creaming of butter and soft dark brown sugar. Butter was always used for this traditional pièce de résistance—*even cooks who disapproved of such extravagance for the rest of the year always put butter in 'the cake'.*

The pan was lined with several layers of parchment paper and protected with a brown paper collar. Our old Aga was coaxed to the correct temperature and soon the seductive smells of home baking filled the house. We could all feel the tension as the cake was tested and retested—there was much examining the bottom of a magical skewer to determine whether it was 'coming out clean'. Then, with a sigh of relief, the cake was reverently carried to a shelf in the cool pantry, after a further blessing of Irish whiskey, or in some households a drop of the 'hard stuff', to help it to mature.

By the time Christmas came round everyone was in a fever of anticipation. The cake was unwrapped, rich marzipan was applied, once more with the help of eager chattering children, and then the royal icing was lathered on to make a convincing snow scene. Finally the 'plaster of Paris' snowmen and Santa were unwrapped from the tissue nests in which they had hidden since the previous Christmas and were placed on top. The cake then graduated to the parlour where it sat in state on the side board until Christmas Eve or Christmas Day.

³/4 cup glacé cherries
¹/4 cup whole almonds
2¹/2 cups best quality golden raisins
2¹/2 cups best quality currants
1¹/2 cups best quality raisins
³/4 cup muscatel raisins, stoned
¹/2 cup ground almonds
grated rind of 1 lemon
grated rind of 1 orange
³/4 cup homemade candied peel
(see page 264)
¹/3 cup Irish whiskey
16 tablespoons (2 sticks) butter
1¹/4 cups light, soft brown sugar
6 eggs, free-range if possible
1 teaspoon mixed spice
2¹/2 cups flour
1 large or 2 small Bramley Seedling apples, grated

Line the base and sides of a 9-inch round, or an 8-inch square pan with parchment paper. Wash the glacé cherries and dry them. Cut in two or four as desired. Blanch the whole almonds in boiling water for 1 or 2 minutes, rub off the skins and chop them finely. Mix the dried fruit, nuts, ground almonds, grated orange and lemon rind and candied peel. Add the whiskey and then leave the mixture for 1 hour to macerate.

Preheat the oven to 325°F.

Cream the butter until very soft. Add the sugar and beat until light and fluffy. Whisk the eggs and add in bit by bit, beating well between each addition so that the mixture doesn't curdle. Mix the spice with the flour and stir in gently. Add the grated apple to the fruit and mix in gently but thoroughly. (Do not beat the mixture again or you will toughen the cake.)

Put the mixture into the prepared pan. Make a slight hollow in the center. Dip your hand into the water and pat it over the surface of the cake: this will ensure that the top is smooth when cooked. Put into the preheated oven; reduce the heat to 300°F after 1 hour. Bake until cooked (about 3 to 3½ hours); test in the center with a skewer—it should come out completely clean. Pour a little whiskey over the cake and leave to cool in the pan.

Next day remove the cake from the pan. Do not remove the lining paper, but wrap in some extra wax paper and foil until required.

Sieve the sugars and mix with the ground almonds. Beat the eggs, add the whiskey and *a drop* of pure almond extract, then add to the other ingredients and mix to a stiff paste. (You may not need all the egg.) Sprinkle the work top with confectioners' sugar, turn out the almond paste and work lightly until the paste is smooth.

Remove the paper from the cake. Put a sheet of wax paper on to the worktop and dust it with some confectioners' sugar. Take about half the almond paste and roll it out on the paper: when rolled, it should be a little less than 1/2 inch thick. Paint the top of the cake with a lightly beaten egg white and put the cake, sticky side down, on to the almond paste. Give the cake a thump to make sure it sticks and then cut round the edge. If the cake is a little 'round-shouldered', cut the almond paste a little larger and press it in against the cake with a palette knife. Then slide a knife underneath the cake or, better still, underneath the paper, and turn the cake the right way up. Gently peel off the wax paper.

Next, measure the circumference of the cake with a piece of string. Roll out two long strips of almond paste; trim both edges to the height of the cake with a palette knife. Paint both the cake and the almond paste lightly with egg white. Press the strips against the side of the cake: do not overlap them or there will be a bulge. Roll a straight-sided water glass along the side of the cake to even the edges and smooth the join. Rub the cake well with your hand to ensure a nice flat surface.

Carefully lift the cake on to a cake board. Allow the almond paste to dry out for several days before applying the royal icing.

Whisk the egg whites in a large bowl just until they begin to froth; then add the sieved confectioners' sugar by the tablespoonful, beating well between each addition. If you are making it in an electric mixer, use the lowest speed. When all the sugar has been incorporated, add the lemon juice, and add a few drops of glycerine if you would like a slightly soft icing. Beat until the icing reaches stiff peaks; scrape down the sides of the bowl. Cover the bowl with a damp cloth for 1 hour until ready to use the icing.

Smear the icing over the top and sides of the cake, using a flexible palette knife. The simplest finish for a Christmas cake, most suitable for those of us not highly skilled in cake decoration, is the snow-scene effect. This is easily achieved by dabbing the palette knife on to the cake at irregular intervals, so the icing comes up in little peaks. While the icing is still wet, stick on some Christmas decorations, e.g. Santas, Christmas trees and robins. If you want to be more ambitious, spread a thinner layer of icing on to the cake so that the top and sides are as smooth as possible. Cover the remainder of the icing with a damp cloth; leave the cake in a cool place or overnight to allow the first coat of icing to set.

With a small star nozzle, pipe rosettes or shell shapes around the base of the cake. Tie a red ribbon around the sides and tie in a flat bow. Decorate the top with rosettes in a star shape or in the shape of a Christmas tree. You could even try writing 'Merry Christmas'. Best of luck—have fun and a Merry Christmas to you too!

To ice the cake

Almond Paste
2/3 cup superfine granulated sugar
2/3 cup confectioners' sugar
2 cups ground almonds
2 small eggs
1 tablespoon Irish whiskey
pure almond extract

Royal Icing
2 egg whites
4 cups confectioners' sugar
2 teaspoons strained lemon juice
glycerine (optional)

Simnel Cake

Simnel was originally a spiced bread, most probably introduced by Elizabethan settlers in the sixteenth century. In and around the Dublin Pale there was a tradition that the mistress of the house provided the ingredients for the maidservants to bake a plum cake, iced with almond paste, to take home on Mothering Sunday—which in Ireland falls on the Sunday before Lent begins.

³/4 cup crystalized cherries
¹/2 cup whole almonds
2¹/2 cups best quality golden raisins
2¹/2 cups best quality currants
2¹/2 cups best quality raisins
³/4 cup homemade candied peel
¹/2 cup ground almonds
rind of 1 lemon
rind of 1 orange
¹/3 cup Irish whiskey
16 tablespoons (2 sticks) butter
1 cup light, soft brown sugar
6 eggs, free-range if possible
1 teaspoon mixed spice
2¹/2 cups flour
1 large or 2 small
apples, peeled and grated

Almond Paste

2¹/2 cups superfine granulated sugar
1 lb ground almonds
2 small eggs
2 tablespoons Irish whiskey
a drop of pure almond extract

Line the base and sides of a 9-inch round, or a 8-inch square pan with parchment paper.

Wash the cherries and dry them. Cut in two or four as desired. Blanch the almonds in boiling water for 1 or 2 minutes, rub off the skins and chop them finely. Mix the dried fruit, peel, cherries, nuts, ground almonds and grated orange and lemon rind. Add about half of the whiskey and leave for 1 hour to macerate.

Next make the almond paste. Sieve the superfine granulated sugar and mix with the ground almonds. Beat the eggs, add the whiskey and a drop of pure almond extract, then add to the other ingredients and mix to a stiff paste. (You may not need all the egg.) Sprinkle a work top with confectioners' sugar. Turn out the almond paste and work lightly until smooth.

Preheat the oven to 325°F.

Cream the butter until very soft. Add the sugar and beat until light and fluffy. Whisk the eggs and add in bit by bit, beating well between each addition so that the mixture doesn't curdle. Mix the spice with the flour and stir in gently. Add the grated apple to the dried fruit, then mix it in gently but thoroughly to the cake batter (do not beat the mixture again or you will toughen the cake).

Put half of the cake mixture into the prepared pan. Roll out about half of the almond paste into a 8¹/2-inch circle and place this on top of the cake mixture in the pan. Cover with the remaining mixture. Make a slight hollow in the center. Dip your hand in water and pat it over the surface of the cake: this will ensure that the top is smooth when cooked. Put into the preheated oven; reduce the heat to 300°F after 1 hour. Bake for about 3 to 3¹/2 hours, until a skewer pushed into the center comes out completely clean. Pour the rest of the whiskey over the cake and leave it to cool overnight in the pan.

Next day remove the cake from the pan. Do not remove the lining paper, but wrap the cake in parchment paper and foil until required.

To ice the cake, roll out about two-thirds of the almond paste into a circle about 9 inches across. Brush the cake with a little lightly beaten egg white and top with the almond paste. Roll the remainder of the paste into eleven balls. The eleven balls represent eleven of the twelve apostles (Judas is absent, being in disgrace for having betrayed Jesus). Score the top of the cake into 1¹/2-inch squares. Brush with beaten egg or egg yolk. Stick the 'apostles' around the outer edge of the top and brush with beaten egg. Toast in a preheated oven 425°F for 15 to 20 minutes or until the almond paste is slightly golden.

Note: nowadays we decorate simnel cake with fluffy Easter chickens.

Porter cake, made with the black stout of Ireland, is now an established Irish cake, rich and moist with 'plenty of cutting'. Either Guinness, Murphy or Beamish can be used, depending on where your loyalties lie.

Preheat the oven to 350°F.

Line the bottom and sides of an 8-inch cake tin, 3 inches deep with parchment paper.

Sieve the flour, salt and baking powder into a bowl. Add the sugar, freshly grated nutmeg and spice. Rub in the butter. Add the fruit, then mix the porter with the beaten eggs. Pour into the other ingredients and mix well. Turn into the lined pan and bake for about 2½ hours. Cool in the pan, then store in an airtight container.

Porter Cake

4 cups plain white flour
pinch of salt
1 teaspoon baking powder
1 cup superfine granulated
   or brown sugar
½ teaspoon freshly ground nutmeg
½ teaspoon mixed spice
16 tablespoons (2 sticks) butter
3 cups golden raisins
⅓ cup chopped candied peel (page 264)
⅓ cup crystalized cherries
1¼ cups porter or stout
2 eggs, free-range if possible

Traditional Porter Cake

This recipe for another porter cake is taken from the manuscript cookbook of Eliza Helena Odell:

4 cups flour
3 cups currants
3 cups raisins
2¹/₂ cups brown sugar
3 sticks butter
8oz citron
4 eggs, broken into the cake not beaten
rind of 1 lemon
half 1 package of mixed spice
and some nutmeg

Rub the butter into the flour, heat ¹/₂ pint of Porter and pour it over a tablespoonful of soda which is to be poured into the above ingredients and mixed with the hand for ³/₄ of an hour, if all put into one tin it takes 3 hours in a slow oven.

Miss Russell

Mixed spice can be made by grinding together 1 tablespoon coriander seeds, 1 crushed cinnamon stick, 1 teaspoon allspice berries and 1 teaspoon whole cloves. Stir in 1 tablespoon freshly grated nutmeg and 2 teaspoons ground ginger.

Boiled Cake

This type of boiled fruit cake is still very popular. Up to recent times many houses did not possess a set of scales, so all the measuring was done in cups.

1 cup water
1 cup butter
1 cup brown sugar
1 cup currants
1 cup golden raisins
3 teaspoons mixed spice
2 cups flour
1 teaspoon baking soda
1 egg, free-range if possible, beaten

Line the base and sides of a 6-inch round cake pan with parchment paper.

Preheat the oven to 350°F.

Put the water, butter, sugar, fruit and spice into a saucepan. Bring to a boil and simmer for about 20 minutes, then turn off the heat and leave to cool. When cold add the flour, stir in the sieved baking soda and beaten egg. Mix thoroughly and turn into the prepared cake pan. Bake in the preheated oven for about 1¹/₂ hours. Cool in the pan and store in an airtight tin. This cake keeps for several weeks.

Slab Cake

Slab cake is sold by weight in many grocers' shops. Recipes vary from plain cakes, such as Madeira or seed cakes, to rich fruit cake. Men often used to bring home a piece of this slab cake after the fair, particularly if they were coming home a little late!

2¹/₂ cups golden raisins
³/₄ cup cherries
1¹/₃ cups candied orange and lemon peel
1 cup chopped almonds
grated rind of 1 orange and 1 lemon
4¹/₂ sticks softened butter
2³/₄ cups superfine granulated sugar
9 eggs, free-range if possible
6¹/₂ cups plain white flour
2 teaspoons baking powder
a little milk

Preheat the oven to 325°F.

Line the base and sides of a rectangular cake pan 10 x 14 x 3 inches with parchment paper. Mix the fruit, peel and nuts with the grated orange and lemon rind. In another bowl cream the butter well, add the sugar and continue to beat until light and pale. Whisk the eggs and beat in bit by bit, adding a little flour if it shows signs of curdling. Stir in the flour and baking powder and finally the mixture of fruit and almonds. If it appears too stiff, add a little milk. Pour into the pan and bake in the preheated oven for 1¹/₂ to 1³/₄ hours. Cool it in the pan. Store in an airtight container.

Hot Cross Buns

Nowadays hot cross buns are traditionally eaten in Ireland on Ash Wednesday and on Good Friday. This practice would have been greatly frowned upon in the past when these were black fast days and the people would scarcely have had enough to eat, let alone spicy, fruit-filled buns. What's the world coming to?

Dissolve the yeast with 1 tablespoon of the sugar in a little tepid milk.

Put the flour into a bowl. Rub in the butter; add the cinnamon, nutmeg, mixed spice, a pinch of salt and the remainder of the sugar. Mix well.

Beat the eggs and add to the milk. Make a well in the center of the flour. Add the yeast and most of the liquid and mix to a soft dough, (add more milk if necessary).

Leave for 2 or 3 minutes, then knead until smooth. Add the currants, sultanas and chopped peel and continue to knead until the dough is shiny. Cover the bowl and let the dough rise in a warm place until it doubles in size. Punch down the dough, by kneading for 3 or 4 minutes. Rest it for a few minutes, then shape it into 1½ inch balls. Put them on to a baking sheet and brush the tops with egg wash. Mark the top of each bun with a cross. Carefully put a cross made of thin strips of shortcrust pastry on to each bun. Leave the buns to rise again to double their size, and brush again carefully with egg wash.

Bake in a preheated oven at 425°F for 5 minutes, then reduce the heat to 400°F for a further 10 minutes or until golden. Cool on a wire rack.

1oz fresh yeast
½ cup superfine granulated sugar
1 to 1¼ cups tepid milk
3¼ cups bread flour
6 tablespoons butter
¼ teaspoon cinnamon
¼ teaspoon nutmeg
1 to 2 teaspoons mixed spice
pinch of salt
2 eggs
½ cup currants
½ cup golden raisins
¼ cup chopped peel
2oz approx. shortcrust pastry (see page 191) or flour and water paste
egg wash - made with milk, sugar and 1 egg yolk to glaze

Protestant Cake

Makes 24

On a Saturday morning in the lobby of the famous old Dublin landmark, the Gresham Hotel, the Dublin folklorist Eamonn MacThomáis shared the food memories of his childhood with me. One of the dainties he spoke of with nostalgic longing was Protestant cake. His family were staunch Dublin Catholics, but he remembers this confection being dished out after Sunday School. 'It was a layer of chocolate and a layer of icing and a layer of mushy stuff, it was very pleasant.' His wife traced the recipe for me; I recognized it as a forerunner to caramel slices.

Make the shortcake base by rubbing the butter into the sugar and flour. Work until it comes together in a ball. Alternatively, blend the three ingredients in a food processor until the mixture comes together. Roll the mixture out evenly and place in a lightly greased roll pan, 10 x 15 inches. Prick the base gently with a fork. Place in a preheated oven at 350°F for 15 to 20 minutes until golden.

Next, make the filling. Melt the butter, over a low heat in a heavy bottomed saucepan. Add the sugar, the corn syrup and lastly the condensed milk, stirring after each addition. Stir continuously for about 20 minutes over a low heat as the toffee forms. The toffee burns very easily if not stirred. When the toffee is a golden brown color, test by placing a drop into a bowl of cold water. A firm ball of toffee indicates that it will make a firm toffee when set. A soft ball of toffee indicates a soft toffee. Pour the toffee mixture over the base, spreading evenly. Allow to cool.

Melt the chocolate slowly in a bowl over hot water and spread evenly over the toffee. Decorate immediately by drawing squiggly lines with the tires of a fork. Cut into squares when the chocolate is firm.

Pastry Base
16 tablespoons (2 sticks) butter
⅔ cup superfine granulated sugar
2½ cups self-rising flour

Toffee Filling
16 tablespoons (2 sticks) butter
1 cup granulated sugar
5 tablespoons corn syrup
16oz fully sweetened condensed milk

Chocolate Top
8oz dark or milk chocolate (approx.)

Caraway Seed Cake

12 tablespoons (1¹/2 sticks) butter
1 cup superfine granulated sugar
3 eggs, free-range if possible
2 cups flour
1 tablespoon ground almonds (optional)
1¹/2 tablespoons caraway seeds
¹/4 teaspoon baking powder
some caraway seeds to sprinkle on top

I hated seed cake as a child, but now it's one of my great favorites. My father had a passion for it, so it was always on offer when we went to visit our Tipperary relations on Sunday afternoons.

Line a round cake pan (7 inches in diameter and 3 inches deep) with parchment paper.

Cream the butter, add the sugar and beat until very soft and light. Beat the eggs and gradually beat into the creamed mixture. Stir in the flour and ground almonds, if using. Add the baking powder and the caraway seeds with the last of the flour. Turn the mixture into the prepared cake pan, scatter a few more caraway seeds on top and bake in a preheated moderate oven, 350°F, for 50 to 60 minutes. Cool on a wire rack. This cake keeps well in an airtight container.

Granny Nicholson's Afternoon Tea

My mother came from just outside the village of Johnstown in Co. Kilkenny. Occasionally, she would receive an invitation from Granny Nicholson, mother of her childhood friends, to bring us all to tea. There was wild excitement when we heard this news, because Granny Nicholson lived in a much grander house than ours and we knew that she served the most sumptuous afternoon teas.

On the appointed day, we all dressed up in our best bib and tucker— quite a performance because we are a large Irish family. I got to wear my smocked dress and angora bolero; the boys wore long pants and ties and had their hair brushed back into a quiff.

On the car journey we were all warned to behave and instructed in the protocol of afternoon tea. (At this time, children were still more or less expected to be seen and not heard!) After we'd played for several hours with Granny Nicholson's grandchildren we were called to tea. We simply couldn't wait, but it was important not to appear too eager. We had to take our places quietly at the long table laid with pretty china and a white embroidered cloth.

We were then warned to wait patiently until one was offered first the thinly sliced bread and butter, then the tiny sandwiches with various fillings—egg and chive, cucumber, salmon, salad or banana. You took the sandwich nearest to you rather than poke through them to find your favorite filling. Eventually we progressed to the buns, cookies crumpets, delectable pastry shells and finally the cake—usually coffee or chocolate. By this time we were in ecstasy, each morsel tasted more delicious than the previous one. These teas, and Granny Nicholson's warm indulgent smile, remain vividly in my memory.

Great Grandmother's Cake

A buttery sponge cake was standard fare for afternoon tea at my grandmother's in Donoghmore, and a great many other Irish houses. When it was taken out of the Aga the cake was cooled on a wire rack by the window in the back kitchen. Thick yellow cream spooned off the top of the milk in the dairy was whipped, and as soon as the cake was cool it was sandwiched together with jam, homemade from the raspberries picked at the top of the haggard.

9 tablespoons butter
3/4 cup superfine granulated sugar
3 eggs, free-range if possible
1 1/4 cups flour
1 teaspoon baking powder
1 tablespoon milk

Filling
8oz homemade raspberry jam
1 1/3 cups whipped cream

superfine granulated sugar to sprinkle

Preheat the oven to 375°F.

Grease and flour two 7-inch round cake pans and line the base of each with a round of parchment paper. Cream the butter and gradually add the sugar. Beat until soft and light and quite pale in color.

Add the eggs one at a time and beat well between each addition. (If the butter and sugar are not creamed properly and if you add the eggs too fast, the mixture will curdle, resulting in a cake with a heavier texture.) Sieve the flour and baking powder and stir in gradually. Mix all together lightly and add 1 tablespoon of milk to moisten.

Divide the mixture evenly between the two pans, hollowing it slightly in the center. Bake for 20 to 25 minutes or until cooked. Turn out onto a wire tray and allow to cool.

Sandwich the cakes together with plenty of homemade raspberry jam and whipped cream. Sprinkle with sieved sugar and serve on an old-fashioned plate with a doily.

Aunt Lil's Wild Strawberry Sponge

5 eggs, free-range if possible
³/4 cup superfine granulated sugar
1¹/4 cups plain white flour

Filling
1¹/2 cups cream
12oz-1lb wild strawberries
or fraises du bois
superfine granulated sugar

1 jelly roll pan 9 inches × 12 inches

When I was a little girl I spent a few weeks of my summer holiday each year on my great-aunt and uncle's farm near Two-Mile-Borris in Co. Tipperary. Noard was a working farm. One of my favorite haunts was the long boreen down to the bog where I picked wild strawberries into a little tin 'ponnie'. I still remember the desperate inner struggle to prevent myself from eating too many of the exquisite wild berries so that Aunt Lil would have enough to sprinkle over her tender sheet of sponge.

Preheat the oven to 375°F. Line the bottom and sides of a roll pan, 9 x 12 inches, with parchment paper. Brush the paper with melted butter; dust with flour and sugar.

Put the eggs and sugar into a bowl over a saucepan of simmering water. Beat the mixture until it is light and fluffy. Take it off the heat and continue to beat until the mixture is cool again. (If you use an electric mixer, no heat is required.) Sieve in about one-third of the flour at a time and fold it into the mixture using a large spatula or metal spoon.

Pour the mixture gently into the pan. Bake in the preheated oven for 12 to 15 minutes. It is cooked when it feels firm to the touch in the center. The edges will have shrunk in slightly from the sides of the pan. Lay a piece of wax paper on the work top and sprinkle it evenly with sugar. Turn the sponge on to the sheet of wax paper. Remove the pan and parchment paper from the bottom of the cake and allow to cool.

Meanwhile beat the cold cream until softly whipped. When the cake is cold, spread whipped cream over the top, cover with wild strawberries, sprinkle with sugar and serve.

Lemon Cheese Cakes

Cheese cakes were a great favorite for afternoon tea or a Sunday treat. This recipe is taken from Annie Kiely's manuscript book:

Make some nice paste ¹/2lb flour and ¹/2lb butter, line some patty pans with it. Cream ¹/4lb butter and ¹/4lb caster sugar, 3 eggs, 6ozs flour, ¹/2 teaspoon baking power, rind and juice of 1 lemon, put one teaspoon of the mixture in each patty pans and bake for ¹/4 of an hour.

Potato Apple Cake

Serves 2

1lb cooked potatoes, mashed
³/4 to 1 cup plain white flour
¹/2 teaspoon salt
2 tablespoons butter
1 or 2 cooking apples, peeled
sugar
butter

This was the highlight of a farmhouse tea in Ulster, particularly in Armagh in the apple growing season. For Halloween night, a ring would be hidden in one of the cakes. The late Monica Sheridan, the much loved television cook of the 1970s, associated this recipe with crisp autumn evenings when she was a child in Tyrone. She put a pinch of cinnamon over the apples, when adding the butter and sugar—a nice touch.

Mix together the potatoes, flour and salt. Roll the potato mixture into a round about ³/4 inch thick. Divide into four patties. Slice a couple of layers of raw apple onto two of the patties and put the other two patties on top. Pinch around the edges to seal. Heat a griddle or a non-stick frying pan or preheat the oven to 350°F.

Cook on both sides until the cake is brown on both sides and the apple is soft in the center (about 20 minutes). Slit each cake crosswise with a knife. Cover the tender apples with slices of butter and sprinkle with sugar. Replace the tops and return to the griddle or oven until the butter and sugar have melted. This forms a delicious sauce. Remove carefully on to warm plates, and serve immediately. Fiddly to make—but delicious!

When my Aunt Florence brings a present of this delicious cake in a tin, lots of people suddenly emerge out of the woodwork pleading for a slice. Without question it's the best orange cake any of us have ever eaten.

Preheat the oven to 350°F.

Grease and flour two round cake pans, 11 inches in diameter and 1½ inches deep. Line the base of each with parchment paper.

Cream the butter and gradually add the sugar. Beat until soft and light and quite pale in color. Add the orange rind. Add the eggs one at a time, beating well between each addition. (If the butter and sugar are not creamed properly, and if you add the eggs too fast, the mixture will curdle, resulting in a cake with a heavier texture.) Sieve the flour and baking powder and stir in gradually. Mix all together lightly; stir in the orange juice.

Divide the mixture evenly between the two pans, hollowing it slightly in the center. Bake the cake in the preheated oven for 35 minutes or until it is cooked. Turn out on to a wire tray and allow to cool.

Meanwhile make the filling. Cream the butter; add the confectioners' sugar and orange rind. Beat in the orange juice bit by bit.

To make the icing, simply squeeze the juice from an orange and add enough to the sugar to make a spreadable icing.

When the cakes are cold, split each one in two halves and spread with a little filling, then sandwich the pieces together. Spread icing over the top and sides and decorate the top, if you like, with little diamonds of candied peel. This cake keeps very well—if you can hide it!

Aunt Florence's Orange Cake

16 tablespoons (2 sticks) butter
1¼ cups superfine granulated sugar
rind of 1 orange
1 tablespoon of orange juice
4 eggs, free-range if possible
1½ cups plain white flour
1 teaspoon baking powder

Orange Filling

8 tablespoons (1 stick) butter
1 cup confectioners' sugar
rind of 1 orange
1 tablespoon orange juice

Orange Glacé Icing

2½ cups confectioners' sugar
orange juice

candied orange peel (see page 264)

Gur Cake

Gur Cake was 'bought in the shops but seldom made in the home', according to the Dublin folklorist Eamonn MacThomáis, who gave me this colorful description. 'You see what happened was this: they sold bread, they sold biscuits, they sold cake, and you know as a cook that if you keep bread and biscuits for a period of time, the bread will go hard but the biscuits will go soft. That's how Jacob's became famous, they used to send them out to the ships, the longer they kept them, the softer the biscuit was getting—that's what made Jacob's famous—they called them sea dog biscuits, the two Jacob brothers made them down in Waterford.

'At the end of the day a shop would have excess bread, excess biscuits, excess cakes. They put them aside for a week, by which time the bread was rock hard and the biscuits were all soft and mushy, so they'd put the whole lot in a barrel, put a bucket of water in on top and stir it all up into a mush. Then they'd throw in a couple of tins of treacle, a bit of candied peel, a few currants or raisins or anything like that and mix it all in. Then they put all the mixture on top of a layer of pastry and then put another layer of pastry on top again. In fact there used to be a lovely marking on top and everyone was convinced in Inchicore that the woman in the shop used her false teeth to mark it, but she maintained that she did it with a fork! Then they'd paint it with egg to give it the shine and sprinkle it with a bit of sugar to give it a glisten. It only took about 10 minutes in the oven because it was all pre-cooked. The smell of that coming out of the oven on a big tray was gorgeous! It was very popular at a halfpenny a slice— nearly as popular as a halfpenny cigarette.

Gur Cake

Makes 12

Most bakeries made a version of these fruity slabs in an effort to recycle stale bread and cake scraps from the previous day's baking. The Dublin cookery writer Honor Moore tells me that they used to be known as 'depth charges' around the docks area of Dublin in the '40s. In Cork they were more elegantly known as Chester cake. Sold at one old penny for a slab between two and three inches square and about one inch or more thick, they were the school dinners of the day. One or two would sustain a pupil 'mitching' from school—or 'on the gur', as it was known in Dublin.

shortcrust pastry(see page 191)
2 cups stale cake, crumbled
4-5 tablespoons plain flour
1/2 teaspoon baking powder
2 teaspoons mixed spice
2/3 cup mixed dried fruit
2 tablespoons candied peel
5-6 tablespoons milk
1 large egg, beaten; free-range if possible

Preheat the oven to 375°F.

Grease a rectangular pan 8 x 12 inches Make the shortcrust pastry, cover and let it rest while you make the filling.

Mix the cake crumbs, flour, baking powder, spice, fruit and candied peel together. Gently heat the milk and mix well with the dry ingredients to make a soft mixture. Whisk the egg and stir in.

Roll out half the pastry and line the pan with it. Spread the fruit mixture over the pastry. Roll out the remaining pastry to cover it and make a few slits in the top. Bake for 45 minutes to 1 hour. When done, cool in the pan and cut into big squares.

Tipsy Cake

Gateaux tipsy cake, which I adored as a child, was a much posher attempt to use up stale cakes. It included cherries, and a dash of some kind of booze as well as dried fruit, and was iced with the most divine pink icing. After Christmas, the tipsy cake was often even more exotic, when the pieces of leftover Christmas cake and icing were added to the mixture.

Margaret O'Connor, an 88-year-old lady from Moyard in Co. Galway, tells me that these biscuits were served at wakes (see page 122) in south Connemara years ago. They are thoroughly delicious.

Mix together the flour and sugar, then rub in the butter. Add the currants, caraway seeds, baking powder and the egg to make a crumbly paste.

Roll out the paste thinly and cut into rounds (we use a 2½ inch cutter). Bake in a moderate oven 350°F for 20 minutes until the cakes are golden brown.

Makes 35 to 40

Wakes Cakes

3 cups plain white flour
1 cup superfine sugar
12 tablespoons (1½ sticks) butter
⅓ cup currants
2 teaspoons caraway seeds
½ teaspoon baking powder
1 egg, free-range if possible.

Funeral Buns

Mrs Marie Kelly of Ballon, Co. Carlow, believes that this recipe is over 130 years old:

About 130 years ago the following recipe for funeral buns was a great favourite and were always given to the mourners at wakes and funerals. They were, of course, washed down with lashings of whiskey which was as easily given then as tea is now.

Take two stones of flour, 1lb of butter and 1lb of sugar rubbed together, 3lbs of currants, ginger, seeds, cinnamon to taste and rosewater mixed with milk. This makes forty eight cakes each weighing 1lb before baking and costing three pence each. Make them round and bake them a fine brown. They will also take one pint of barm in the mixing.

Makes 12

Queen Cakes & Other Dainties

8 tablespoons (1 stick) butter
²/₃ cup superfine granulated sugar
2 eggs, free-range if possible
vanilla extract, orange or lemon rind
1¼ cups flour
³/₄ teaspoon baking powder
1 tablespoon approx. milk or water

Queen cakes, butterfly buns and the like were often served for tea on Nollaig na mBan —Women's Christmas—which was celebrated on the twelfth day of Christmas. This was the women's own feast day. There would be a splendid high tea when all the dainties that the women really enjoyed were served. Pretty little buns like these are often the first recipe that children attempt and they are still as adorable as ever.

Cream the butter until really soft. Add the sugar and beat until white and creamy, either with your hand, as many of our ancestors did, or with a wooden spoon.

Beat the eggs and flavoring and add gradually to the creamed butter and sugar. Beat well. If preferred, the eggs may be broken and beaten into the mixture one at a time. A little sieved flour may be added between each addition of egg if liked.

Stir in the remainder of the flour, mixed with the baking powder, adding a little water or milk if necessary for a dropping consistency. Put the mixture in spoonfuls into well greased muffin pans and bake for about 20 minutes at 400°F. Cool on a wire rack.

Fairy Cakes

Follow the recipe for queen cakes, adding ¹/₃ cup plump golden raisins.

Cherry Cakes

Follow the recipe for queen cakes, adding ¹/₃ cup chopped glacé cherries.

Butterfly Buns

Follow the recipe for queen cakes. Cut the tops off each of the baked queen cakes. Cut these pieces in half and keep aside. Put a little homemade raspberry jam and a dollop of cream on to the bottom part of the bun. Replace the two little pieces, arranging them like butterfly wings. Dredge with confectioners' sugar. Serve on a pretty plate with a doily underneath.

Coffee Cake

16 tablespoons (2 sticks) butter
1 cup superfine granulated sugar
2 cups plain white flour
1 teaspoon baking powder
4 eggs, free-range if possible
¹/₄ to ¹/₃ cup coffee essence
(Irel or Camp)

Coffee Butter Cream Filling
4 tablespoons butter
1 cup confectioners' sugar
1 to 2 teaspoons coffee essence

Coffee Glacé Icing
2 cups confectioners' sugar
1 tablespoon coffee essence
2 tablespoons boiling water

Decoration
hazelnuts or chocolate coffee beans

Little square bottles of Irel or Camp coffee essence are on sale in almost every village shop in Ireland. It makes the best coffee cake.

Preheat the oven to 350°F.

Line the bottom of two 8-inch pans with parchment paper. Brush the bottom and sides with melted butter and dust with flour.

Cream the butter until soft. Add the sugar and beat until pale and light in texture. Beat the eggs and add to the mixture, bit by bit, beating well between each addition. Sieve the flour with the baking powder and stir gently into the cake mixture. Finally add the coffee essence. Spoon the mixture into the prepared pans and bake for about 30 minutes. Cool the cakes on a wire rack.

To make the filling, cream the butter with the sieved confectioners' sugar and add coffee essence to taste.

To make the icing, sieve the confectioners' sugar into a bowl. Add coffee essence and enough boiling water to make icing the consistency of thick cream.

When the cakes are cold, sandwich them together with coffee butter cream. Ice the top and sides with coffee glacé icing. Decorate with hazelnuts or chocolate coffee beans.

Cake Dances

Irish country people were always happy to have an excuse for festivity, and the tradition of the cake dance goes back to medieval times or even earlier. It is still vivid in folk memory in many parts of the country.

On fine Summer evenings from Easter Sunday onwards they would gather at cross roads and dance to the lively tunes of local musicians. The cake in question might have been a currant bread, barmbrack or even a simple loaf of griddle bread, depending on the occasion. If it was a special feast—for example, Easter, Whitsun or midsummer—the crust of the cake might have been decorated with birds or animals.The cake was proudly laid out on a white linen cloth on top of a milk churn and decorated with wild flowers and whatever fruit was in season.

As soon as the musicians struck up, dancing began and the couples swirled for hours and hours. The winners might be the handsomest young couple who were lightest on their feet, or those who danced the longest, or a pair who announced their engagement. The winners who had the honor of 'taking the cake' cheerfully shared it with their friends.

The earliest written account of a cake dance that we know of was in Co. Westmeath in 1682:

> On the patron day in most parishes, as also on the feasts of Easter and Whitsuntide, the more ordinary sort of people meet near the ale house in the afternoon at some convenient spot of ground and dance for a cake. The cake is provided at the charge of the ale wife and is advanced on a board on top of a pike about ten foot high; this board is round and from it rises a kind of garland, tied with meadow flowers if it be early summer. If later the garland has the addition of apples set in round pegs fastened into it. All dance in a large ring around the bushes they call the garland, and they that hold out the longest win the cake and the apples.

Queen Cakes, Fairy Cakes,
Cherry Cakes and Buterfly Buns

Makes 24 to 32, depending on size

Shortbread

3 cups plain white flour
20 tablespoons (2¹/2 sticks) butter
²/3 cup superfine granulated sugar
²/3 cup farina
good pinch of salt
good pinch of baking powder

vanilla or superfine granulated
sugar for sprinkling

For some reason it has become a tradition in Kinoith always to have shortbread in the Aga! Many years ago when I was attempting to hide the shortbread from the children, who seemed to devour it as fast as it was made, I discovered quite by accident that it keeps beautifully for days in the coolest oven of our four-door Aga. Now it is not only the children, but also all our friends who know where to look!

Sieve the dry ingredients into a bowl. Cut the butter into cubes and rub in until the whole mixture comes together. Spread evenly into a roll pan, approximately 10 x 15 ins.

Our unorthodox but very effective way of doing this is to spread the shortbread mixture roughly in the pan, cover the whole tray with plastic wrap, then roll the mixture flat with a rolling pin. Remove the plastic wrap and prick with a fork. Bake the shortbread for 1 to 1¹/2 hours in a low oven, 275°-300°F. It should be pale golden but fully cooked through. Cut into squares or fingers while still hot. Sprinkle with superfine granulated or vanilla sugar and allow to cool in the pan.

Some of the shortbread recipes I came across suggested substituting ¹/4 cup ground almonds for some of the flour, while others included some caraway seeds and even a little candied peel. Caraway seeds were exceedingly popular in Ireland in the eighteenth and nineteenth centuries.

Gingerbread

2 tablespoons milk
¹/2 teaspoon baking soda
2 tablespoons golden raisins
¹/3 cup ginger, preserved in
syrup, chopped
8 tablespoons (1 stick) butter
²/3 cup soft brown sugar
2 eggs, free-range if possible
1¹/2 cups molasses
2 cups flour
1 teaspoon ground ginger
2 tablespoons raisins

A much loved spicy bread, gingerbread was sold at fairs and markets and given to children as a treat. There are many references in old cookery books to it—in fact ground ginger was almost as popular as caraway seeds. This recipe is particularly delicious.

Warm the milk gently with the baking soda and take off the heat. Add the golden raisins and preserved ginger.

Cream the butter, add the sugar and beat until light and fluffy.

Add in the eggs, one by one. Stir in the molasses and fruit, then add the flour and ground ginger. Mix well. Pour into a large loaf pan which has been lined with parchment paper.

Bake at 325°F for 1 to 1¹/2 hours. Cool on a wire rack.

Note: *gingerbread keeps well in an airtight tin.*

Mrs Ray's Meringues

Florence Ray was one of my friends at the village school. She lived in a very grand house called Phillipsburg. Occasionally she asked me home to play. It was a more formal arrangement than with some of my other friends, for her mother would have afternoon tea spread out on the drawing-room table. It was here that I first tasted meringues, light, crisp little blobs, green, palest pink and white, deliciously chewy in the center and crisp on the outside. I longed to know how to make them so I could tell Mummy, but at that time was far too timid and overawed to ask.

4 egg whites
1¼ cups superfine granulated sugar
pink and green food coloring (optional)
whipped cream

Beat the egg whites until stiff but not yet dry. Fold in half the sugar. Beat again until the mixture will stand in a firm dry peak. Fold the remaining sugar in carefully. If you wish, divide the mixture into three bowls. Add a few drops of pink food coloring to one and a few drops of green to the second, leaving the third one white. Mix both to a delicate pale color. Line a baking tray with parchment paper. Spoon blobs of mixture on to the tray. Bake in a preheated oven at 200°F for about 4 hours. Allow to cool, then sandwich together in pairs with whipped cream.

Granny Nicholson's Pastry Shells

2 cups plain white flour
pinch of salt
10 to 12 tablespoons butter
$1/2$ to $2/3$ cup very cold water
homemade raspberry jam
softly whipped cream

Nothing disappears so fast as these little cakes! They crackle in your mouth and taste utterly irresistible.

To make the pastry, sieve the flour and salt into a cold bowl. Cut the butter into knobs about the size of a sugar lump and add to the flour. Do not rub in, but add just enough cold water to bind the pastry together. Mix first with a fork then bring together with your hand.

Wrap the pastry in plastic wrap and leave it to relax in the fridge for 10 minutes. Flour a board and roll the pastry into a strip. This should be done carefully—do not over-stretch or break the pastry surface. Fold the strip into three and turn, so the folded edge is to your left, like a closed book.

Roll out again into a strip $1/2$ inch thick. Fold in three again, cover and leave in the fridge for a further 15 minutes. Roll and fold the pastry twice as before, then chill again for 15 minutes. Roll and fold again, by which time the pastry should be ready for use, with no signs of streakiness. If it does still appear streaky, give it another roll immediately and rest for a further 15 minutes. Roll the pastry out thinly and stamp out 4-inch rounds, (this is most successfully done using the top of a glass). Fit the pastry circles into round-bottomed bun trays. Fill with little squares of parchment paper (years ago we used the tissue paper that wrapped oranges) and dried peas or baking beans. Chill again before baking.

Bake in a preheated moderate oven at 350°F for about 15 minutes or until crispy and lightly browned. Remove the paper and beans and cool the pastry shells on a wire rack. They can then be piled into each other and kept in an airtight tin. Just before serving, fill each pastry shell with a teaspoonful of raspberry jam and put a blob of cream on top. Serve on a cake plate on a pretty paper doily.

Raspberry Buns

$1^1/2$ cups plain white flour
pinch of salt
4 tablespoons butter
$1/3$ cup superfine granulated sugar
1 teaspoon baking powder
1 egg, free-range if possible
a little milk
1 tablespoon raspberry jam
egg wash and sugar to glaze

I'm not at all sure that this is traditional food, but raspberry buns have a very special place in my heart because they were the very first thing I learned to cook under the watchful eye of my Aunt Florence.

Preheat the oven to 400°F.

Sieve the flour and salt into a bowl. Rub the butter into the flour, add the sugar and baking powder. Beat the egg and add a little milk. Mix with the dry ingredients to form a stiffish dough. Divide the dough into 10 equal portions and roll into balls, using a little flour.

Lay the balls of dough on a greased tray and make a hole in the top of each with a floured thumb. Fill with a small quantity of raspberry jam and pinch the dough together again. Flatten the buns slightly. Brush with a little egg wash and sprinkle with sugar. Bake in the preheated oven for about 15 minutes. When the buns are ready they will crack on top and the jam will peep out. They are quite delicious eaten straight from the oven.

The Irish Pantry

The more rural parts of Ireland did not get electricity until quite recently, and it is therefore only in the latter part of this century that such conveniences as refrigerators, never mind freezers, have been installed in most houses. Perhaps for this reason, the traditional arts of preserving are still very much alive in Ireland, to keep food from a time when it is plentiful for consumption during the lean months of the year. Every household, whether a large country house or the cottage of a laborer's family, would have had its larder or pantry of jams, preserves, bottled fruits and cordials to provide a welcome touch of interest, and also some vitamins, to a monotonous winter diet.

Sugar is now used widely, but the traditional sweetening was honey, and beekeeping has a long and honorable history in Ireland—one I like to carry on, with my own hives of bees making Ballymaloe honey. I have included a recipe here for mead, made from honey, as drunk by the heroes of the early Irish legends. I cannot guarantee that your exploits will be as great as theirs!

No book about Irish food would be complete without mention of our other great traditional drinks—buttermilk, tea and, of course, whiskey. Many accounts from the eighteenth and nineteenth centuries attest not only to the quantities of food consumed in Ireland, but also to the prodigious drinking. Amhlaoibh Uí Shúileabháin records a meal in 1835 which was accompanied by 'strong brown ale and above proof whiskey in the shape of punch'.

Old Fashioned Marmalade

Makes about 7lb

2lb Seville oranges
9 cups water
1 lemon
10 cups granulated sugar

Seville and Malaga oranges give a distinctive flavor to the marmalade. They come into the shops after Christmas and are around for 4 to 5 weeks. The peel of the oranges must be absolutely soft before the sugar is added, otherwise it will become very hard at that point and impossible to soften.

Wash the fruit, cut in half and squeeze out the juice. Remove the membrane with a spoon, put with the seeds, tie them in a piece of muslin and soak for half an hour in cold water. Slice the peel finely or coarsely, depending on how you like your marmalade. Put the peel, orange and lemon juice, bag of seeds and water into a non-reactive bowl or saucepan and leave overnight.

Next day, bring everything to a boil and simmer gently for about 2 hours until the peel is really soft and the liquid is reduced by half or even more. Squeeze all the liquid from the bag of seeds and remove it. Add the warmed sugar and stir until all the sugar has been dissolved. Increase the heat and bring to a full rolling boil, then cook rapidly, uncovered, until setting point is reached—about 5 to 10 minutes. Test for a set, either with a sugar thermometer (it should register 220°F), or on a saucer. You should put a little marmalade on a cold saucer and leave it to cool for a few minutes. If it wrinkles when you push it with your finger, it's done.

Stir well and pot immediately into hot sterilized jars. Cover, seal and store in a cool, dry, dark place.

Homemade Candied Peel

5 oranges
5 lemons
1 teaspoon salt
7½ cups sugar
water

Elizabeth Murphy from Kenmare, Co. Kerry recalled the ritual of making candied peel for the cakes and pudding in her childhood. Oranges and lemons were scarcer and more highly valued then.

Cut the fruit in half and squeeze out the juice. Reserve the juice for another use, perhaps home-made lemonade. Put the peel into a large bowl (not aluminum), add salt and cover with cold water. Leave to soak for 24 hours.

Next day, discard the soaking water, put the peel in a saucepan and cover with fresh cold water. Bring to a boil. Cover and simmer very gently until the peel is soft, about 3 hours. Remove the peel and discard the water. Scrape out any remaining flesh and membranes from inside the cut fruit, leaving the white pith and rind intact. (You could do the next step the next day if that were more convenient.)

Dissolve the sugar in 3¾ cups water, bring to a boil, add the peel and simmer gently until it becomes translucent, about 30 minutes. Remove the peel, drain and leave it to cool. Boil down the remaining syrup until it becomes thick and syrupy, but don't stir or it will crystallize. Remove from the heat and put the peel in again to soak up the syrup. Leave for 30 minutes.

Pack the candied peel into sterilized glass jars and pour the syrup over. Cover and store in a cold place or refrigerate.. Alternatively, cool the peel on a wire rack and pour any remaining syrup into the centers. Finally pack into sterilized glass jars and cover and seal. It should keep for 6 to 8 weeks, or longer under refrigeration.

Raspberry Jam

1lb of fruit to 1lb of sugar

This recipe was also in the Kitchen Book of Clonbrock, *in which it is attributed to Mrs. Howard Guinness and dated 1931:*

Put the fruit into a preserving pan and bring it to boiling point only.

The sugar should be placed in a dish on a tray in the oven to get as hot as [possible] but not melted.

When the fruit has come to boiling point, remove the preserving pan off the fire, and add the sugar, stir till quite melted.

Replace the preserving pan on the fire, and again bring only to boiling point. Remove from fire, and cover when hot.

It should keep for years and retain the flavor and color of fresh raspberries.

The advantage of this receipt is the 1lb of fruit and 1lb of sugar produces 2lbs of jam.

Makes 7 to 8lb

Rhubarb & Fig Jam

6lb red rhubarb
1¼ cups sugar
8oz dried figs, previously cut in small pieces and soaked in 2½ cups tepid water overnight

A recipe for this jam appears in several old books. It would appear to have been a great favorite years ago, and was sent to me by a number of people.

Wash and dry the rhubarb if necessary. Cut into ½ inch pieces. Put into a preserving pan and stir until the juice begins to flow. Warm the sugar and add it with the figs. Continue to stir the liquid until it comes to the boil. Boil for 30 minutes or until it looks even in texture all the way through. The jam mixture tends to stick to the pot, so stir frequently. Turn into sterilized glass jars and cover and seal at once.

Rhubarb & Fig Jam and Medlar Jelly

Raspberry Vinegar

use 2¹/₂ cups vinegar to 6lb raspberries

This recipe was given to me about ten years ago by Mrs. Mackey of Ringduffrin in Co. Down, as she presided over a wonderful afternoon tea on the long mahogany table in her dining room.

Put in crock or container and add same ratio for larger quantities fruit and vinegar. Stir occasionally and add more fruit etc. for 2 to 3 days if necessary. Strain through cloth bag. Boil juice for ¹/₂ hour allowing 2¹/₂ cups sugar to each 2 cups of liquid.

Skim well until juice is fairly free of thick skim, (if you put the skimmings into a wide jug, this settles and can be used later). It is important to keep skimming and to take the thick part out of the juice, as it may thicken in bottles if too much is allowed to remain in the juice. It should keep indefinitely. Serve diluted with cold water as a refreshing sumer drink.

The recipe below is from Eliza Helena Odell's manuscript receipt book of 1851:

Put the raspberries into a calico bag and let them strain till all the juice is gone, then put 1lb of sugar to 1 pint of juice, boil and skim it well, when nearly boiled put the vinegar to sour taste.

Cowslip Vinegar

Another recipe taken from Eliza Helena Odell's manuscript receipt book. It is dated 26 August 1851:

To 4 gallons of water with the chill just taken off add 6lb of sugar and half a peck of cowslips, flowers and stalks together, put all into a cask with 3 tablespoonfuls of barm put a piece of glass or slate over the bung hole an let it in a warm place till the vinegar turns sour when the bung hole may be fastened down. This is a cheap and excellent vinegar keeping pickles nice and crisp. If kept in a warm place it will be ready in 6 weeks for use ¹/₄ ounce of gelatin or isinglas will help to clear it.

Honey

Ireland has been described by many poets and storytellers as 'the land of milk and honey', and there is little doubt that there was milk and honey in abundance from earliest times. Numerous references and legends refer to Ireland's sweet honey. Up the end of the twelfth century, when sugar was introduced by an Anglo-Norman baron, honey was the only sweetener in Ireland. However, it took until the sixteenth century before sugar was widely available to the poorer people.

Honey was so important in early Ireland that a whole section in the Brehon Laws was devoted to bees and beekeeping. Tributes were paid in honey, and no banquet was complete without honey and mead, the legendary drink made from it. Honey was used not just for cooking, but also for basting, and as a condiment to dip meat, fowl and fish in at the table.

I have always had a great love for bees and I keep a few hives in the apple orchard. My bees gather their pollen from the apple blossom and the flowers in the gardens nearby, and reward me with more than enough delicious comb honey for family and friends, even in a poor year. There's still a charming, if poignant, custom in many parts of Ireland that if a death occurs in the family, one must go down to the hive to 'tell the bees', otherwise they would swarm or die in the hives.

Drinks

In early times the Irish enjoyed many home-brewed beverages. St. Brigid had the reputation for making the best ale in Ireland and St. Patrick is said to have had his favorite brewer who traveled around the country with him as he converted the pagan Irish. We certainly got the message about the beer! Anyone could brew ale who wished to, but the Brehon Laws laid down regulations for the sale and the proper running of ale houses.

It has been suggested that the Irish also drank *nenadmin*, a cider made from wild or crab apples, *fraochan* (see page 183) made from *fraughans* or wild blueberries or blackberries, and bragget, made by fermenting ale and honey together. But of all the drinks mead, a wine made from honey and said to be both potent and delicious, was the favorite—the drink of celebration. It was served at every banquet. In Brid Mahon's book *Land of Milk and Honey*, there are vivid descriptions of two feasts which tell us of the kind of food and drink served at princely banquets. The first one concerns Bricriu, a wealthy and malicious chieftain who decided to give a feast and for that purpose built a house big enough to accommodate the Ulster heroes and their wives; the meal included 'beef broth, roast boar, salmon, honey cakes and many other dishes; to drink the guests had the finest of ale, the choicest of mead and the rarest of wines…' In another story, 'The Wooing of Etain', we read how King Eochaidh made a great feast at Tara, during which mead, fine wines and barrels of ale were served.

Haymaking Drink

Mrs. Frances Dillane from Ladytown, Newbridge, Co. Kildare told me that for haymaking, the most satisfying drink was ice-cold milk and ice-cold spring water—in equal parts.

Sowans

Sowans is made from the husk and chaff residue (the 'sids') of milled oatmeal, steeped in hot or cold water for any period between four days and three weeks. During the period of steeping, the mixture ferments and when this fermentation subsides it is strained to yield a whitish liquid, known as 'bull's milk'. This was used in baking and was drunk on church black fast days. It has a decidedly sour taste.

Sowans were traditionally prepared at Halloween, specifically for the returning dead, who, it was believed, visited their former homes at that time. It was customary to prepare a bed by the fire and to leave out some tobacco and sowans for their visit.

In *Old Days, Old Ways,* Olive Sharkey recalls the popularity of sowans in her father's day:

> Sowans were a drink made from the husks of oats, a widely acclaimed thirst-quencher when my father was a boy. It was made for the hay-making season when mouths were bone dry, if the weather was particularly dry. The husks were poured into a large earthenware pot, together with some whole oats and left to soak in water for up to a week. The liquid was then strained through a rush mat, ready for drinking.

Buttermilk

At least since the eighth century, buttermilk (the thin milk left in the churn after buttermaking) has been a popular drink in Ireland. The Brehon Laws stipulate that it is a legal duty to provide hospitality to anyone who calls at one's door, and buttermilk is listed as an appropriate drink to offer. Centuries later, while touring Ireland in 1825, Sir Walter Scott found the same hospitable tradition: 'perpetual kindness in the Irish cabin: buttermilk, potatoes, a stool is offered or a stone is rolled that your honour may sit down'.

Buttermilk has remained one of the foundations of Irish cooking to this day. During the eighteenth and nineteenth centuries it was part of the staple diet of the peasantry. C. Valey, in *A New System of Husbandry* (1770), writes 'at the time of the year when potatoes are out of season [May, June and July] their whole living is oat bread and buttermilk.'

Margaret Breen, of Lahard Upper, near Beaufort, Co. Kerry wrote to me with the following memory of buttermilk:

Each house had its own Cow. She was fierce important entirely as before the tea was popular full cream sour milk was the drink with the Bastible Bread and Boiled Egg for the Breakfast. That fine thick sour milk was served at dinner also.

Then the Butter was made from the milk which was set in pans for the cream to rise on it. A calf got the skim milk usually. The Buttermilk was wonderful for a Special Drink and for Breadmaking.

Buttermilk was believed to cure eczema. It was also common for girls and women to wash their faces with buttermilk to improve their complexions.

Tea

Tea was first introduced into Ireland in the late seventeenth century and grew very quickly in popularity, though it was an expensive commodity. In September 1719 a duty of twelve pence per pound was imposed on tea imported from England. Household books from the prosperous Carew family of Castleboro estate in Co. Wexford show that in 1769 a pound of breakfast green tea cost 6s 6d.

There was a major increase in tea-drinking in the rural communities in the second half of the nineteenth century, as small grocery shops began to be established in small towns and villages. These grocers were willing to exchange tea and sugar for farm-produced butter and eggs.

There is a common belief that tea is useful as a cure for sore eyes, and in fact the Irish drink more *per capita* than any other nation.

Dandelion Coffee

Wash the root of the dandelion with a coarse brush and cut in small pieces. Roast it in the oven until it is crisp and dark brown. It will then go in powder when crushed. Use 1 teaspoon of this to each cup of coffee required. Brew or draw it like tea and then add boiled milk and sugar to taste.

Dandelion has very valuable medicinal properties.

Florence Irwin, *Irish Country Recipes*

This recipe is from the Kitchen Book of Clonbrock:

> Put all ingredients into a pan which holds 6 gallons of water. Fill up with boiling water—be very careful that the water does boil—cover—when cold strain off—Take a large round of toast, on which put 2 teaspoonfuls of good yeast, cover, let it stand till next day—strain again, and bottle.

Ginger Beer

5lb lump sugar
3oz bruised ginger
rind and juice of 5 lemons

An old lady who did service in one of Ireland's big houses gave me this recipe which she called Protestant lemonade.

Squeeze the juice from the lemons and add the syrup and water. Taste and add a little more water or syrup if necessary. Add ice, garnish with sprigs of fresh mint or lemon balm and serve.

To make the syrup, first dissolve the sugar in the water and bring to a boil. Boil for 2 minutes, then allow it to cool. Store it in the refrigerator until needed.

Protestant Lemonade

4 lemons
1¼ cups syrup (see below)
3¼ cups water
sprigs of fresh mint or lemon balm

Basic Syrup
Makes 3½ cups
2½ cups sugar
2½ cups water

Mead

Boil eight quarts of water in a preserving pan and dissolve in it two pounds of honey. Add thin slices of lemon with skin, pith and pips removed. Remove pan from cooker and when the mixture is nearly cold, add one pint of pale ale and quarter of a teaspoon of yeast dissolved in a little tepid water. Leave overnight. Strain into bottles, putting two washed raisins and a teaspoon of sugar in each bottle. Seal bottles and leave in a warm room for four or five hours. Store in a cool dark place. The mead is ready for drinking in a week.

Apple Wine

Recipes for apple wine regularly appear in old manuscripts and cookbooks. This recipe was given to Máire Ní Mhurchu by Nora Peter Paul O'Sullivan.

Wash the apples thoroughly. Cut them into slices or chunks, do not peel or core them. Allow a gallon of water to each gallon of cut-up apples. Leave them steeping for ten days. Stir occasionally and strain through a clean cloth (fine nylon or a gauze). Add about 3lb sugar to the strained juice and stir until dissolved. Cream $1/2$oz yeast with a teaspoonful of sugar and add to the mixture.

Place this mixture in a large jar or big bottle. Keep in a moderately hot place while fermenting, covering the container with a one thickness of cloth.

It will take 10 to 15 days to finish and you will know when it is finished as soon as the liquid stops bubbling and hissing. Filter it through fine filter paper or use 3 or 4 thicknesses of nylon. Cork in sterilised bottles making sure that the corks have been boiled for 15 minutes. Cork tightly so that no air gets through.

Store on its side and keep the corks moist.

Note: *apple wine takes about 3 months to mature; it will keep indefinitely.*

Whiskey

Ireland has a long and colorful history of distilling and Irish whiskey is now famous the world over. The earliest references to whiskey date to the fifteenth century; *The Annals of Connaught*, *The Annals of Clonmacnoise* and *The Annals of the Four Masters* each record a tragic incident which occurred in 1405:

Risderd Mag Ragnaill, eligible for chieftainship of Muintir Eolais, entered into rest after drinking *usci bethad* [water of life—i.e. whiskey] to excess, it was a deadly water to him.

During the eighteenth century the first commercial distilleries were established; Kilbeggan Distillery was founded in 1757, followed by Jameson in 1780, Bushmills in 1784 and Powers in 1791. At the close of the century there are estimated to have been more than 2,000 whiskey stills in Ireland, most of them illegal!

Illegal poteen is still made in clandestine stills in remote country areas and distributed to eager customers by an underground network.

Cordials

Orange Cordial

These three recipes are taken from Eliza Helena Odell's manuscript receipt book dated 26 August 1851:

To 1 quart of Whiskey, put the peel cut very thin, and juice of 3 sweet oranges, 1 oz of whole ginger sliced, the rind of 1 lemon and a little of the juices, put all into a crock with a close cover and let it stand for a week stirring it frequently, then strain it through a hair sieve, add 1 lb of white sugar to each quart and filter it when ready.

Blackcurrant Cordial

Steep a gallon of blackcurrants in a gallon of whiskey, with 2 oz of bitter almonds and 1 oz of cloves (both pounded). Let them remain in a jar for three weeks shaking them occasionally then strain off the juice and to every quart put ½ lb of loaf sugar. When the sugar is dissolved bottle for use.

Ginger Cordial

Pick bruise and strain 1 lb of white currants and 1 lb of white sugar and 3 ounces of grated ginger, steep the rind of a Lemon overnight in a quart of good Whisky or Brandy after which take out the Lemon peel, add the whisky to the above ingredients let them stand for a fortnight shaking the vessel daily then strain and filter, it must be closely corked.

Punch

Visitors in the sixteenth and seventeenth centuries regularly comment on the Irish custom of flavoring and sweetening their whiskey—for example, Luke Gerron, in *A Discourse of Ireland* (1620), comments that 'the aquavitae or usquebath of Ireland is not such an extraction as is made in England, but far more qualified and sweetened with licorish'. After the establishment of the distilling industry, whiskey became more widely available, at least to more affluent households, and several writers attest to the popularity of punch during the nineteenth century. Amhlaoibh Uí Shúileabháin (unsurprisingly) seems to have relished it, recording, for example, the night of October 19, 1830 as 'a mild night which I passed happily at Michael Hickey's drinking sweet strong punch till midnight...' In a fictional story, which he retells in his diary, he describes 'a tumbler of punch, strong in whiskey and weak in hot water, sweetened with sugar and acid with lemon'.

Thomas Carlyle, staying in the Imperial Hotel, Sackville Street, Dublin in 1849, recounts in his *Reminiscences of my Irish Journey* how he enjoyed 'punch...and after a silent pipe...tumbled into bed'. Punch continues to have that effect!

Serves 1

Trish Archer's Gaelic Coffee

1 measure of Irish whiskey
2 teaspoons soft brown sugar
strong black coffee
softly whipped cream

Gaelic coffee always puts me in mind of my father-in-law, who always manages to end up with a white moustache as he carefully sips it, much to the general hilarity of his grandchildren!

The most irresistible velvety Gaelic coffee I've ever tasted was made not by an Irish person at all, but by Trish Archer, an English girl who fell for a Corkman and ended up in Ballycotton.

Sláinte agus saol agat—*Health and long life to you!*

Warm a medium sized wine glass with hot water. Pour out the water and put the sugar and whiskey into the glass. Add the coffee and stir well. Pour the softly whipped cream out of a pitcher over the back of a spoon on to the top of the coffee. The cream should float on top of the coffee so don't attempt to stir. The hot whiskey flavored coffee is drunk through the cold cream—one of the very best Irish traditions!

Dairy Produce

Milk and all milk products, known as *banbidh* or white meats, were important features in the Irish diet. The Irish were incredibly innovative with their variations on this much loved food; there was fresh milk, sour milk, buttermilk, thick or ropy milk, cream, butter, curds and cheese. Sheep's milk cheese was still made in Kilkenny up to the end of the nineteenth century. Goats' milk was always highly valued as being the most nutritious of all. Curds, eaten with cream and honey, were also very important; a variety are mentioned in the eleventh century tale *Aislinge Meic Con Glinne*.

It is only a small step from curds to cheese and for many centuries the Irish were considered to be among the world's great cheesemakers. Both hard and soft cheeses were made in Ireland from pre-Christian times onwards, and both types appear in the country's early literature. Queen Maeve, the legendary warrior queen of Connaught, who features in the *Tain Bo Cuailgne*, finally met her demise when she was hit on the forehead by a lump of hard cheese thrown by her nasty nephew Furbaidhe!

Traditional cheeses ranged from simple curds, made by boiling sour and sweet milk together, to *tanach*—a hard-pressed skim milk cheese. A variation of this was known as *tanach torrach* ('pregnant' cheese). Other kinds included *tath*, a soft cheese made from warmed sour milk curds, *gruth* and *mulchan*, curd cheeses made from buttermilk and *millsen*, made from sweet milk curds. *Millsen* was traditionally eaten at the end of a feast or harvest festival.

Before the establishment of rural creameries in the late nineteenth century, every farmhouse dairy had its own churn to make butter. In my childhood people were still so involved with the land that they knew which field 'made the best butter'. I remember Sheila Delaney on the Rocks skimming the cream off the pails of milk in the cool dairy and putting it into the big wooden churn. We all took turns to turn the handle and peep in through the little glass window on top to see how the butter was progressing. It seemed to take an eternity, but eventually one heard the sloshing sound which indicated that the butter was forming. That was the really exciting bit for us children because we could watch the butter being 'gathered' after it was washed with icy cold water from the well. The butter was then salted and shaped into blocks for the house and market.

If we were very good we were allowed to make our own pats of butter with wet butter 'hands'. We made tiny blocks with a criss-cross pattern specially to fit the small glass butter dishes for the house. Occasionally I was given one to take home. We were more accustomed to the flavor of 'creamery butter', however, so it was really the shaping of the butter which was the novelty. As children, we couldn't be persuaded to drink the buttermilk, marvelling at how the men on the farm could drink it with such relish. In the late 1950s I also made butter with my aunt in Tipperary, but at that stage, after rural electrification, they were very up to date with an electric separator and churn.

There were many superstitions about buttermaking in early times, several of which remained up to the time of my childhood. The fairies could jinx the whole procedure if not placated regularly; a successful butter maker needed to know various ways to counteract their spells.

The biggest butter market in the world between 1759 and 1870 was in Cork and Irish butter is still exported widely today. It is much sought after because of its high quality. Farmhouse cheesemaking has had an enormous revival during the past seventeen years, and Ireland can once again take its place among the most important cheese makers in the world.

Makes 1lb (450g) cheese (approximately)

Curd Cheese

10 cups full-cream milk
¹/2 to 1 teaspoon liquid rennet
good quality muslin or cheesecloth

Put the milk into a spotlessly clean stainless steel saucepan. Heat it very gently until it is barely tepid. Stir the rennet well into the milk, not more than one teaspoon—too much will result in a tough acid curd.

Cover the saucepan with a clean tea towel and the lid. The cloth prevents the steam from condensing on the lid of the pan and falling back on to the curd. Put the pan to one side and leave undisturbed in your kitchen for 2 to 4 hours. The milk should then have coagulated and will be solid.

Cut the curd and heat gently until the whey starts to run out. It must not get too hot or the curd will tighten and toughen too much. Ladle into a muslin-lined colander over a bowl. Tie the corners of the muslin and allow the curd to drip overnight. Next day it can be eaten with soft brown sugar and cream, or freshly picked soft fruit from the garden.

Traditional Cream Cheese

The present Marquis of Waterford writes:

The requirements are to have at least two cows in milk, preferably a Jersey and a Friesan. They must be hand milked into one container and the milk skimmed by hand, the resulting cream placed in a double muslin bag and left to hang until it stops dropping, which will probably be two days. It is then ready to eat. Salt, pepper, chives etc. may subsequently be added according to personal taste, though in my opinion the pure cream cheese is the best. We used to have a cream cheese to the house twice a week in the days when we had cows in the dairy and a dairymaid to look after them.

Cream Cheese

made with Rennet

This charming recipe appears on the very first page of the receipt book of Mrs Dot Drew from Mocollop Castle, Ballyduff, Co. Waterford, dated 1804:

Take a pottle of new milk, a quart of sweet cream and a quart of boiling water, put into a pan and when just milk warm put a teaspoon of rennet to it more or less according to the strength of the rennet, cover it with a napkin for about an hour. Put a napkin in hoop or vat or take up your junket with a saucer and lay it in a hoop or board with holes in it till 'tis about half full then throw spring water over it cover it with one part of the napkin and lay the saucer on it for a while to press it then put in more of your junket and spring water as before so until all is in let it lie till quite drained, then turn it out on another board with holes in it and put a swatch round it keep it in form, put nettles over it and under it. Next day put it on another board with fresh nettles, do this every day for eight or ten days when it will be fit for use.

Yellowman

Yellowman, a sweet crunchy confection, has always been associated with the Ould Lammas Fair of Ballycastle, which takes place in August. Like other favorite Irish foods it was celebrated in song:

Did you treat your Mary Ann to dulse and yellowman,
At the Ould Lammas Fair at Ballycastle—oh?

Dick Murray from Lurgan, a famous yellowman-maker of bygone days, sometimes hid a halfpenny or two in the mixture before it set, which generated a great deal of anticipation and excitement. The coin usually came back to him in exchange for more supplies of his yellowman!

Melt the butter in a heavy-bottomed saucepan. Swirl the saucepan around in order to grease it well. Add the water, sugar and syrup and stir until the sugar has melted. Boil steadily without stirring until a little of the syrup will go crispy and crackly when dropped into cold water. When it reaches this stage stir in the sieved bread soda and pour it immediately onto a greased marble slab or baking sheet. Turn the edges into the center with a spatula and continue to work and pull it until it turns a paleish colour. Traditionally at the fairs it was in one large lump, from which pieces were broken off as required.

2 tablespoons butter
2 tablespoons water
1¼ cups brown sugar
1 lb corn syrup
1 teaspoon baking soda

Ballymaloe Fudge

Makes approx. 96 pieces

Melt the butter in a heavy-bottomed saucepan over a low heat. Add the milk, water, sugar and vanilla. Stir with a whisk until the sugar is dissolved. Turn up the heat and simmer, stirring constantly, until it reaches the soft ball stage. To test, put a little of the fudge in a bowl of cold water. Pull the pan off the heat and stir until the fudge thickens and reaches the required consistency. Pour into a 9 x 13 inch roll pan and smooth out with a spatula.

Allow to cool and then cut before completely cold.

16 tablespoons (2 sticks) butter
5 cups light brown sugar or superfine granulated sugar
1 can evaporated milk (16oz)
¾ cup water
vanilla extract

Candied Peel for Petits Fours

Cut the freshly made candied peel (see page 264) into ¼ to ½ inch thin slices. Roll in sugar and serve with coffee.

Alternatively, dip one end of candied orange peel into melted dark chocolate. Allow to set and serve.

Appendix 1:
Cheeses & Cheesemaking in Ireland

In early medieval times there was a thriving cheesemaking tradition in Ireland. Cheese even features in an account of a foiled attempt on the life of St. Patrick, almost poisoned by some contaminated pressed curds.

Veronica Steele, matriarch of the latest generation of Irish cheesemakers, believes that it was Irish monks who taught the French how to make cheese in the first place when they set up monasteries on the Continent. From the seventh century the monasteries in Ireland were renowned centers of culture and learning. Many had their own farms and made their own cheese. The monastery at St. Gallen in Switzerland was founded in 620 by Irish monks who introduced cheesemaking techniques to local farmers. Münster cheese is also thought to have an Irish connection, through the Irish monks who founded a monastery in the Münster valley in Germany in 668.

In his book on French cheeses Patrick Rance echoes the theory:

'There is, however, a stronger tradition that the first preaching of the Gospel here was by Irish monks from the following of Columban… The lower farms and the *chaumes*, as the high pastures became known, were let to farmers or *marcaires* who paid at least part of their rent in the cheese the monks had taught them how to make.'

Veronica believes that the dissolution of the Irish monasteries in the twelfth century was a major factor in the gradual demise of the cheesemaking tradition in Ireland. Although dairy produce remained a firm staple of the Irish diet, indigenous cheesemaking was to lose its momentum over the following centuries.

During my childhood cheese was a highly processed product which could be bought, foil-wrapped, in little boxes in the village shop. The only real cheeses available were the truckles of red and white Cheddar, which were wrapped in cheesecloth. This kind of cheese was sold only by high-class grocers or delicatessens.

My first taste of real cheese was when I came to Ballymaloe in 1969. We occasionally received a parcel of delicious *Pont l'Evêque* type cheese made by the Franciscan Missionary sisters at Loughglynn near Castlereagh in Co. Roscommon. We were saddened when the nuns eventually discontinued the cheesemaking.

Then we heard that a young Dutch girl, Anneliese Bartelink, was making a cheese in the heart of the Burren which she called Poulcoin. This excellent cheese, sometimes made from cows' milk, sometimes from goats', depending on the time of year, came by post wrapped up in brown paper and recycled twine. We greatly looked forward to it at Ballymaloe and relished every morsel.

In the 1960s Veronica Steele and her husband, Norman, moved down to the Beara Peninsula on the southwest coast of Ireland to live on a farm they had inherited. They grew vegetables, had a cow and reared a pig. Inevitably they had surplus milk, so Veronica tried her hand at cheese-making. A unique new cheese was born which was eventually christened "Milleens" after the beautiful area where the Steeles live. Veronica encouraged others to make cheese, she did much research and was enormously generous with her help and information. In 1982 she taught a cheesemaking class at the Lavistown Study Centre in Co. Kilkenny, and many of the people who came to that and subsequent classes are still active in the Irish farmhouse cheese business today.

University College Cork also ran excellent courses and so a new generation of cheesemakers has sprung up all over the country with an initial predominance in the southwest. Irish cheeses—Milleens, Cashel Blue, Gubbeen, to mention but a few—can now once again take their places proudly among the best in the world.

For further details contact:
The Irish Farmhouse Cheesemakers' Association
38 Molesworth Street, Dublin 2, Eire

Irish Farmhouse Cheeses

A Guide to Irish Handmade Cheeses

1. Abbey Blue
2. Ardrahan
3. Ardsallagh
4. Ballingeary— Carraig Goats Cheese
5. Bartelink
6. Baylough
7. Beal Lodge
8. Boley Hill Cheddar
9. Brekish Dairy
10. Caora
11. Capparoe
12. Carrigbyrne Farmhouse Cheeses: St Killian/St Brendan
13. Carrigaline
14. Carrowholly
15. Cashel Blue/(Cashel White)
16. Castle Farm Goats Cheese
17. Chatwynd Irish Blue
18. Cooleeney
19. Coolea
20. Corleggy
21. Cliffony
22. Cratloe
23. Creeshia
24. Crimlin
25. Croghan
26. Culimore Blue
27. Dunbarra
28. Dunbeacon
29. Durrus
30. Glen-O-Sheen
31. Gubbeen
32. Inagh Farmhouse Cheeese: St Tola/Laugh Caum
33. Kerry Farmhouse Cheese
34. Killorglin
35. Kilshanny
36. Knockalara
37. Knockanore/(Ballyneety)
38. Lavistown
39. Maughnaclea
40. Milleens
41. Mary Morrin's Cheese
42. Old Ardagh
43. Ring
44. Round Tower
45. Ryefield/Boilie
46. St Martin
47. Waterville
48. West Cork Natural Cheeses: Desmond/Gabriel

Appendix 2:
The Potato & the Famine

There is some controversy as to when and by whom the potato was introduced into Ireland. Legend has it that Sir Walter Raleigh, or rather his gardener, planted the first one in Ireland, on his estate, Myrtle Grove, in Youghal, Co. Cork in 1586. The popular nineteenth century ditty 'The Pratie Song' echoes this legendary claim:

> The brave Sir Walter Raleigh, Queen
> Bess's own knight
> Brought here from Virginia
> The root of delight
> By him it was planted
> At Youghal so gay
> An' sure Munster's praties
> Are farmed to this day.

An alternative suggestion is that in the days following the wreck of the Spanish Armada, stocks of potatoes from Spanish ships were cast on to Irish shores, picked up and planted by the Irish.

Whatever its origin, the potato was certainly in Ireland by the close of the sixteenth century. It had already made its way to Europe and England at an earlier date, where it was viewed as a botanical curiosity for some time and was only slowly embraced as a novel vegetable. By contrast the potato in Ireland quickly gained phenomenal popularity.

The Irish climate is ideally suited to potato cultivation. The crop thrives in a cool damp environment and delights in the dark and crumbly soils of Ireland. Potato growing, when compared to cereal husbandry, was less laborious and infinitely more rewarding. Once set, the potato crop looked after itself and needed little attention until the harvest in August. It also returned greater yields per acre than grain crop.

The potato was also welcomed as a comforting crop offering food security after famine and plague had wreaked havoc throughout Ireland in the late sixteenth and seventeenth centuries. The clash of the Gaelic Irish with incoming settlers had seen the destruction of property, crops and cattle. In addition, there had been catastrophic rains in the 1580s, which destroyed much of the corn harvest.

The insipid, abrasive oatencake was quickly usurped by the superior taste and texture of potatoes laced with buttermilk and melting butter. Such was the taste for potatoes that in pre-Famine Ireland the average cottier, or landless laborer, consumed anything between seven and fourteen pounds of potatoes per day. Arthur Young, writing his *Tour in Ireland* in the late eighteenth century, observed 'six people, a man, his wife and four children, will eat eighteen stone of potatoes a week or 252lb'. The Poor Enquiry Commission recorded the following sentiment from a small Co. Down farmer in the 1830s: 'a stone of potatoes is little enough for a man in a day and he'd want something with it to work upon'.

Usually potatoes were simply boiled over the open fire and delivered to the table ungarnished. Many peasants cultivated an extra long thumbnail with which to peel the potatoes. The potato could then be perched upon the nail point and conveniently dipped into buttermilk or other condiments. All the historical references highlight that potatoes were most commonly eaten with buttermilk or milk. Mustard was also popular and onion dip, a simply prepared sauce of onions, milk, flour and butter, was served as an accompaniment to potatoes well into this century. For those who could afford it, a herring or piece of meat was boiled with the potatoes to stretch the dish and impart additional flavor. Pots of boiling meat and broth were nothing strange to the Irish, but once the potato was added, the country's most famous traditional dish, Irish Stew, was born. Similarly, introducing the potato to the iron griddle heralded the arrival of the equally traditional potato cakes, boxty and fadge.

Potatoes were even recommended as a remedy against infertility. Reverend Maunsell, writing in his treatise *On the Culture of Potatoes from the Shoots* (1794) describes the potato as 'the most fruitful root we have; its fructifying quality is visible in every cabbin you pass by... Doctor Lloyd... frequently recommended potatoes as a supper to those ladies whom providence had not yet blessed with children, and an heir has often been the consequence.'

On a more serious note, the evidence strongly suggests that the potato was indeed responsible for the staggering expansion of the Irish population between the late eighteenth century and the 1840s. In 1780, the population was around four million. By the 1841 Census, the figure had risen to 8,175,125. This unprecedented growth in the population is attributed to improved diet; potatoes and buttermilk, though monotonous and bland, were an excellent source of protein, fat and carbohydrate and also supplied most of the minerals and vitamins, particularly vitamin C, necessary for health and vigor.

The monotony of the potato diet was offset by the abundance of the crop. However, by the early nineteenth century, the demands of a swelling population, coupled with soil exhaustion and years of severe frost, resulted in poor potato yields and severe food shortages. By 1845 the people were accustomed to recurrent crop failures and when one-third of the crop was lost in that year, it was viewed as just another bad harvest. However, recognizing the impending crisis, Sir Robert Peel, the British Prime Minister, purchased £100,000 worth of maize in the autumn of 1845. The corn went on sale in March 1846 and those who could afford it could buy it for a penny a pound. Nicknamed 'Peel's Brimstone', it was not popular. People did not know how to prepare it. Many died of dysentery after eating improperly cooked corn and the Government was forced to issue cooking instruction pamphlets warning against these dangers.

In 1846, the people once again set their tubers and looked forward to an improved harvest. However, the fungal disease *Phytophthora infestans,* which had destroyed much of the crop in 1845, was to deliver its worst blow. By September 1846, over two-thirds of the entire crop was lost. Further bad harvests in 1847 and 1848 saw famine and disease sweep through the laboring and poorer classes.

Deprived of their sole means of existence, the peasantry were forced to exploit the food resources of the wild. Starving bands, if they had the energy to do so, migrated to coastal regions and picked the shores bare of shellfish and edible seaweeds. Others scavenged the woods and fields, collecting nuts, wild vegetation and roots. Often the pulp of rotting potatoes was squeezed out and mixed with meal in a vain attempt to make boxty bread on the griddle. The cattle of wealthy farmers were stolen and slaughtered for food at nighttime, so that the smell of boiled meat would go undetected. Inland waterways were drained of all they could offer, but effective fishing, in particular deep-sea fishing, was impossible, for many people had been obliged to pawn or sell their boats and fishing tackle for cash, following the 1845 crisis.

In 1847 the Temporary Relief Act or Soup Kitchen Act saved many from starvation and death, but it was ill equipped to cope with the enormous numbers of distressed and destitute. Scenes of unprecedented suffering, like those described by Mr Nicholas Cummins, a leading Cork merchant, were nationwide. He describes his visit to West Cork in 1846:

> I entered some of the hovels... In the first, six famished and ghastly skeletons, to all appearance dead, were huddled in a corner in some filthy straw, their sole covering what seemed to be a ragged horsecloth and their wretched legs hanging about, naked above the knees. I approached with horror and found by a low moaning they were alive; they were in fever—four children, a woman and what once had been a man... in a few minutes I was surrounded by at least 200 of such phantoms, such frightful spectres as no words can describe. By far the greater number were delirious, either from famine or from fever.

By the time of the 1851 Census the population of Ireland was reduced to six million. Over one million people had died as a direct result of famine and fever and a further two million had been forced to emigrate. The tragic consequences of dependence upon one key foodstuff had been realized only too graphically.

Appendix 3:
Cooking Pits of the Fianna

All over Ireland, but particularly in Munster and Connaught, can be found the remains of ancient cooking pits known as *Fulachta Fiadh*. They date back to the Bronze Age, but are traditionally associated with Fionn Mac Cumhaill and his heroic band of warriors, the Fianna, who, according to legend, lived in Ireland around the third century A.D.

The ancient burnt mounds and cooking pits are usually found near water—rivers, streams or wells. They consist of a boiling pit, a hearth and an enclosing mound of burnt stone. The boiling pits seem to have been lined with stone slabs or timber, depending on the area, and then filled with fresh spring water.

According to a description in G. Keating's *The History of Ireland:*

>...from Bealltaine [1 May] until Samhain [1 November] the Fian were obliged to depend solely on the products of their hunting and of the chase as maintenance and wages from the kings of Ireland... And it was their custom to send their attendants about noon with whatever they had killed in the morning's hunt to an appointed hill, having wood and moorland in the neighbourhood, and to kindle raging fires thereon, and to put into them a large number of emery stones; and to dig two pits in the yellow clay of the moorland, and put some of the meat on spits to roast before the fire; and to bind another portion of it with sugans in dry bundles, and set it to boil in the larger of the two pits and keep plying them with stones that were in the fire, making them seethe often until they were cooked.

Modern-day reconstructions of the cooking pits have demonstrated that meat cooked in this way would have been moist and juicy—cooked to perfection in about the same time as it would take in a moderate oven today.

An Irish Food Chronology

c.7,000 B.C.	Ireland inhabited by hunter-gatherers.
4,000–3,000 B.C.	Agricultural development and introduction of domestic herds. Farming economy established.
c.2,000 B.C. (Bronze Age)	Introduction of metal. It is used for making cooking pots.
800 B.C. (Iron Age)	Emergence of hunting warrior aristocracy.
5th–7th centuries A.D.	Introduction of Christianity and literacy to Ireland. Cereals and dairy produce staples of Irish diet.
12th century A.D	Anglo-Norman conquest of south and east Ireland. Increased agriculture, introduction of built-up ovens and use of spices in food.
13th century A.D	Growth of towns and overseas trade including importation of foodstuffs.
16th and 17th centuries	Tudor and Stuart conquests of Ireland. Introduction of pheasant, turkey and potato. Emergence of Anglo-Irish upper class cuisine influenced by French and Italian dishes.
18th century	Era of the 'Big House'. Refined cosmopolitan cuisine of gentry co-exists with peasant diet of oats and dairy produce in which potato is becoming increasingly dominant.
1845	One third of potato crop lost. Great Famine begins.
1846–7	Two-thirds of entire potato crop fails. Famine and disease hit poorer classes.
1851	Census shows 1 million died and 2 million emigrated during Famine.
Late 19th century	Rapid commercialization means availability of processed goods in rural areas, especially tea, sugar and white bread.
1914–18	War Tea and white bread staples in many households.
Early 20th century	Restaurants or eating-houses on the increase in urban areas. Reluctance to eat traditional dishes seen as 'famine foods'.
1960s	Economic prosperity means package holidays and encounters with ethnic foods.
1980s and 90s	Irish supermarkets stock diversity of multicultural foods from Mediterranean and the East. Resurgence of traditional Irish products: seaweeds, shellfish and farmhouse cheeses.

Index

Bibliography

Bell, Jonathan **& Watson,** Mervyn, *Irish Farming Implements and Techniques 1750-1900,* John Donald, Edinburgh, 1986

Cambrensis, Giraldus, *The History and Topography of Ireland,* (trans. by John J. O'Meara), Penguin Books, London, 1982

Cambrensis, Giraldus, *Expugnatio Hibernica* (The Conquest of Ireland), edited with trans. by A. B. Scott & F. X. Martin, Royal Irish Academy, Dublin, 1978

Carberry, Mary, *The Farm by Lough Gur,* Mercier Press, Cork and Dublin, 1973

Cosmopolite, A., *The Sportsman in Ireland,* vol. I & II, Henry Colburn, London, 1897

Crosbie, Paddy, *Your Dinner's Poured Out,* O'Brien Press, Dublin, 1991

Crohan, Tomas O, *The Islandman* (trans. by Robin Flower), Oxford University Press, Oxford, 1978

Cullen, L. M., *The Emergence of Modern Ireland, 1600–1900,* Gill & Macmillan, Dublin, 1983

Danaher, Kevin, *The Quarter Days in Irish Tradition,* Mercier Press, Cork and Dublin, 1959

Danaher, Kevin, *In Ireland Long Ago,* Mercier Press, Cork and Dublin, 1970

Danaher, Kevin, *The Pleasant Land of Ireland,* Mercier Press, Cork and Dublin, 1972

Danaher, Kevin, *The Year in Ireland,* Mercier Press, Cork and Dublin, 1972

Derricke, John, *The Image of Ireland,* John Day, London, 1581

Donnelly, James S., Jr., 'Cork Market: Its Role in the Nineteenth Century Irish Butter Trade', *Studia Hibernica* No. II, 1971

Evans, E. Estyn, *Irish Folk Ways,* Routledge & Kegan, London, 1957

Fitzgibbon, Theodora, *Irish Traditional Food,* Gill & Macmillan, Dublin, 1983

Fox, Robin, *The Tory Islanders,* Cambridge University Press, London, 1978

Hall, Mr & Mrs C. S., Ireland, *Its Scenery and Character,* 3 vols, How and Parsons, London, 1841

Irwin, Florence, *The Cooking Woman,* Oliver & Boyd, Edinburgh, 1949

Jackson, Kenneth (trans. & ed.), *Aislinge Meic Con Glinne,* Dublin, 1991

Joyce P. W., *A Social History of Ancient Ireland,* vols I & II, M H Gill & Son, Dublin, 1920

Keane, J. B., *Strong Tea,* Mercier Press, Cork and Dublin, 1972

Lucas, A. T. 'Nettles and Charlock as Famine Food', *Breifne,* vol I, no. 2, Cumann Seanchais Bhreifne, 1958

Lucas, A. T., 'Irish Food Before the Potato', *Gwerin,* vol. iii, no. 3, Denbigh, Gee and Son, 1960–2

Lysaght, Patricia, 'When I makes Tea, I makes Tea, *Ulster Folk Life,* vol. 33, 1987

McKinney, Jack, 'They came in Cars and Carts: A History of the Fairs and Markets of Ballyclare', Area Resource Centre, Antrim, 1989

MacLysaght, E., *Irish Life in the Seventeenth Century,* Cork University Press, Cork, 1939

Maguire, W. A., *Caught in Time,* Friars Bush Press, Belfast, 1986

Mahon, Bríd, *Land of Milk and Honey,* Poolbeg, Dublin, 1991

Maxwell, Constantia, *The Stranger in Ireland,* Jonathan Cape, London, 1954

Maxwell, W. H., *Wild Sports of the West,* Richard Bentley, London, 1843

Meyer, Kuno (ed.), *The Vision of MacConglinne* (trans by Aisling MacConglinne), Lemma Publishing Corporation, New York, 1974

Mitchell, Frank, *The Shell Guide to Reading the Irish Landscape,* Country House, Dublin, 1986

Moryson, Fynes, *Itinerary, 1605,* John Beale, London, 1617

O'Donovan, John ed., *Annals of Ireland by the Four Masters,* 7 vols, Dublin, 1856

O'Drisceoil, Diarmuid, '*Fulachta Fiadh:* the Value of Early Irish Literature', *Burnt Offerings; International Contributions to Burnt Mound Archaeology,* compiled by Victor Buckley, Dublin, 1990, 157–164

O Hógáin, Dáthí, *Myth, Legend and Romance,* London, 1990

O'Kelly, M. J., 'Excavations and experiments in ancient Irish cooking places', *JRSAI 84,* 1954, 105–155

O'Loan, J., 'A History of Early Irish Farming.', *Journal of the Dept. of Agriculture and Fisheries 62,* Dublin, 1965, 131–98

O'Mara, Veronica **& O'Reilly,** Fionnuala, **An Irish Literary Cookbook,** Town House, Dublin, 1991

O'Neill, Timothy, *Merchants and Mariners in Medieval Ireland,* Irish Academic Press, Dublin, 1987

O'Sé, Micheál, 'Old Irish Buttermaking', *Journal of Cork Historical and Archaeological Society 54,* 1959, 61–67

O Shúileabháin, Amhlaoibh, *Cinnlae Amhlaoibh Uí Shúileabháin,* edited by Michael McGrath, Irish Texts Society, 4 vols., 1936

O Tuama, Sean **& Kinsella,** Thomas, *An Duannaire 1600–1900: Poems of the Dispossessed,* Dolmen Press, Portlaoise, 1981

Petty, Sir William, *The Political Anatomy of Ireland,* Irish University Press, 1691

Póirtear, Cathal (ed.) *The Great Irish Famine,* Mercier Press, Dublin, 1995.

Power, Catryn, 'Dental Anthropology', *Archaeology Ireland,* 4/3, 1990, 36–28

Proudfoot, V. B. 'The Economy of the Irish Rath', *Medieval Archaeology 5,* 1966, 94–122

Ryan, Michael (ed.), *Treasures of Ireland,* Royal Irish Academy, Dublin, 1983

Salaman, Redcliffe, *The History and Social Influence of the Potato,* Cambridge University Press, Cambridge, 1949

Sayers, Peig, *Machnamh Sean-Mhna* (An Old Woman's Reflections), Oxford University Press, Oxford, 1962

Sexton, Regina, *Cereals and Cereal Foodstuff of the Early Historic Period in Ireland,* Unpublished Thesis, Cork, 1992

Sexton, Regina, ' "I'd ate it like Chocolate": The Disappearing Offal Food Traditions of Cork City' in *Proceedings of the Oxford Symposium on Food and Cookery 1994,* Oxford, 1995

Sharkey, Olive, *Old Days Old Ways,* O Brien Press, Dublin, 1985

Thackeray, William Makepeace, *The Irish Sketch Book,* vol. XVIII, Smith Elder & Co. London, 1879

Wakefield, Edward, *An Account of Ireland,* Statistical and Political, vols & II, London, 1812

Watson, Mervyn, 'Standardisation of Pig Production: The Case of the Large White Ulster', *Ulster Folk Life,* vol. 34, 1988

Went, Arthur E. J., 'The Irish Hake Fishery 1504–1824'. *Journal of The Cork Historical and Archaeological Society,* vol. 51, 1946

Wilson, Anne, *Food and Drink in Britain,* Constable, London, 1973

Young, Arthur, *A Tour in Ireland,* vols I & II, Cadell, London

Photographic Acknowledgments

Nancy Ellis showing Darina how to cook griddle bread, Glin Castle, Co. Limerick (see page 218).

All food photography by Michelle Garrett, unless otherwise specified.

The photographs on the following pages are by Kevin Dunne:
6&7, Ballymaloe Cookery School, Co. Cork; 8, Lana Pringle and Darina Allen making Barm Brack; 16/17, Bealaclugga, Co. Clare; 20, St Brendan's Well, Birr Castle, Co. Offaly; 36/37, Connemara, Co. Galway; 42, Ballyheigue, Co. Kerry; 53, Eddy Sheehan, fishmonger, in the Old English Market, Cork; 54, *bairneachs* by the sea, Ballyheigue, Co. Kerry; 57, Darina Allen picking perinkles at Ballycotton, Co. Cork; 63, Bealaclugga, Co. Clare; 70/71, Lady's View, Killarney, Co. Kerry; 77, Glendollach Lake, Co. Galway; 79, George Gossip hunting at Birr, Co. Offaly; 81, hanging game at the Dower House of George Gossip, Birr, Co. Offaly; 84, George Gossip's game pie at Bir; 86/87, ducks in bog pond, Roundstone, Co. Galway; 90, Hill Farm in Magillycuddy Reeks, Co. Kerry; 94/95, sheep in Magillicuddy Reeks, Co. Kerry; 104/105, Bealaclugga, Co. Clare; 130, Simon O'Flynn with pigs' trotters (crubeens) in the Old English Market, Co. Cork; 135, Darina Allen buying tripe and drisheen in the Old English Market, Co. Cork; 140/141, 'lazy beds' for potatoes, Ballyconneely, Co. Galway; 160, market at Moore Street, Dublin; 169, Seakale at Glin Castle, Co. Limerick; 174/175, Glentrasna, Co. Galway; 208/209, lake near Clifden, Co. Galway; 221, Joan Twomey and Darina Allen baking bread in a bastible; 225, bastible over an open fire; 226, table laid for afternoon tea, Glin Castle, Co. Limerick; 232/233, turf pile, Lough Inagh, Co. Galway; 238/239, hill farm near Killarney, Co. Kerry; 262/263, Connemara, Co. Galway.

The photographs on the pages below are by the photographers specified:
30/31, Gannet colony, Saltees, Co. Wexford, Stuart Smyth; 82, red deer, NHPA/Laurie Campbell; 112/113, Burren, Co. Donegal, Stuart Smyth; 124/125, stubble burning, Co. Kilkenny, Stuart Smyth; 156/157, Bray, Co. Wicklow, Stuart Smyth; 188/189, Ballinaskeagh Pass, Co. Kerry, NHPA/Robert Thompson; 212/213, bales of straw, Co. Wicklow, Stuart Smyth; 261, Glen Malure, Co. Wicklow, Stuart Smyth.